BASIC PROGRAMMING FOR THE
FINANCIAL EXECUTIVE

BASIC PROGRAMMING FOR THE
FINANCIAL EXECUTIVE

THOMAS J. HUMPHREY

A WILEY-INTERSCIENCE PUBLICATION

John Wiley & Sons • New York • Chichester • Brisbane • Toronto

Library of Congress Cataloging in Publication Data:

Humphrey, Thomas Junior, 1932-
    Basic programming for the financial executive.

    "A Wiley-Interscience publication."
    Includes index.
    1. Corporations—Finance—Data processing.
    2. Corporations—Finance—Computer programs.
    3. Basic (Computer program language) I. Title.
    HG4026.H79   658.1'5'0285424   78-5670
    ISBN 0-471-03020-1

Printed in the United States of America

10 9 8 7 6 5 4 3 2

To my wife, Terpsy

Preface

This book demonstrates how to develop computer programs for financial analysis. It should be of use to both the financial executive who desires to develop analytical tools and the professional programmer who wants to gain insight into financial concepts.

The approach used is to develop, step-by-step and line-by-line, four programs that are basic to the analysis of the cash flows associated with various financial and financing alternatives. In this way, both programming techniques and financial techniques are demonstrated simultaneously with the assembly of working, practical programs.

LOAN is a program that produces loan amortization tables for one loan or a package of any number of loans combined. It can handle both mortgage-type and sinking-fund loans, with or without balloon payments, with payments in advance or arrears, and will automatically solve for the payment amounts if not given. It can also handle changes in either or both the interest rate and the amortization rate including deferred amortization. For the mortgage-type loan there are two floating interest rate options—with fixed amortization and floating amortization.

DISC is a general purpose discounting program. It accepts any number of cash flows categorized by type—single, series of equal, and series of unequal—so as to avoid tedious period-by-period input. It solves for present values, discount rates (rates of return), and future payments at any practical discount frequency.

LEAS is designed for use by lessors for structuring leases but is of equal value to lessees for evaluating leases. It solves for present values, rates, and rentals for one lease or a package of any number of leases. Leveraged leases can be evaluated or rentals calculated using either the internal rate of return or sinking-fund methods.

LEASBUY is designed from the lessee's viewpoint and produces a complete economic comparison between purchasing an asset and leasing it. Based on concepts drawn from the prior programs and some new concepts, it compares the two alternatives in terms of pretax rates, after-tax rates, present values, impact on cash flow, and impact on profit.

These programs provide the opportunity to explore programming techniques for all the three sections into which a program is divided. Input techniques include accordion input, piggyback input, open-end loops, testing input data for errors, and many more.

Computational techniques include deriving such financial functions as interest, principal repayments, depreciation (including ADR), and deferred taxes. A whole chapter is devoted to exploring the concepts and developing the equations for compounding and discounting. Two methods for calculating rate of return are covered, one of which can be used to solve for both rates possible when a stream of cash flows reverses polarity.

Output techniques include formatting terminal printouts, selecting a portion of a table for printing, adding payment dates (with adjustment for February 29th), and multiple selections in any sequence.

The programming language used is BASIC, which is well suited for the person who programs on a casual basis and cannot spend the time required to learn the more complicated languages. BASIC uses nothing more than a few simple English words and elementary algebra. Anyone who can read this paragraph and has completed a course in high school algebra can quickly learn to write quite powerful programs, as the book demonstrates. Consider the following program:

```
1 INPUT A
2 LET B=A+5
3 PRINT B
4 END
```

This is a complete program and consists of a series of instructions which the computer will perform step by step in sequence. The program contains all three required sections. The first line inputs the data, the second line performs a computation, and the third line prints the answer. The fourth line merely tells the computer that the end of the program has been reached.

The program contains four separate instructions or statements—INPUT, LET, PRINT, and END. The book uses only 23 such statements, although more are available in BASIC, which means that one-sixth of the book's programming vocabulary is used above.

The book is relatively free of computer jargon, and nothing is said of what a computer is or how it works. It is treated as a "black box" that slavishly follows the instructions entered by the user/programmer from a typewriter/terminal. Indeed the author found that he was unconsciously referring to programs as though they were the machine rather than a set of instructions to the machine. For this lapse he begs the indulgence of those readers who may be professional programmers.

The main goal of the book is to develop the logic for financial programs. It is not a teaching text for BASIC. Although each BASIC statement is briefly described when it is introduced, it is assumed that the reader will refer to the BASIC manual provided by the time-sharing supplier for a full discussion. The Appendix contains a summary comparison of the BASIC dialects offered by 23 time-sharing companies and computer manufacturers.

THOMAS J. HUMPHREY

Port Jefferson Station, New York
January 1978

Acknowledgments

The author is indebted to Mr. J. J. Tierney, American Airlines, Inc., for reviewing the manuscript and making many helpful suggestions. Any errors in the text are, however, solely the responsibility of the author.

Thanks are also sincerely extended to the following firms for providing copies of their BASIC manuals or other information used in compiling the Appendix: Chi Corporation; Computer Sciences Corporation; Control Data Corporation; Cybershare Limited; The Kiewit Computation Center of Dartmouth College; Dataline Systems Limited; First Data Corporation; The Information Services Business Division of General Electric Company; Interactive Sciences Corporation; International Business Machines Corporation; Multiple Access Computer Group; National CSS, Inc.; Polycom Systems Limited; Remote Computing Corporation; The Service Bureau Company; Standard Information Systems, Inc.; Tymshare, Inc.; Uni-Coll Corporation; The Information Network Division of United Computing Systems, Inc.; Wang Computer Services; and Xerox Computer Services.

T.J.H.

Contents

BASIC PROGRAMMING FOR THE
FINANCIAL EXECUTIVE

1

The Sinking-Fund Loan

One of the most basic tools for financial analysis is a program that will produce a loan amortization schedule. This is a table that presents, period-by-period, the amount of each loan payment, its division between principal and interest, and each new loan balance.

Any loan that requires partial, periodic repayments of principal before the maturity date of the loan can be categorized as either a sinking-fund loan or a mortgage-type loan. The sinking-fund loan is characterized by equal, or level, installments of principal, plus interest. That is, the principal component of the payment is the same from period to period. Since the interest component declines as the loan balance declines, the total periodic payment also declines over time. The mortgage-type loan, on the other hand, has equal payments divided between a declining interest component and an increasing principal component. This chapter is devoted to the sinking-fund loan.

THE LOAN AMORTIZATION SCHEDULE

Since the loan program produces a table, a good place to begin is at the end, that is, with the printout.

The first thing to do is to lay out the format of the table in pencil to determine exactly what has to be produced. The layout for a loan amortization schedule will look like this:

AMORTIZATION SCHEDULE FOR $ _____ LOAN

Year	Payment	Interest	Principal	Balance

Total

Now identify the variables to be printed out and name them. In this case the output variables are the same as the column headings.

> *Year is* T
> *Payment is* N
> *Interest is* L
> *Principal is* M
> *Balance is* P

The three columns for payment, interest, and principal also have totals. The balance column does not need a total because its final value will be the same figure as the last periodic amount. So three more variables are needed.

> *Total Payment is* N1
> *Total Interest is* L1
> *Total Principal is* M1

The table's title has a space for the original amount of the loan. This does not require a separate variable as it can be the declining balance P before it starts declining. If the original loan balance were to be printed after printing the body of the table then another variable would be required to "remember" the original amount.

Once the table's format has been decided upon, the program statements that produce that format, the IMAGE statements, can be written.

The basic determinant of the table's format is the repeating line in the table's body. This is the line that determines the position and spacing of all the other IMAGE statements. So this line should be written first. The number of columns, the number of digits in each column, and the number of spaces between columns determine the width of the table. The number of columns is fixed by the nature of the table, but the number of digits to be printed deserves some thought.

For multimillion-dollar loans and accuracy to the penny, many digits are required. For example, $123,456,789.01 requires 12 characters including the decimal point but excluding the commas and the dollar sign. If the loans to be analyzed never reach a million dollars then no more than nine characters per column are required and perhaps less. Or if large loans are analyzed but they are used for planning purposes where complete accuracy is not required, then the answers can be rounded, say, to the nearest thousand and only six characters per column are required.

The significance of this is that a table with columns 12 characters wide will take almost twice as much time to print out as a table of columns that are six characters wide. For this chapter, eight digits plus the decimal point will be sufficient.

The Year column requires only two digits to accommodate the number of years as it is the rare loan that has a term in excess of 99 years. This would mean, however, that the abbreviation "YR" would have to be used as the column heading. If the whole word is desired in the heading then one merely accepts a wider column than the numbers require.

The final determinant of the table width is the number of blank spaces. For this chapter, indent the table one space and use two spaces between columns.

The whole table is now 48 characters wide, consisting of one field of four characters, four fields of nine characters each, and eight spaces for separating columns. In addition, there is one space for identation.

FORMAT SPECIFICATION

The IMAGE statement for the lines in the body of the table can now be written. Choose a line number high enough that the rest of the program can be inserted before the IMAGE statements.

320 :   ①#### ②######.## (4X)

This is the pencil-draft version and contains a couple of suggested shortcuts. The circled numbers indicate the number of blank spaces. Such a guide is needed for typing at the terminal as it is difficult to judge spacing from a handwritten scrawl. The (4X) means that the preceding field, and its spacing, is to be written four times. Writing a series of crosshatches across the paper can become tedious. If there is a repeating pattern it is easier to write it once and then indicate how many times it is to be used.

This is what is actually typed at the terminal:

320 : #### ######.## ######.## ######.## ######.##

Now add the underlining for the headings. This IMAGE statement will also serve as the overlining for the totals. The number of characters and spacing will be identical to the above line.

310 : ____ _____ _____ _____ _____

Now add the heading. The spacing between the words should be adjusted so that each word is centered above the underlining of its column as closely as practicable.

300 : YEAR PAYMENT INTEREST PRINCIPAL BALANCE

Now add the totals line. The only difference between this line and the repeating line used in the body of the table is the substitution of the word "total" for the year field.

330 : TOTAL ######.## ######.## ######.## ######.##

Finally the title line can be written. It is last so that the other lines can serve as a guide when centering the title over the table. Since it has 41 characters compared to 48 for the table, it should be indented from the edge of the table by either three or four spaces which represents one-half of the difference.

290 : AMORTIZATION SCHEDULE FOR $######.## LOAN

The line numbers of the IMAGE statements were assigned in the order in which they will be used by the program rather than in the order of writing. When presented together in numerical order, as they will be in a listing of the program, they compose a picture of the table's format.

```
290 :          AMORTIZATION SCHEDULE FOR $######.## LOAN
300 :  YEAR      PAYMENT       INTEREST       PRINCIPAL      BALANCE
310 :  — —      — — — —       — — — —         — — — —        — — — —
320 : ####  ######.##     ######.##      ######.##      ######.##
330 : TOTAL ######.##     ######.##      ######.##      ######.##
```

ANALYZING THE PROBLEM

Before the computational part of the program is developed the problem should be analyzed manually. In most cases the program steps will closely follow the manual steps.

Assume a $1000 loan, bearing interest at 10%, that will be repaid in five equal annual installments. This provides three input data for which the variables can now be named.

Interest rate is	A1
Loan term is	B2
Loan balance is	P

Dividing the loan amount by the number of payments produces the amount of each principal payment, in this case, $200.

$$\frac{\$1000}{5} = \$200$$

In BASIC this would be expressed as LET M = P/B2.

During the first year the entire amount of the loan is outstanding and accruing interest at 10% so that at the end of the year the interest payment is $100.

$$\$1000 \times .1 = \$100$$

LET L = P * A1

The principal payment of $200 plus the interest payment of $100 results in a total payment of $300.

$$\$200 + \$100 = \$300$$

LET N = L + M

Since the loan is being reduced by $200 the outstanding balance at the end of the first year is $800.

$$\$1000 - \$200 = \$800$$

LET P = P − M

This BASIC expression is not an equation in the arithmetic sense because something cannot equal itself minus something else. It is a valid BASIC statement, however, for it is really an instruction that the machine will perform in rigid sequence. The machine will take the value of P, whatever it is, subtract from it the value of M, and then call the result P. The original value of P will be lost or "forgotten."

This expression should not be used if the original value of P is to be used again elsewhere in the program. In that case an additional variable will have to be used so that both values can be remembered.

LET P1 = P − M

For the second year there is no need to calculate the principal payment because that remains constant each year and has already been calculated.

The amount outstanding during the second year is $800 so interest for the year is $800 × .1 = $80. The total payment for the year is $200 + $80 = $280. The new balance is $800 − $200 = $600.

The calculations for the second year and all subsequent years are the same as for the first year. The only difference is that they apply to a lower loan balance each year.

Once the values for each year are known the totals are calculated by summing each column. The resulting amortization table looks like this:

Year	Payment	Interest	Principal	Balance
1	300.00	100.00	200.00	800.00
2	280.00	80.00	200.00	600.00
3	260.00	60.00	200.00	400.00
4	240.00	40.00	200.00	200.00
5	220.00	20.00	200.00	0.00
Total	1300.00	300.00	1000.00	0.00

There is considerable flexibility as to the sequence in which the program is developed. It can be written straight through from the first line to the END statement. Or it can be written section by section, perhaps the computational expressions first, then the input lines, and then the print statements.

Whatever approach is taken, spaces should be left between the line numbers. This permits the later insertion of an overlooked statement or the addition of a complete section if necessary. A good way to provide for these eventualities is to mentally reserve blocks of line numbers for specific purposes. For instance the input statements can start at line number 100, the first set of computations at 1000, the second set of computations at 2000, the IMAGE statements at 4000, and so on. Use 9999 for the END statement. This way whenever another set of statements is required there will be space available. When the program is completed and debugged the RENUMBER command will eliminate the gaps caused by unused line numbers.

The line numbers specified in this book will be those of the final sample program. This is to make it easier to cross-reference between the explanatory text and the program listings in the figures. These line numbers will always be in multiples of 10. When an illustrative statement is used that does not appear in the final program then the line number will end in a digit other than zero, usually five.

THE PROGRAM'S FRONT END

So far the format of the output table has been designed, the IMAGE statements written, and the variables named. A sample problem has been analyzed manually and the computational expressions developed. It is now time to write the program.

The program will be named LOAN1. A flowchart showing the logic of the completed program appears in Figure 1.1.

The first thing the program is going to do is print the title of the table. Since the title includes the loan amount, that particular piece of information must be inputted. There are various methods for inputting data to a program, and these will be discussed in detail in a later chapter. For now the simple READ / DATA approach will be used.

```
100 READ P
```

Print the title, the column headings, and the underlining.

```
110 PRINT
120 PRINT USING 290,P
130 PRINT
140 PRINT USING 300
150 PRINT USING 310
```

The two dummy PRINT statements, lines 110 and 130, do not result in any actual printing but cause the paper to advance one line each. This provides spacing before and after the title so that it stands out from the body of the table.

Now the program has to start calculating. That means the remaining loan parameters, namely the interest rate and the loan term, must be inputted.

```
160 READ A1,B2
```

The corresponding DATA line can be anywhere in the program for the machine will ignore it during program execution until it encounters a READ statement. Then it will find the DATA line wherever it is. For now place the data at the end of the program.

```
340 DATA 1000,.1,5
```

The input data must be in the same sequence as that in which the corresponding variables are read in the READ statements. That is, the first value in the DATA line must correspond to the first variable that is READ, P. The sequence thus is loan amount, interest rate, and loan term.

The first calculation is the amount of the annual principal payment as this value is needed for each year's computations.

```
170 LET M=P/B2
```

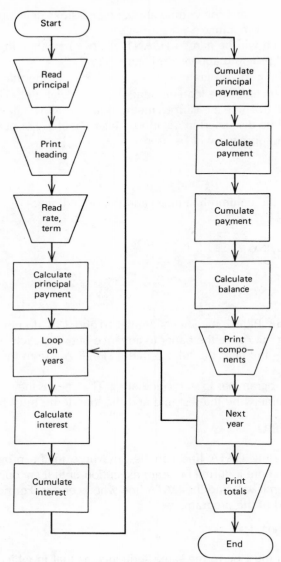

Figure 1.1   Flowchart of LOAN1.

LOOPS

The next step is to calculate the values for each year of the loan. Since the arithmetic is the same for each year, the obvious approach is to use a loop defined by FOR / NEXT statements.

```
180 FOR T=1 TO B2
190 LET L=P*A1
```

. . .

```
220 LET N=L+M
```

. . .

```
240 LET P=P−M
```

. . .

```
260 NEXT T
```

Loops are so important to so many financial programs that they deserve discussion in some detail.

A FOR / NEXT loop begins with a FOR statement, ends with a NEXT statement, and contains any number of expressions in between. In the above loop the FOR statement tells the machine to use T as the variable that counts the number of passes through the loop, tells it to set T equal to one for the first pass, and to exit from the loop when T equals B2. Thus the machine will set T = 1 and calculate the values of L, N, and P in sequence. When it reaches the NEXT statement it will increase T by one (to the next higher integer unless instructed otherwise) and return to the beginning of the loop for another pass. When the assigned limit of T is reached, that is, when T = B2, the machine will calculate L, N, and P for the last time and then go on to the line following the NEXT statement.

A FOR / NEXT loop is not indispensable because the same results can be obtained by using an IF . . . GOTO loop.

```
175 LET T=0
185 LET T=T+1
190 LET L=P*A1
```

. . .

220 LET N=L+M

. . .

240 LET P=P−M

. . .

255 IF T>=B2 GOTO 270
265 GOTO 185

Line 175 is not part of the loop but ensures that T is set to an initial value of zero. If this is the first time that T is used by the program, or the only time, then line 175 is not necessary as the machine automatically sets all variables to an initial value of zero when the program is run. But if there is any chance that T might have a carryover value from some prior use, then it should be explicitly reset to zero.

Line 255 provides excape from the loop not only when T equals B2 but also if T should exceed B2. This is purely a precaution as T would normally never exceed B2 if T were properly set to zero before the loop were entered. But there is at least the conceptual possibility that a momentary aberration in the machine, due perhaps to a line voltage surge, could cause the program to miss its exit cue if that cue is too narrowly defined. The result would be that the program would go around the loop indefinitely, or at least until the user became impatient and stopped execution.

The prudent approach is never to test and decide on the basis of equality unless that is exactly what is meant. Otherwise use > = or < =.

The FOR / NEXT loop is simpler to use than the IF . . . GOTO loop and requires fewer lines. Also, since the loop is bracketed by the FOR and NEXT statements it stands out visually so that the program listing is easier to read. But on some occasions the IF . . . GOTO approach is preferable; for example, when the number of passes through the loop cannot be predetermined.

PRINTING THE OUTPUT

The PRINT statement for each year's calculations will have to be placed after the last calculation but before the exit from the loop so that the printing will also be repetitive. The table format has already determined the sequence in which the variables are to be printed—year, payment amount, interest, principal repayment, and remaining balance.

250 PRINT USING 320,T,N,L,M,P

The column totals must also be printed but these amounts will not be known until all of the years have been calculated, that is, after the loop. But the cumulation itself must be done within the loop.

```
200 LET L1=L1+L
210 LET M1=M1+M

. . .

230 LET N1=N1+N
```

Each pass through the loop results in the new values of L, M, and N being added respectively to the old totals of L1, M1, and N1. The final totals should be printed after leaving the loop and after printing the underlining.

```
270 PRINT USING 310
280 PRINT USING 330, N1,L1,M1,P
```

LOAN1 is now complete. The program's listing and a run of the sample loan are presented in Figure 1.2.

VARYING THE PAYMENT FREQUENCY

LOAN1 is a program that works but it is a very inflexible one. It assumes, for example, that the loan payments are made annually. It would be of more practical use if provision were made for handling loans with semiannual, quarterly, or monthly payments. So a more sophisticated version called LOAN2 will be developed. Its flowchart appears in Figure 1.3.

The loan term B2 has been treated until now as though it referred to years. Actually it can refer to any regular period of time, such as months or quarters. Once its definition is broadened, however, the treatment of the interest rate A1 must be examined more closely. It would not do to have the program calculate interest at 10% per quarter when what is meant is 10% per annum.

The easiest approach for the programmer, which would not require any change in the program, would be to define A1 as the periodic interest rate rather than the annual interest rate. Users would be on notice that for a quarterly loan they would have to divide the annual interest rate by four. They would thus enter .025 rather than .1. This approach, however, makes for overworked analysts and lazy programmers.

Whenever there is a choice between working the programmer and work-

```
LIST

LOAN1          8:53    THURSDAY JAN.27,1977

100 READ P
110 PRINT
120 PRINT USING 290,P
130 PRINT
140 PRINT USING 300
150 PRINT USING 310
160 READ A1,B2
170 LET M=P/B2
180 FOR T=1 TO B2
190 LET L=P*A1
200 LET L1=L1+L
210 LET M1=M1+M
220 LET N=L+M
230 LET N1=N1+N
240 LET P=P-M
250 PRINT USING 320,T,N,L,M,P
260 NEXT T
270 PRINT USING 310
280 PRINT USING 330,N1,L1,M1,P
290 :    AMORTIZATION SCHEDULE FOR $######.## LOAN
300 : YEAR    PAYMENT    INTEREST   PRINCIPAL   BALANCE
310 : ----    --------   --------   --------   --------
320 : ####   ######.##   ######.##  ######.##  ######.##
330 : TOTAL ######.##   ######.##  ######.##  ######.##
340 DATA 1000,.1,5
350 END


RUN

LOAN1          8:54    THURSDAY JAN.27,1977

          AMORTIZATION SCHEDULE FOR $  1000.00 LOAN
```

YEAR	PAYMENT	INTEREST	PRINCIPAL	BALANCE
----	--------	--------	---------	-------
1	300.00	100.00	200.00	800.00
2	280.00	80.00	200.00	600.00
3	260.00	60.00	200.00	400.00
4	240.00	40.00	200.00	200.00
5	220.00	20.00	200.00	0.00
----	--------	--------	---------	-------
TOTAL	1300.00	300.00	1000.00	0.00

```
TIME 0 SECS.
```

Figure 1.2   List and run of LOAN1.

ing the user, always favor the user. After all, the programmer will only write the program once. The analyst will be using it hundreds of times.

So let the program do the dividing. This will require an additional bit of input, namely, the number of payments per year. Name this variable B1. The conversion from an annual interest rate to a periodic interest rate is simple division.

    145 LET A1=A1/B1

So far the user has been required to enter the annual interest rate in decimal form, that is, as .1. Mentally, however, the user is probably visualizing "10 percent" and not "point one." This means that there is a chance that some day he or she will inadvertently type "10" in error.

When designing the input format, conform as closely as possible to the terms in which the user thinks of the data.

Since the user is thinking "10" but the machine has to use .1, insert a statement that will divide the input by 100. Then the input datum can be entered in percentage form and the machine will immediately convert it to its decimal equivalent.

    147 LET A1=A1/100

Both conversions—from annual rate to periodic rate and from percentage form to deciimal form—can be combined in the same statement.

    140 LET A1=A1/(B1*100)

Or, if the original value must be remembered,

    145 LET A=A1/(B1*100)

Notice the use of parentheses in this expression. Without parentheses how would the machine interpret A1/B1*100? Would it calculate A1/(B1*100) or (A1/B1) *100? The answers would be quite different. The machine would not find the lack of parentheses ambiguous for it would automatically perform the operations in a rigid, predetermined order. The sequence is operations within parentheses, exponentiation, multiplication or division, and then addition or subtraction. Operations on the same level are performed from left to right. Even so, it would be prudent to err on the side of too many parentheses rather than too few. Use parentheses whenever there is the slightest chance of ambiguity.

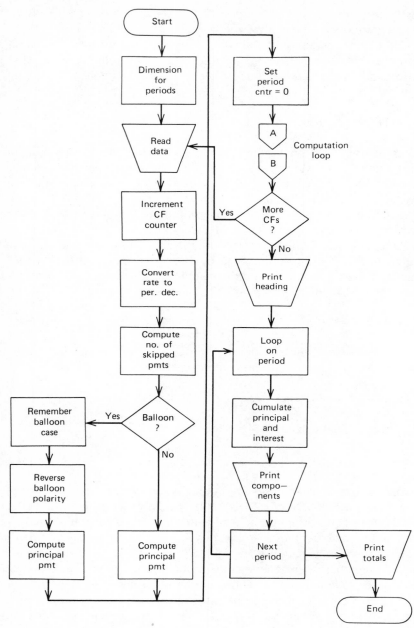

Figure 1.3   Flowchart of LOAN2.

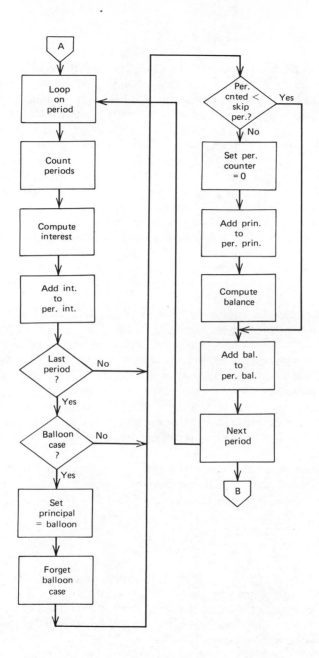

VARYING PRINCIPAL PAYMENTS

LOAN1 also assumed that the loan's principal installments would remain the same throughout the term of the loan. Many loans, however, provide that the amount of the sinking-fund payment varies over the term. Or the early payments may be interest only and sinking-fund payments are deferred for several years. And there is often a balloon payment in which the final installment is several times as large as the preceding periodic payments. If the program cannot handle these cases its use will be very restricted.

The common characteristic of the above cases is that the amortization rate changes abruptly, or breaks, at some time. It is necessary only to identify the time periods applicable to the term of each segment of the loan. Call the beginning of the term J1 and the end of the term J2.

The sample loan had a five-year term with annual payments. For this loan J1, the time at which the loan is drawn down and interest begins accruing, is zero. Time J2, the point at which the loan ends, is five. If the loan had quarterly payments rather than annual then J2 would be 20 (5 × 4 = 20). Time J1 would still be zero.

Keeping the payments on a quarterly basis, assume that the payments are interest-only for the first two years and that the loan is fully amortized over the last three years. The first, or nonamortizing segment, would have J1 = 0 and J2 = 8. The second, or amortizing, segment begins at the very instant that the first segment ends, so that its J1 = 8. Its J2, of course, equals 20.

There are other ways of defining the time periods involved but one of the advantages of this approach is that the difference between J2 and J1 equals the number of payments. Thus the number of payments for the first segment is J2 − J1 = 8 − 0 = 8. The number of payments for the second segment is J2 − J1 = 20 − 8 = 12.

With the loan divided into two segments each segment can be treated as a separate loan. This is done by running the segments through the program's loop separately with J1 and J2 being used to define the limits of the loop's counter T.

    230 FOR T= (J1+1) TO J2

Counter T starts at one greater than J1 because although J1 marks the beginning of the term the first payment occurs one period later.

In the input data the balance outstanding at the end of each segment's term must now be specified for it can no longer be taken for granted that the ending balance will be zero.

Ending balance is I2

The periodic principal payment will be the difference between the beginning and ending balances divided by the number of payments.

    175 LET S6=(H1−I2)/(J2−J1)

The principal payment has been renamed S6 because P will be used for a related variable later.

    For each loan segment five pieces of information are now required—interest rate A1, beginning balance H1, ending balance I2, beginning of term J1, and end of term J2. The DATA lines for the example look like this:

    565 DATA 10,1000,1000,0,8
    575 DATA 10,1000,0,8,20

The nonamortizing segment, line 565, has the beginning and ending balances the same, $1000. The amortizing segment, line 575, starts with the full $1000 and amortizes it down to zero.

    The interest rate of 10% appears in both lines. This may appear to be unnecessary since the interest rate is the same for both segments. However specifying the interest rate in each DATA line increases the scope and flexibility of the program in two ways. First, the program can now accommodate loans with a floating interest rate. Many loans today have an interest rate that varies up or down with some index, often a bank's prime rate. Such a loan can be broken into segments according to forecasted changes in its interest rate. Second, the program can now handle more than one loan at a time. Several loans of differing interest rates and terms can be combined into a single amortization table. To the program, it makes no difference whether a given DATA line represents a segment of a loan or a different loan entirely.

    The use of multiple DATA lines also enables the program to handle multiple takedowns. In this situation only a portion of the loan is drawn down immediately and the rest of the loan is drawn down later. If each takedown is entered as a separate loan the program will combine them into a single amortization table.

    But the program must be told how many DATA lines to expect. Otherwise the machine will just keep processing until it runs out of data, and then it will print an error message and stop. This requires another input variable. Each DATA line describing a loan or loan segment will be referred to by the general term "cash flow line."

    Number of cash flow lines is B

In summary, three pieces of information are needed in addition to those in the cash flow lines—total number of periods B2, number of periods per year

B1, and number of cash flow lines B. The DATA line for these variables looks like this:

    555 DATA 20,4,2

The program will have to count each cash flow line as it inputs it. It will then go through the loop to process the cash flow, and then compare the count with B to determine whether there is another cash flow line to be processed. Call the cash flow counter T2.

    110 READ B2,B1,B
    125 READ A1,H1,I2,J1,J2
    130 LET T2=T2+1

    . . .

    230 FOR T=(J1+1) TO J2

    . . .

    360 NEXT T
    370 IF T2 < B GOTO 125

By this means any number of loans or loan segments can be incorporated in the amortization table, from one up to whatever the capacity of the machine is. And there is no need for the loans to have the same terms. They can be of any term as long as B2 has a value at least as high as the value of J2 for the longest-lived loan.

THE PERIOD VARIABLES

This raises another complication. To avoid printing a series of amortization tables, one for each cash flow line as it goes through the loop, the PRINT statement has to be moved out of the loop so that the table is not printed until after all the calculations are completed. This requires some provision for remembering the calculated values for each period until it is time to print them. This can be done by using dimensioned variables to cumulate the total amount of each component for each period. The subscripts of the dimensioned variables will correspond with the time periods. The DIMENSION statement looks like this:

    100 DIM L (360),M(360),P(360)

Now the specified variables can have as many as 360 subscripts—
$L_1, L_2, L_3 \ldots L_{360}$, or in BASIC L(1), L(2), L(3) . . . L(360). Because the subscripts refer to periods, the dimensioned variables can accommodate
monthly loans of up to 30-year terms (360 ÷ 12 = 30), quarterly loans of up
to 90-year terms, and so on.

As each cash flow line is processed by the loop its interest Q1 for each
period will be added to the total interest L for that period. Thus, for quarterly
transactions, the first loan will have its interest for the first quarter added to
L(1), and the second loan will also have its interest for the first quarter added
to L(1), so that eventually L(1) will equal the total interest during quarter one
of all loans combined. The principal payment and the balance outstanding
are handled in the same manner.

260 LET L(T)=L(T)+Q1

. . .

330 LET M(T)=M(T)+S6

. . .

350 LET P(T)=P(T)+H1

The number of variables has increased because of the need to keep the
calculations separate from the intraperiod accumulations, and they can be
summarized as follows:

	Payment	Interest	Principal	Balance
One loan for period	Q1+S6	Q1	S6	H1
All loans for period	L(T)+M(T)	L(T)	M(T)	P(T)
All loans and periods	L1+M1	L1	M1	—

The use of separate variables for the payment has been discontinued. The
payment is always equal to the sum of the interest and principal components, and the summation can be done just as well by the PRINT statements.

460 PRINT USING 530,T,L(T)+M(T),L(T),M(T),P(T)

. . .

490 PRINT USING 540,L1+M1,L1,M1,P(T)

It would be possible to drop another variable by combining the two interest lines

    250 LET Q1=H1*A1
    260 LET L(T)=L(T)+Q1

into one. As the interest is calculated in only one expression and is used in only one expression, the same result could be achieved by

    255 LET L(T)=L(T)+(H1*A1)

The principal payment is not amenable to the same simplification because in the final version of LOAN2 the value of S6 will be determined by three separate expressions.

It is often helpful while conceptualizing and writing a program to keep the various components separate even though this may lead to a temporary proliferation of expressions. After the program has been completed and debugged it can be reviewed carefully for opportunities to combine expressions and eliminate unnecessary variables.

THE BALLOON PAYMENT

The balloon payment case must still be incorporated. At present, LOAN2 will amortize a loan down to a remaining balance I2. But the final principal payment, at time J2, is the same amount as the prior principal payments. A balloon payment, on the other hand, requires that the loan be amortized down to some balance at term end, but before the final principal payment, and then the final payment takes it down to zero.

The problem would be solved if there were a means of indicating whether I2 is the balance before or after the final principal payment. The direct way to do this would be to use a separate input variable for the balloon. But this would mean that one or the other of the two variables, remaining balance and balloon, would always be zero but the user would have to input both. A more subtle approach is to use the polarity of I2 to indicate its nature. If remaining balance is meant, then use a positive I2. If balloon is meant, then use a negative I2. The program can test to determine whether I2 is positive or negative and treat it accordingly. This approach can be used because I2 would never be negative ordinarily.

    160 IF I2<0 GOTO 190
    175 LET S6=(H1−I2)/(J2−J1)

```
180 GOTO 220
190 LET C4=1
200 LET I2=−I2
215 LET S6=(H1−I2)/(J2−J1−1)
. . .
270 IF T<J2 GOTO 310
280 IF C4<1 GOTO 310
290 LET S6=I2
300 LET C4=0
```

Line 160 tests I2 for negative polarity. If I2 is not negative then the principal payment S6 is calculated in the same manner as before in line 175. Line 180 then jumps the program around the negative polarity section.

If I2 is negative then the program jumps to line 190 where C4 is set to one. The function of variable C4 is to remember the nature of I2. If C4 = 1 then I2 is a balloon payment, and if C4 = 0 then I2 is not a balloon payment but a remaining balance. Once the nature of I2 is "remembered" its polarity is reversed back to positive in line 200. Now when the principal payment is calculated in line 215 it is based on one less than the number of payments because the final payment will be I2 itself.

The principal payment is made equal to I2 in line 290 within the loop. Since this should not occur until the final period line 270 causes the program to bypass the change for all periods before J2. Further, line 280 causes the bypass if C4 says that I2 is not a balloon payment. Thus the principal payment is made equal to I2 only if two conditions are met—the program is working on the last period of the loan, and it has been specifically told that there is a balloon payment. Line 300 "disremembers" the balloon payment by resetting C4 to zero in preparation for processing the next cash flow line.

An additional variable C4 had to be used after all, but the user of the program was saved from having to worry about it. Figure 1.4 is a run to illustrate changes in amortization.

SKIPPED PRINCIPAL PAYMENTS

So far it has been assumed that the interest payments and the principal payments are made at the same frequency, but this is not always the case. For example, both publicly traded issues and private placements often provide for annual sinking-fund payments while the interest payments are made semiannually. That is, every other payment is interest only. In the program this case can be handled by periodically bypassing the statement controlling the principal payment within the computation loop.

```
FIND ALL,"DATA"
550 DATA 12,4,3
560 DATA 4,10,1000,1000,0,4
570 DATA 4,10,1000,800,4,8
580 DATA 4,10,800,-500,8,12

READY


RUN

LOAN2          8:50    MONDAY FEB 28,1977
```

```
                LOAN AMORTIZATION SCHEDULE

    PER    PAYMENT    INTEREST  PRINCIPAL   BALANCE
    ---   ---------- ---------- ---------- ----------
     1       25.00      25.00       0.00    1000.00
     2       25.00      25.00       0.00    1000.00
     3       25.00      25.00       0.00    1000.00
     4       25.00      25.00       0.00    1000.00
     5       75.00      25.00      50.00     950.00
     6       73.75      23.75      50.00     900.00
     7       72.50      22.50      50.00     850.00
     8       71.25      21.25      50.00     800.00
     9      120.00      20.00     100.00     700.00
    10      117.50      17.50     100.00     600.00
    11      115.00      15.00     100.00     500.00
    12      512.50      12.50     500.00       0.00
    ---   ---------- ---------- ---------- ----------
    TOT    1257.50     257.50    1000.00       0.00

TIME 0 SECS.
```

Figure 1.4   Run of LOAN2. The input data are for a three-year $1000 10%
loan with quarterly payments. The loan is amortized 20% in the second year,
30% in the third year, and has a 50% balloon.

Another input variable is required. For computational purposes this variable should be the number of interest payments made for each principal
payment. For input purposes, however, it should be the number of principal
payments per year in order to conform to the manner in which the user
probably thinks of it and to be consistent with the form of the basic payment
frequency B1.

   *Number of principal payments per year/Number
   of interest payments per principal payment is* K1

This double definition can be accomplished by inputting the variable under the first definition and then having the program convert it to the second.

    120 READ K1,A1,H1,I2,J1,J2

    . . .

    150 LET K1=B1/K1

The expressions for calculating the amount of the principal payments must now be rewritten. Remember that they divided the amount to be amortized H1−I2 by the number of payments J2−J1. But J1 and J2 still define the loan term in terms of interest payment periods. So the number of interest payments must be divided by the number of interest payments per principal payment in order to obtain the number of principal payments over the term.

    170 LET S6=(H1−I2)/((J2−J1)/K1)

    . . .

    210 LET S6=(H1−I2)/(((J2−J1)/K1)−1)

Should the frequency of the interest and principal payments be the same then K1 will equal one and the calculated principal payment amounts will be the same as before.

The number of periods being bypassed must be counted so the program will know when to permit a principal payment. Call this counter X1 and increment it by one within the computation loop for each period. The principal payment statements will be bypassed as long as X1 is less than K1. When a principal payment is made X1 must be reset to zero in preparation for counting periods for the next principal payment. In addition X1 is set to zero before entering the loop to eliminate any carryover value from prior cash flow lines.

    220 LET X1=0
    230 FOR T=(J1+1) TO J2
    240 LET X1=X1+1

    . . .

    310 IF X1<K1 GOTO 350
    320 LET X1=0
    330 LET M(T)=M(T)+S6
    340 LET H1=H1−S6
    350 LET P(T)=P(T)+H1
    360 NEXT T

THE PRINT LOOP

Only one task remains—to print out the results of the calculations. This can be done by setting up another loop. Since both loops will not be used at the same time, the same counter T can be used for the second loop as for the first. This time, however, the limit of T will be the maximum number of periods B2 as the values for each and every period of the various loans or loan segments must be printed. The print loop will both cumulate the period values to obtain the totals and perform the printing for the periods.

```
430 FOR T=1 TO B2
440 LET L1=L1+L(T)
450 LET M1=M1+M(T)
460 PRINT USING 530,T,L(T)+M(T),L(T),M(T),P(T)
470 NEXT T
```

The headings and totals are printed in the same manner as for LOAN1.

This completes LOAN2. A sample run appears in Figure 1.5 to illustrate the case of semiannual interest payments combined with annual sinking-fund payments. Figure 1.6 is a listing of the program.

```
FIND ALL,"DATA"
550 DATA 6,2,1
560 DATA 1,10,100000,0,0,6

READY


RUN

LOAN2        8:55   MONDAY FEB 28,1977


                 LOAN AMORTIZATION SCHEDULE

   PER    PAYMENT    INTEREST  PRINCIPAL   BALANCE

     1    5000.00    5000.00       0.00  100000.00
     2   38333.33    5000.00   33333.33   66666.67
     3    3333.33    3333.33       0.00   66666.67
     4   36666.67    3333.33   33333.33   33333.33
     5    1666.67    1666.67       0.00   33333.33
     6   35000.00    1666.67   33333.33      -0.00
   ---  ---------- ---------- ----------  ----------
   TOT  120000.00   20000.00  100000.00      -0.00

TIME 0 SECS.
```

Figure 1.5   Run of LOAN2. The input data are for a three-year $100,000 10% loan with semiannual interest payments and annual principal repayments.

```
100 DIM L(360),M(360),P(360)
110 READ B2,B1,B
120 READ K1,A1,H1,I2,J1,J2
130 LET T2=T2+1
140 LET A1=A1/(B1*100)
150 LET K1=B1/K1
160 IF I2<0 GOTO 190
170 LET S6=(H1-I2)/((J2-J1)/K1)
180 GOTO 220
190 LET C4=1
200 LET I2=-I2
210 LET S6=(H1-I2)/(((J2-J1)/K1)-1)
220 LET X1=0
230 FOR T=(J1+1) TO J2
240 LET X1=X1+1
250 LET Q1=H1*A1
260 LET L(T)=L(T)+Q1
270 IF T<J2 GOTO 310
280 IF C4<1 GOTO 310
290 LET S6=I2
300 LET C4=0
310 IF X1<K1 GOTO 350
320 LET X1=0
330 LET M(T)=M(T)+S6
340 LET H1=H1-S6
350 LET P(T)=P(T)+H1
360 NEXT T
370 IF T2<B GOTO 120
380 PRINT
390 PRINT USING 500
400 PRINT
410 PRINT USING 510
420 PRINT USING 520
430 FOR T=1 TO B2
440 LET L1=L1+L(T)
450 LET M1=M1+M(T)
460 PRINT USING 530,T,L(T)+M(T),L(T),M(T),P(T)
470 NEXT T
480 PRINT USING 520
490 PRINT USING 540,L1+M1,L1,M1,P(T)
500 :          LOAN AMORTIZATION SCHEDULE
510 : PER    PAYMENT     INTEREST    PRINCIPAL     BALANCE
520 : ---    ---------   ---------   ---------   ---------
530 : ###    ######.##   ######.##   ######.##   ######.##
540 : TOT    ######.##   ######.##   ######.##   ######.##
550 DATA 12,4,3
560 DATA 4,10,1000,1000,0,4
570 DATA 4,10,1000,800,4,8
580 DATA 4,10,800,-500,8,12
590 END
```

Figure 1.6   List of LOAN2.

This program has considerable flexibility as it can produce an amortization table for a single loan or any number of loans combined, for loans of any term and payment frequency, for loans whose sinking-fund payments vary over the term, for loans with floating interest rates, and for those whose interest payments are more frequent than the principal payments.

The next chapter examines the mortgage-type loan.

2

The Mortgage-Type Loan

The mortgage-type loan is characterized by equal periodic payments of principal and interest, with the principal installments increasing over time. This means that the program for mortgage-type loans must know the payment amount before entering the computation loop, as opposed to knowing the principal installment for a sinking-fund loan program.

Since the sinking fund and mortgage-type loan programs will eventually be combined into a single compound program, their input variables should be as alike in name, definition, and form as practicable. Here are the input variables for a simple mortgage-type loan program, which shall be named LOAN3. The variables are identical to those for LOAN2 in the last chapter except for I2 and the temporary absence of K1.

Total number of periods is	B2
Periods per year is	B1
Number of cash flow lines is	B
Annual interest rate is	A1
Amount of loan is	H1
Amount of periodic payment is	I2
Beginning of term is	J1
End of term is	J2

PAYMENTS IN ARREARS

The DIM statement, the READ statements, the cash flow counter, and the interest rate conversion expression are also the same as for LOAN2.

```
105 DIM L(360), M(360), P(360)
110 READ B2,B1,B
```

```
125 READ A1,H1,I2,J1,J2
130 LET T2=T2+1
```

. . .

```
290 LET A1=A1/(B1*100)
```

With the payment amount I2 given the program can then enter the computation loop. Within the loop the periodic payment will be the known variable rather than the principal installment. The principal installment will be the unknown variable and will be calculated by subtracting the interest component from the payment.

```
550 FOR T=(J1+1) TO J2
```

. . .

```
600 LET Q1=H1*A1
```

. . .

```
635 LET L(T) = L(T)+Q1
```

. . .

```
725 LET S6=I2−Q1
735 LET M(T)=M(T)+S6
740 LET H1=H1−S6
755 LET P(T)=P(T)+H1
760 NEXT T
795 IF T2<B GOTO 125
```

Line 725 calculates the principal installment S6. All the other lines above are exactly the same as their counterparts in LOAN2. The PRINT statements, print loop, and IMAGE statements would also be the same.

Figure 2.1 presents a sample run of LOAN3 at this stage in its development. Note that in contrast to the sinking-fund loan the periodic payments are the same each period, while the principal component of the payment increases from period to period.

```
FIND ALL,"DATA"
980 DATA 6,1,1
990 DATA 2,10,100000,22960.74,0,6

READY


RUN

LOAN3        8:38   TUESDAY MAR. 01, 1977


          LOAN AMORTIZATION SCHEDULE

  PER    PAYMENT    INTEREST   PRINCIPAL   BALANCE
  ---   ---------  ---------  ----------  ---------
   0       0.00       0.00        0.00    100000.00
   1    22960.74   10000.00    12960.74    87039.26
   2    22960.74    8703.93    14256.81    72782.45
   3    22960.74    7278.24    15682.50    57099.95
   4    22960.74    5710.00    17250.74    39849.21
   5    22960.74    3984.92    18975.82    20873.39
   6    22960.74    2087.34    20873.40       -0.02
  ---   ---------  ---------  ----------  ---------
  TOT  137764.44   37764.42   100000.02      -0.02

TIME 1 SECS.
```

Figure 2.1   Run of LOAN3. Six-year $100,000 10% loan with annual payments of $22,960.74 in arrears.

ZERO SUBSCRIPTS

The above discussion assumed that the payments would be made in arrears, that is, at the end of each period. For the sample run in Figure 2.1, which had six annual payments, the payments occurred at times 1, 2, 3, 4, 5, 6.

But with a mortgage-type loan payments are sometimes due in advance. This means that each payment occurs at the beginning of its period rather than at the end. In this case the first payment of the sample loan would occur immediately upon takedown and the sixth payment would occur at the beginning of the sixth year rather than at the end. The total number of annual payments would still be six. Since the beginning of one period is, for practical purposes, the same as the end of the prior period, the six payments would occur at times 0, 1, 2, 3, 4, 5.

The program must therefore be capable of handling a time period of zero. For loops this presents no problem as the FOR statement can merely be rewritten so that the loop starts at zero rather than one. The print loop would appear as follows.

```
850 FOR T=0 TO B2
```

. . .

```
890 NEXT T
```

The period variables may present a problem, depending on which BASIC system is being used. The period variables are dimensioned, or subscripted, variables. Most versions of BASIC are sophisticated enough that they will accept zero subscripts. The system in which this book is written, IBM's CALL-OS, will not accept zero subscripts. So a subterfuge is required.

The subscripts for the period variables will have to be one greater than the periods to which they relate. Thus period zero will be specified by a subscript of one, period one by a subscript of two, and so on. This means that each statement containing a dimensioned variable must be rewritten. This is not really difficult. It merely requires replacing each (T) with (T+1) because the counter T is the variable that defines the periods and thus the subscripts.

```
630 LET L(T+1)=L(T+1)+Q1
```

. . .

```
730 LET M(T+1)=M(T+1)÷S6
```

. . .

```
750 LET P(T+1)=P(T+1)+H1
```

. . .

```
860 LET L1=L1+L(T+1)
870 LET M1=M1+M(T+1)
880 PRINT USING 960,T,L(T+1)+M(T+1),L(T+1),M(T+1),P(T+1)
```

. . .

```
910 PRINT USING 970,L1+M1,L1,M1,P(T+1)
```

The DIM statement must also be rewritten. If it is desired that the program handle 360 periods, then the period variables must be redimensioned to 361.

    105 DIM L(361),M(361),P(361)

Just remember that this cumbersome "plus one" device will not be required for the majority of BASIC systems which do accept zero subscripts.

PAYMENTS IN ADVANCE

Advance payments also require some additions to the mechanics of the program. For one thing, another input variable is required to specify whether the payments are in advance or arrears.

   Timing of payments is $K1$

A simple code can be used to specify the timing. If $K1 = 1$ then the payments are in advance. If $K1 = 2$ then payments are in arrears. This additional variable must be inserted into the READ statement.

    125 READ K1,A1,H1,I2,J1,J2

Since the first payment occurs immediately upon takedown, no time has passed, no interest has accrued, and the interest component of the first payment is zero. This means that the entire payment I2 is composed of principal repayment which is immediately deducted from the loan balance H1. The new balance is then added to the period balance P and the payment is added to the period principal component M. The period is the beginning of the term J1 but the subscript must be specified as $J1 + 1$ because of the zero subscript problem. This is all done before entering the computation loop.

    480 IF K1>1 GOTO 530
    495 LET H1=H1−I2
    500 LET P(J1+1)=P(J1+1)+H1
    515 LET M(J1+1)=M(J1+1)+I2
    520 GOTO 550

Line 480 causes the program to bypass the application of the payment to the balance if the payment is in arrears.

The print loop will now start its printing at period zero and the above statements will ensure that the payment, principal installment, and loan balance will all be properly recorded for the advance payment case. The interest component will be zero. The arrears payment case, however, will cause the entire row to be printed with zeros, when actually there is an initial loan balance. A statement must be inserted to add the initial balance to the period balance variable P at time zero. This will not be necessary when the loan or loan segment begins at some time in the future so a bypass statement is also included.

```
530 IF J1>0 GOTO 550
540 LET P(1)=P(1)+H1
```

The advance payment case not only means that there is a payment at the very beginning of the term J1, but also that there is not a payment at the very end of the term J2. Within the computation loop there must be a statement that sets the payment I2 to zero at the end of the last period.

```
650 IF K1>1 GOTO 690
660 IF T<J2 GOTO 715
675 LET I2=0
```

The two IF statements ensure that the payment will be set to zero only if the payment is an advance payment and only if the loop is in the last period. Three lines are required because of the constraints of the CALL-OS system. Other verisons of BASIC may permit a series of tests to be conducted within a single statement so that only one line would be required to accomplish the same result.

```
655 IF K1=1 THEN IF T=J2 THEN I2=0
```

Figure 2.2 presents a sample run of the advance payments case. Comparing it with Figure 2.1 reveals that the effect of advance payments is to shift one principal installment from the end of the term to the beginning. This lowers the average balance over the term and reduces the total interest to be paid. This means that the amount of the periodic payment necessary to amortize the loan is less when payments are in advance than when payments are in arrears, even though the stated loan amount and interest rate are the same.

On the other hand, the borrowing firm receives less in net proceeds,

```
FIND ALL, "DATA"
980 DATA 6,1,1
990 DATA 1,10,100000,20873.40,0,6
```

READY

RUN

LOAN3   8:50   TUESDAY MAR. 01, 1977

LOAN AMORTIZATION SCHEDULE

PER	PAYMENT	INTEREST	PRINCIPAL	BALANCE
0	20873.40	0.00	20873.40	79126.60
1	20873.40	7912.66	12960.74	66165.86
2	20873.40	6616.59	14256.81	51909.05
3	20873.40	5190.90	15682.50	36226.55
4	20873.40	3622.66	17250.74	18975.81
5	20873.40	1897.58	18975.82	-0.01
6	0.00	-0.00	0.00	-0.02
---	---	---	---	---
TOT	125240.40	25240.38	100000.02	-0.02

TIME 1 SECS.

Figure 2.2   Run of LOAN3. Same as Figure 2.1 except payments are $20,873.40 in advance.

$79,126.60 instead of $100,000, and must borrow a larger amount, $126,379.75, in order to receive the desired net amount of $100,000.

Under the approach developed above, the parameters describing the beginning of the term J1 and the end of the term J2 are the same regardless of whether the payments are in advance or arrears. It is K1 that specifies the relative timing of the payments.

An alternative approach would be to use J1 and J2 to indicate payment timing as well as defining the term. Thus for a six-year loan with annual payments, J1 and J2 would be one and six, respectively, if payments were in arrears and zero and five if payments were in advance. Then K1 would not be necessary.

This approach has two disadvantages. First, the difference between J1 and J2 would no longer equal the number of payments. However, the difference plus one would equal the number of payments and the programmer would merely have to keep this in mind while writing the program. But the user would be deprived of a simple way to check the correctness of the term parameters.

Second, the user would have to do some mental juggling with the term parameters. Although it would be relatively simple to adjust from one and six to zero and five for J1 and J2, some confusion could arise with a more complex loan. For example, if the loan term were 15 years and payments were quarterly, then there would be 60 periods. If the loan were divided into three segments of four, six, and five years because of changes in the interest or amortization rate, then the term specifications are considerably more complex without K1 than with it.

| | With K1 | | Without K1 | | | |
| | Arrears or Advance | | Arrears | | Advance | |
	J1	J2	J1	J2	J1	J2
1st Segment	0	16	1	16	0	15
2nd Segment	16	40	17	40	16	39
3rd Segment	40	60	41	60	40	59

Programmers will often be faced with alternative approaches to performing a given function. Their choices, and even their perceptions of the alternatives, will be influenced by their experiences and temperaments. They should, however, strive to adopt that approach which is easiest for the user of the program.

ROUNDING

Figure 2.1 contains several apparent arithmetical errors. If the columns are added manually, it will be found that the total of the interest column is 37,764.43 and not the printed total of 37,764.42. Similarly, the manual total of the principal column is 100,000.01 rather than the printed total of 100,000.02. The machine has not made a mistake. It has merely done what it was told. The error is a rounding error, caused by the IMAGE statements specifying that the numbers be rounded to the nearest 1/100 for printing while the machine calculates and remembers the numbers to 15 significant digits. The machine does not subtract the six-digit printed interest figure for the period from the payment, but the full 15-digit calculated value. In the real world the firm will be recording interest, and all other amounts, rounded to the nearest cent, that is, to the nearest 1/100 of a dollar. The solution to the problem is to ensure that the machine uses the rounded amount in its calculations. This rounding must be done after the period's interest is calculated but before it is used anywhere.

```
600 LET Q1=H1*A1
610 LET Q1=INT (100*(Q1+.005))/100
```

The INTEGER statement causes the machine to truncate the value of the specified variable to its integer. That is, 2.054 would be truncated to 2. Since the value is desired to the 1/100, the variable must be multiplied by 100, then the integer taken, and then divided by 100 to move the decimal point back into position. This results in 2.054 becoming 205.4, being truncated to 205, and then becoming 2.05.

This procedure would also result in 2.058 being converted to 2.05. In order to obtain rounding rather than truncation, the variable must be increased by ½ the amount of required precision. Thus for precision to the nearest .01 the value of Q1 must be increased by .005. Then the 2.058 example would become 2.063, would be divided by 100 to become 206.3, would be truncated to 206, and then would be divided by 100 to become 2.06, the desired rounded value.

Variations of the expression in line 610 can be used to obtain rounding to any desired decimal place. To round to the nearest 1/10 use INT(10 * (Q1 + .05))/10, and to the nearest 1/1000 use INT(1000 * (Q1 + .0005))/1000.

There is no need to round the principal component or the balance as these are derived from the payment less the interest component, and the payment was entered already rounded to the nearest cent.

Figure 2.3 presents a run of the same loan as in Figure 2.1 but with the rounding statement added to the program. The result is that the interest for the fourth period is now 5709.99 instead of 5710.00 and the principal for that period is now 17,250.75 instead of 17,250.74. The columns now add to the correct totals.

This rounding refinement is also applicable to the sinking-fund loan program developed in Chapter 1.

ADJUSTING THE FINAL PAYMENT

An examination of Figure 2.3 reveals that the loan is being overamortized by 2 cents. The given payments result in $100,000.02 of principal being repaid rather than exactly $100,000.00. The smallest amount by which the periodic payments can be reduced is 1 cent. But since there are six payments, this would result in 6 cents less of total payments and the loan would then be

```
FIND ALL,"DATA"
980 DATA 6,1,1
990 DATA 2,10,100000,22960.74,0,6

READY


RUN

LOAN3          8:42   WEDNESDAY, MAR. 2, 1977



                    LOAN AMORTIZATION SCHEDULE

    PER    PAYMENT    INTEREST   PRINCIPAL    BALANCE
    ---   --------   --------    --------    --------
     0       0.00       0.00        0.00    100000.00
     1    22960.74   10000.00    12960.74     87039.26
     2    22960.74    8703.93    14256.81     72782.45
     3    22960.74    7278.24    15682.50     57099.95
     4    22960.74    5709.99    17250.75     39849.20
     5    22960.74    3984.92    18975.82     20873.38
     6    22960.74    2087.34    20873.40        -0.02
    ---   --------   --------    --------    --------
    TOT  137764.44   37764.42   100000.02        -0.02

TIME 1 SECS.
```

Figure 2.3   Run of LOAN3. Same as Figure 2.1 except that interest payments are rounded to nearest cent.

underamortized by 4 cents. This illustrates the fact that it is seldom possible to find a payment amount that will exactly amortize a loan when the payments of necessity can only be specified to the nearest cent.

In lieu of revamping the currency system, the financial community has adopted the convention of adjusting the final loan payment to that amount which is just sufficient to provide interest for the period plus repayment of the exact amount of the remaining loan balance. This means that the final payment will usually be a few cents more or less than the prior periodic payments.

In the program this can be done by setting the last payment I2 equal to the interest Q1 plus the balance H1. The last payment will occur at time J2 for the arrears payment case and at time J2 − 1 for the advance payment case.

```
640 IF T<J2−1 GOTO 720
650 IF K1>1 GOTO 690
665 IF T<J2 GOTO 715
```

675 LET I2=0
680 GOTO 720
690 IF T<J2 GOTO 720
715 LET I2=Q1+H1

Lines 650, 665, and 675 were developed earlier and are repeated here because they interlock with the present operation.

Figure 2.4 presents a run of the same loan as in Figures 2.1 and 2.3. The final payment is now 2 cents less than the prior payments and the loan is amortized exactly.

CALCULATING PAYMENTS

LOAN3 represents the basic structure for handling mortgage-type loans. But it cannot handle cases in which the payment amount is unknown, nor can it handle remaining balances. To do these LOAN3 will be expanded further.

The remaining balance and the payment amount are mutually exclusive as given variables. If the payment is known then the remaining balance is the dependent variable and will be the residual balance, if any, after the given payments are applied to interest and principal over the term. Conversely, if the remaining balance is known, then the payment is the dependent variable and will be that amount necessary to amortize the beginning balance down to the given ending balance.

This means that the same input variable can be used for both with the polarity of the variable indicating its nature. This is the approach that was used for the remaining balance/balloon variable in LOAN2.

Remaining balance (positive polarity)/
Payment amount (negative polarity) is I2

The program will test the polarity of I2 and branch accordingly. If the polarity is negative then it will be reversed to positive and renamed.

Payment amount is U3

The payment amount will be U3 for calculation purposes and I2 for input purposes. The statements are

360 IF I2<0 GOTO 470

. . .

470 LET U3=−I2

```
FIND ALL,"DATA"
980 DATA 6,1,1
990 DATA 2,10,100000,22960.74,0,6

READY


RUN

LOAN3        8:44   WEDNESDAY, MAR. 2, 1977


            LOAN AMORTIZATION SCHEDULE

PER    PAYMENT    INTEREST   PRINCIPAL   BALANCE
---    --------   --------   ---------   -------
 0        0.00       0.00        0.00   100000.00
 1     22960.74   10000.00    12960.74    87039.26
 2     22960.74    8703.93    14256.81    72782.45
 3     22960.74    7278.24    15682.50    57099.95
 4     22960.74    5709.99    17250.75    39849.20
 5     22960.74    3984.92    18975.82    20873.38
 6     22960.72    2087.34    20873.38        0.00
---    --------   --------   ---------   -------
TOT   137764.42   37764.42   100000.00        0.00

TIME 1 SECS.
```

Figure 2.4   Run of LOAN3. Same as Figure 2.3 except that the last payment is adjusted for exact amortization of the remaining balance.

If I2 is zero or greater than zero then the program will have to calculate the payment amount. The payment will have two components, one for the portion of the loan that will be amortized over the term and one for the nonamortizing portion, which is the remaining balance.

The amortizing portion of the payment is that periodic amount which, when discounted at the interest rate A1, equals the amount of the loan to be amortized. It is determined by dividing the amortizing portion H1−I2 of the loan by the appropriate payment factor.

Payment factor is U1

The factor is a present value factor and is a function not only of the interest rate A1 but also of the number of periods J2−J1. For arrears payments the equation is

$$U1 = \frac{1 - \dfrac{1}{(1 + A1) \uparrow (J2 - J1)}}{A1}$$

If the payments are in advance then the first payment is taken at full value and has a factor of one and the number of remaining payments is one less than the difference between J2 and J1.

$$U1 = 1 + \frac{1 - \dfrac{1}{(1 + A1) \uparrow (J2 - J1 - 1)}}{A1}$$

These equations are from Figure 7.3 and are developed in Chapter 7.

The nonamortizing portion of the loan will not require any principal repayments, but will require interest. The second component of the loan payment thus will be interest-only payments on the constant amount of the remaining balance. For payments in arrears the payment amount will be calculated as the remaining balance I2 times the interest rate A1. For payments in advance the payment amount will be the remaining balance times the interest rate divided by one plus the interest rate.

Nonamortizing portion of payment is U2

The total loan payment U3 will be the sum of the amortizing payment (H1 − I2) / U1 and the interest-only payment U2.

```
375 IF K1>1 GOTO 415
385 LET U1=1+((1−(1/(1+A1)↑(J2−J1−1)))/A1)
390 LET U2=I2*A1/(1+A1)
400 GOTO 430
415 LET U1=(1−(1/(1+A1)↑(J2−J1)))/A1
420 LET U2=I2*A1
430 LET U3=((H1−I2)/U1)+U2
440 LET U3=INT(100*(U3+.005))/100
450 PRINT USING 920,U3
460 GOTO 480
```

. . .

```
920 : PAYMENT IS $######.##
```

40　The Mortgage-Type Loan

Since the machine calculates the payment to 15 significant digits (the exact number will vary depending on the BASIC system used), the payment is rounded to the nearest cent in line 440. The calculated payment is then printed by line 450 in the format specified by line 920.

Figure 2.5 presents the same loan as Figure 2.4 but with the payments calculated by the program.

SUPPRESSION OF FINAL PAYMENT ADJUSTMENT

The program currently has a provision for adjusting the final payment to that amount necessary to ensure that the loan is amortized exactly to zero. Thus it is impossible to have a remaining balance. But in the case of a compound

```
FIND ALL."DATA"
980 DATA 6,1,1
990 DATA 2,10,100000,0,0,6

READY

RUN

LOAN3        8:39   THURSDAY, MAR. 3, 1977

  PAYMENT IS $ 22960.74
              LOAN AMORTIZATION SCHEDULE

   PER    PAYMENT    INTEREST   PRINCIPAL   BALANCE
   ---   ---------   ---------  ---------  ---------
    0        0.00       0.00        0.00  100000.00
    1    22960.74   10000.00    12960.74   87039.26
    2    22960.74    8703.93    14256.81   72782.45
    3    22960.74    7278.24    15682.50   57099.95
    4    22960.74    5709.99    17250.75   39849.20
    5    22960.74    3984.92    18975.82   20873.38
    6    22960.72    2087.34    20873.38       0.00
   ---   ---------   ---------  ---------  ---------
  TOT  137764.42   37764.42   100000.00       0.00

  TIME 1 SECS.
```

Figure 2.5　Run of LOAN3. Same as Figure 2.4 except that the payment amount is calculated by the program instead of being entered as input.

loan broken into several segments, the individual segments, except for the last one, must have a remaining balance. So the final payment adjustment must be suppressed when a remaining balance is desired.

A test must be devised to determine whether a residual balance is desired or is to be eliminated. A simple IF I2> 0 inserted shortly after the READ statement would suffice if the loan is defined by balances. But this would not work if it is defined by payments.

The purpose of the final payment adjustment is to compensate for the inability to vary the payment in amounts of less than 1 cent. The maximum residual balance arising from this cause would be 1 cent times the number of payments, assuming the given payment was calculated correctly. It follows then that a greater residual balance than this indicates a desired remaining balance and the adjustment statement should be bypassed.

```
705 IF (H1−U3+Q1)> (J2−J1)/100 GOTO 720
710 LET U3=Q1+H1
```

Since the balance H1 is being tested before the final principal installment U3 − Q1 is made, the principal payment must be hypothetically deducted from the balance for the purpose of the test. If the result is greater than the number of payments J2 − J1 divided by 100 (which is the same as multiplying by .01) then the adjustment statement in line 710 will be bypassed and the remaining balance will not be eliminated.

UNKNOWN BALANCES

For a sinking-fund loan it is relatively simple to determine the beginning and ending balances for each segment of a compound loan and include them as input data. This is because the loan is defined in terms of either principal repayments or loan balances and the loan segments are amortized over their terms on a straight-line basis.

The mortgage-type loan, however, is defined in terms of level payments, of which the principal component is but part, and a changing part at that. If this type of loan is compound its terms may specify payments of, say, $10,000 per year for the first three years, $15,000 per year for the next three years, and $20,000 per year for the last four years. The initial amount of the loan will be known, as will be the balance at the end of the term. But the unamortized balances at the segment breakpoints will not be known, nor can they be determined by a simple examination of the payment amounts. Indeed, the need to know the balance at various times is often the very reason for running the amortization table. It is impracticable then for the analyst to use balances to define the loan segments for a mortgage-type loan. The facility to do so will be retained in the program, but a more feasible approach must be included as well.

With the initial loan amount and the payment known, the program will enter the computation loop where it will calculate the period's interest, subtract it from the payment, and apply the remainder of the payment to the loan balance. After the specified number of periods have been processed, the loan balance will either be zero for a simple loan or will have some residual value for any but the last segment of a compound loan. This residual value must be remembered and then used as the beginning balance of the next segment when its cash flow line is inputted.

Residual loan balance is H2

The cash flow line for the next segment must be coded so that the program will know that there is a residual balance to be picked up. Since the beginning balance H1 of the next segment is unknown to the analyst, this variable is the logical one to use for the coding. If the cash flow line is for a segment, other than the first segment, of a compound loan, then H1 will be entered as zero.

```
125 READ K1,A1,H1,I2,J1,J2

. . .

320 IF H1<>0 GOTO 360
330 LET H1=H2

. . .

550 FOR T=(J1+1) TO J2

. . .

760 NEXT T
770 LET H2=H1

. . .

795 IF T2<B GOTO 125
```

The first loan segment will have a known beginning balance. Its H1 will thus be greater than zero and line 320 will cause the program to bypass line 330 to go on to the computation loop. After leaving the loop, line 770 will set H2 to the final balance H1 of the segment and the program will then input the next cash flow line. Being the next segment of a compound loan, this cash flow line will have an H1 of zero. So line 330 will set H1 equal to H2, thus assigning a value to the beginning balance of the new segment.

This procedure has now, for the first time, placed a constraint upon the sequence in which cash flow lines must be inputted and processed. The loan segments of a compound loan must be entered in correct chronological order with no other DATA lines intervening. Simple loans can continue to be entered in any order, and a compound loan as an entity can be in any position relative to simple loans and other compound loans. But within a compound loan the cash flow lines representing its segments must be in sequence as indicated by their term periods J1 and J2.

Two segments of a compound loan are run and shown as though they were separate loans in Figures 2.6 and 2.7. Payments are in advance.

An examination of Figure 2.6 reveals an interesting characteristic of a loan that requires payments in advance and has a remaining balance. The payments actually overamortize the loan at one point. That is, the final payment reduces the balance below the desired remaining balance of $50,000. But this occurs one period before the end of the term. During the last period the balance continues to accrue interest. But there is no payment at the end of the term to pay this accrued interest, so it is added to the loan balance. This accrued but unpaid interest is the exact amount necessary to bring the balance up to the desired end-of-term amount.

Figure 2.6 shows that the balance of the first segment at the end of the third year is $50,000. The second segment, shown in Figure 2.7, will pick up that balance as its balance for the beginning of the fourth year and, since the payments are in advance, will immediately apply its first payment to it for a resulting balance of $31,722.05. But the end of the third year is the same point in time as the beginning of the fourth year and both balances will be added to P(3). As a result the program will print their sum of $81,722.05 as the balance at that time. This double-counting error can be eliminated by deducting the first segment's remaining balance H2 from P at the time that the second segment picks it up. This will only be necessary in the case of advance payments so the statement is bypassed in the event that payments are in arrears.

```
340 IF K1>1 GOTO 360
350 LET P(J1+1)=P(J1+1)−H2
```

Figure 2.8 combines the two segments into one loan.

```
FIND ALL,"DATA"
980 DATA 6,1,1
990 DATA 1,10,100000,50000,0,3

READY


RUN

LOAN3          8:44   FRIDAY MAR.4,1977

   PAYMENT IS $ 22823.40
```

LOAN AMORTIZATION SCHEDULE

PER	PAYMENT	INTEREST	PRINCIPAL	BALANCE
0	22823.40	0.00	22823.40	77176.60
1	22823.40	7717.66	15105.74	62070.86
2	22823.40	6207.09	16616.31	45454.55
3	0.00	4545.45	-4545.45	50000.00
4	0.00	0.00	0.00	0.00
5	0.00	0.00	0.00	0.00
6	0.00	0.00	0.00	0.00
TOT	68470.20	18470.20	50000.00	0.00

```
TIME 1 SECS.
```

Figure 2.6   Run of LOAN3. First segment of a compound loan. The annual in advance payments are calculated to leave a remaining balance of $50,000.

A lender, in structuring a compound loan, will know the amounts to be amortized over the terms of the several segments and will want to calculate the appropriate payments. The borrower, on the other hand, will have been presented with the payment terms and will wish to determine the balances. LOAN3 can satisfy both needs with equal facility.

FLOATING INTEREST RATE
WITH FLOATING AMORTIZATION

The program will adequately handle a compound loan when the loan segments are discrete units. This is the case when the loan is prestructured; that is, the breakpoints and the payments or balances are predetermined and written into the terms of the loan agreement. An example would be when the

```
FIND ALL,"DATA"
980 DATA 6,1,1
990 DATA 1,10,50000,0,3,6
```

READY

RUN

LOAN3   8:47   FRIDAY MAR.4,1977

PAYMENT IS $ 18277.95

LOAN AMORTIZATION SCHEDULE

PER	PAYMENT	INTEREST	PRINCIPAL	BALANCE
0	0.00	0.00	0.00	0.00
1	0.00	0.00	0.00	0.00
2	0.00	0.00	0.00	0.00
3	18277.95	0.00	18277.95	31722.05
4	18277.95	3172.20	15105.75	16616.30
5	18277.93	1661.63	16616.30	0.00
6	0.00	0.00	0.00	0.00
TOT	54833.83	4833.83	50000.00	0.00

TIME 1 SECS.

Figure 2.7   Run of LOAN3. Second segment of a compound loan.

payments are increased or decreased ("stepped payments") over the term to meet the cash flow requirements of the borrower.

When the loan has a floating interest rate, however, the evaluation of the impact of changing interest rates is a bit more complex. In such a case the loan agreement must specify exactly how the payments are to be calculated when the interest rate changes and yet without knowing when the interest rate will change again. This means that the payment calculation cannot be based on the term of the loan segment, which is only a hypothetical term that is assumed for forecasting purposes. Instead it must be based on the full remaining term of the loan.

There are two methods of accomplishing this. The first is to determine the level payment required over the term remaining to amortize the remaining balance at the new interest rate. When the interest rate is assumed to change again, a new level payment is calculated to amortize the then lower

```
FIND ALL,"DATA"
980 DATA 6,1,2
990 DATA 1,10,100000,50000,0,3
1000 DATA 1,10,0,0,3,6

READY


RUN

LOAN3          8:50    FRIDAY MAR.4,1977

PAYMENT IS $ 22823.40
PAYMENT IS $ 18277.95
```

	LOAN AMORTIZATION SCHEDULE			
PER	PAYMENT	INTEREST	PRINCIPAL	BALANCE
---	---------	---------	---------	---------
0	22823.40	0.00	22823.40	77176.60
1	22823.40	7717.66	15105.74	62070.86
2	22823.40	6207.09	16616.31	45454.55
3	18277.95	4545.45	13732.50	31722.05
4	18277.95	3172.20	15105.75	16616.30
5	18277.93	1661.63	16616.30	0.00
6	0.00	0.00	0.00	0.00
---	---------	---------	---------	---------
TOT	123304.03	23304.03	100000.00	0.00

```
TIME 1 SECS.
```

Figure 2.8   Run of LOAN3. Combination of the two loan segments of Figures 2.6 and 2.7.

balance over the then shorter remaining term at the subsequent interest rate. The result is a series of loan payments that step up or down between segments but each is calculated as though there would be no subsequent steps. Another result is that the amortization rate will change with each change in the interest rate. The loan will shift from one amortization curve to another.

Figure 2.9 presents the amortization schedule for a three-year loan with quarterly payments in which the interest rate remains constant over the term. This will be the base case for comparison purposes.

Figure 2.10 presents the same loan but with the interest rate changing each year. The payments for the first year are calculated to amortize the beginning balance of $100,000 over the full 12 quarters of the loan term at 10% interest. The payments for the second year are calculated to amortize the $69,899.61 balance outstanding at the beginning of the year at 12% interest over the remaining eight quarters of the loan term, and not over the

```
FIND ALL, "DATA"
980 DATA 12,4,1
990 DATA 2,10,100000,0,0,12,0

READY

RUN

LOAN3          8:44   THURSDAY, MAR. 3, 1977

   PAYMENT IS $  9748.71

              LOAN AMORTIZATION SCHEDULE

   PER    PAYMENT     INTEREST   PRINCIPAL    BALANCE
   ---   ---------   ---------   ---------   ---------
    0       0.00        0.00        0.00    100000.00
    1     9748.71     2500.00     7248.71    92751.29
    2     9748.71     2318.78     7429.93    85321.36
    3     9748.71     2133.03     7615.68    77705.68
    4     9748.71     1942.64     7806.07    69899.61
    5     9748.71     1747.49     8001.22    61898.39
    6     9748.71     1547.46     8201.25    53697.14
    7     9748.71     1342.43     8406.28    45290.86
    8     9748.71     1132.27     8616.44    36674.42
    9     9748.71      916.86     8831.85    27842.57
   10     9748.71      696.06     9052.65    18789.92
   11     9748.71      469.75     9278.96     9510.96
   12     9748.73      237.77     9510.96        0.00
   ---   ---------   ---------   ---------   ---------
  TOT   116984.54    16984.54   100000.00        0.00

  TIME 1 SECS.
```

Figure 2.9   Run of LOAN3. Base case loan with constant 10% interest rate over the three-year term.

four quarters of the segment. In other words, the payment is calculated as though the interest rate were not going to change again.

Note in the principal column that when the interest rate changes the principal repayments change from what they were in the base case loan. The amortization rate changes every time the interest rate changes. And, further, a return to the original interest rate will not result in a return to the original amortization curve because the balance will have changed from what it otherwise would have been at the same point in time. This means that for this type of floating-interest-rate loan the actual principal repayment schedule cannot be predetermined and will not even be known until after

```
FIND ALL,"DATA"
980 DATA 12,4,3
990 DATA 2,10,100000,0,0,4,12
1000 DATA 2,12,0,0,4,8,12
1010 DATA 2,14,0,0,8,12,12

READY


RUN

LOAN3        8:46    THURSDAY, MAR. 3, 1977

    PAYMENT IS $  9748.71
    PAYMENT IS $  9957.65
    PAYMENT IS $ 10076.98
```

LOAN AMORTIZATION SCHEDULE

PER	PAYMENT	INTEREST	PRINCIPAL	BALANCE
0	0.00	0.00	0.00	100000.00
1	9748.71	2500.00	7248.71	92751.29
2	9748.71	2318.78	7429.93	85321.36
3	9748.71	2133.03	7615.68	77705.68
4	9748.71	1942.64	7806.07	69899.61
5	9957.65	2096.99	7860.66	62038.95
6	9957.65	1861.17	8096.48	53942.47
7	9957.65	1618.27	8339.38	45603.09
8	9957.65	1368.09	8589.56	37013.53
9	10076.98	1295.47	8781.51	28232.02
10	10076.98	988.12	9088.86	19143.16
11	10076.98	670.01	9406.97	9736.19
12	10076.96	340.77	9736.19	0.00

TOT	119133.34	19133.34	100000.00	0.00

```
TIME 1 SECS.
```

Figure 2.10   Run of LOAN3. Floating interest, floating amortization case. The interest rate is 10% the first year, 12% the second, and 14% the last year.

the loan has been completely repaid. Any run of a before-the-fact amortization schedule will be but one of an infinite number of possible cases.

To handle this situation the program must base the payment calculations on the total number of remaining loan payments and not on the number of payments in a segment of the loan. This requires that the final period of the loan be defined in the segment's cash flow line.

Period at the end of which the loan ends is J3

Variable J3 will be inputted in addition to the variables J1 and J2, which define the beginning and end of the segment. The value of J3 will be used instead of J2 in the payment calculation expressions.

```
120 READ K1,A1,H1,I2,J1,J2,J3
```

. . .

```
300 IF J3>J2 GOTO 320
310 LET J3=J2
```

. . .

```
370 IF K1>1 GOTO 410
380 LET U1=1+ ((1−(1/(1+A1)↑(J3−J1−1)))/A1)
```

. . .

```
410 LET U1=(1−(1/(1+A1)↑(J3−J1)))/A1
```

Line 380 now calculates the advance payment factor on the basis of remaining loan payments J3 − J1 and line 410 does the same for arrears payments. The computation loop will still have its limit defined by the end of the segment's term J2. In the case of a simple nonsegmented loan, or the final segment of a compound loan, the analyst will enter J2 and J3 with the same value. Lines 300 and 310 ensure that J3 will not inadvertently be less than J2 as the loan cannot mature before the end of its segment. This also permits the user to enter J3 as zero when it does not exceed J2, which is a little faster and easier than entering a two- or three-digit number. Zero can very often be used in such manner as a code for "not applicable" when the variable would otherwise never have a zero value.

The above statements are the ones that produced the schedule in Figure 2.10

The addition of J3 now enables a more direct method of suppressing the final payment adjustment. Since J3 will exceed J2 for the loan segments for which a remaining balance is desired it is no longer necessary to compare the residual balance with the number of payments times 1 cent. The statement that bypasses the final payment adjustment can be based on a comparison between J3 and J2.

```
700 IF J3>J2 GOTO 720
710 LET U3=Q1+H1
```

FLOATING INTEREST RATE WITH FIXED AMORTIZATION

The second method of calculating the payments for a floating-interest-rate loan is to keep the principal installments to a fixed schedule and allow only the interest payments to vary. The initial interest rate of the loan will determine the principal installments throughout the term.

Figure 2.11 presents a run of the fixed-amortization-rate case. The principal installments are the same as those of the base case loan in Figure 2.9 for all periods. The interest payments vary with the interest rate. Given that the amortization rate is fixed if the interest rate changes the payments will no longer be level. They will change from period to period.

```
FIND ALL,"DATA"
980 DATA 12,4,1
990 DATA 2,-10,100000,0,0,4,12
1000 DATA 4,12,4,14,0

READY


RUN

LOAN3        8:49   THURSDAY, MAR. 3, 1977

PAYMENT IS $  9748.71

          LOAN AMORTIZATION SCHEDULE

   PER    PAYMENT    INTEREST   PRINCIPAL   BALANCE
   ---    --------   --------   ---------   --------
    0       0.00       0.00       0.00    100000.00
    1     9748.71    2500.00    7248.71    92751.29
    2     9748.71    2318.78    7429.93    85321.36
    3     9748.71    2133.03    7615.68    77705.68
    4     9748.71    1942.64    7806.07    69899.61
    5    10098.21    2096.99    8001.22    61898.39
    6    10058.20    1856.95    8201.25    53697.14
    7    10017.19    1610.91    8406.28    45290.86
    8     9975.17    1358.73    8616.44    36674.42
    9    10115.45    1283.60    8831.85    27842.57
   10    10027.14     974.49    9052.65    18789.92
   11     9936.61     657.65    9278.96     9510.96
   12     9843.84     332.88    9510.96        0.00
   ---   --------   --------   ---------   --------
   TOT  119066.65   19066.65  100000.00        0.00

TIME 1 SECS.
```

Figure 2.11 Run of LOAN3. Floating interest, fixed amortization case. The interest rates are the same as Figure 2.10 and the principal installments are the same as Figure 2.9.

An approach to handling this case which would maintain the practice of breaking the loan into segments would be to calculate all the principal installments for the full loan term with the first segment. This would require extending the computation loop for the first segment only to the loan term end J3. The interest calculations would be suppressed for periods after the segment end J2. The subsequent segments would then provide the interest components for the time between J2 and J3 with the principal calculations being suppressed.

There is another approach that reduces the number of input data required. This approach treats the loan as a whole without breaking it into segments and only requires sufficient additional data to specify the interest rates and the periods to which they apply.

> *Secondary interest rate is* A2
> *Number of periods for secondary interest rate is* B3

There must be a means of indicating to the program that this is a floating-interest-rate case. A convenient way to do this is to use the polarity of the interest rate A1. If A1 is positive then the loan has a constant interest rate. If A1 is negative then the interest rate will vary. In the latter case C4 will be used to remember the floating case and A1 will be reversed to positive.

```
140 IF A1>=0 GOTO 290
150 LET C4=1
160 LET A1=-A1/(B1*100)
```

This approach requires the use of a dimensioned variable to remember the interest rate for each period of the loan term.

> *Interest rate for period is* N

This variable must be added to the DIMENSION statement.

```
100 DIM L(361),M(361),N(361),P(361)
```

If the loan is floating the program will enter a short loop where the value of the initial interest rate A1 will be assigned to N for each period through J2.

```
170 FOR T=0 TO J2
180 LET N(T+1)=A1
190 NEXT T
200 LET J2=J3
```

Variable J2 is set equal to J3 so that the limit of the computation loop will be the end of the loan term and not the end of the segment.

The program will then input the number of periods B3 to which the second interest rate applies and the value of the second interest rate A2. A second short loop assigns the value of the second interest rate to the appropriate periods of N. This second loop uses the same period counter T as the first loop and begins with a value of T that is one greater than the final value of T in the first loop.

```
210 READ B3
220 IF B3=0 GOTO 320
230 READ A2
240 LET A2=A2/(B1*100)
250 FOR T=T+1 TO T+B3
260 LET N(T+1)=A2
270 NEXT T
280 GOTO 210
```

After leaving the loop the program returns to line 210 to input the number of periods for the next interest rate. This way any number of interest rates can be specified over the loan term and the program will assign them to the appropriate periods in order. It will continue to input succeeding interest rates until it encounters a number of periods B3 value that equals zero. This trailing code will cause the program to cease inputting and to proceed to the next stage in the calculations.

This type of input loop is useful whenever an input variable may change in a value several times over the term of the transaction and the number of changes is also variable. Without it the analyst would have the chore of typing in each period's value individually.

After leaving the input loops the program will continue on to the computation loop as usual, calculating the payment or picking up a beginning balance along the way if required.

Because J2 has been set equal to J3 the computation loop will extend through the end of the loan term.

Within the loop the program not only has to calculate the interest Q1 based on the initial interest rate A1, but also a new interest component based on the interest rate specified by N.

Interest for varying interest rate case is Q2

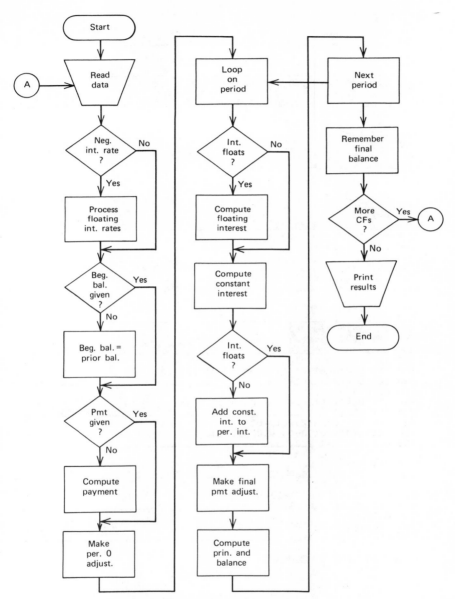

Figure 2.12   Condensed flowchart of LOAN3.

```
100 DIM L(361),M(361),N(361),P(361)
110 READ B2,B1,B
120 READ K1,A1,H1,I2,J1,J2,J3
130 LET T2=T2+1
140 IF A1>=0 GOTO 290
150 LET C4=1
160 LET A1=-A1/(B1*100)
170 FOR T=0 TO J2
180 LET N(T+1)=A1
190 NEXT T
200 LET J2=J3
210 READ B3
220 IF B3=0 GOTO 320
230 READ A2
240 LET A2=A2/(B1*100)
250 FOR T=T+1 TO T+B3
260 LET N(T+1)=A2
270 NEXT T
280 GOTO 210
290 LET A1=A1/(B1*100)
300 IF J3>J2 GOTO 320
310 LET J3=J2
320 IF H1<>0 GOTO 360
330 LET H1=H2
340 IF K1>1 GOTO 360
350 LET P(J1+1)=P(J1+1)-H2
360 IF I2<0 GOTO 470
370 IF K1>1 GOTO 410
380 LET U1=1+((1-(1/(1+A1)↑(J3-J1-1)))/A1)
390 LET U2=I2*A1/(1+A1)
400 GOTO 430
410 LET U1=(1-(1/(1+A1)↑(J3-J1)))/A1
420 LET U2=I2*A1
430 LET U3=((H1-I2)/U1)+U2
440 LET U3=INT(100*(U3+.005))/100
450 PRINT USING 920,U3
460 GOTO 480
470 LET U3=-I2
480 IF K1>1 GOTO 530
490 LET H1=H1-U3
500 LET P(J1+1)=P(J1+1)+H1
510 LET M(J1+1)=M(J1+1)+U3
520 GOTO 550
530 IF J1>0 GOTO 550
540 LET P(1)=P(1)+H1
```

Figure 2.13 List of LOAN3.

```
550 FOR T=(J1+1) TO J2
560 IF C4=0 GOTO 600
570 LET Q2=H1*N(T+1)
580 LET Q2=INT(100*(Q2+.005))/100
590 LET L(T+1)=L(T+1)+Q2
600 LET Q1=H1*A1
610 LET Q1=INT(100*(Q1+.005))/100
620 IF C4<>0 GOTO 640
630 LET L(T+1)=L(T+1)+Q1
640 IF T<J2-1 GOTO 720
650 IF K1>1 GOTO 690
660 IF T<J2 GOTO 700
670 LET U3=0
680 GOTO 720
690 IF T<J2 GOTO 720
700 IF J3>J2 GOTO 720
710 LET U3=Q1+H1
720 LET S6=U3-Q1
730 LET M(T+1)=M(T+1)+S6
740 LET H1=H1-S6
750 LET P(T+1)=P(T+1)+H1
760 NEXT T
770 LET H2=H1
780 LET C4=0
790 IF T2<B GOTO 120
800 PRINT
810 PRINT USING 930
820 PRINT
830 PRINT USING 940
840 PRINT USING 950
850 FOR T=0 TO B2
860 LET L1=L1+L(T+1)
870 LET M1=M1+M(T+1)
880 PRINT USING 960,T,L(T+1)+M(T+1),L(T+1),M(T+1),P(T+1)
890 NEXT T
900 PRINT USING 950
910 PRINT USING 970,L1+M1,L1,M1,P(T+1)
920 : PAYMENT IS $######.##
930 :            LOAN AMORTIZATION SCHEDULE
940 : PER    PAYMENT     INTEREST  PRINCIPAL    BALANCE
950 : ---    --------    --------   --------    --------
960 : ###  ######.##   ######.##  ######.##   ######.##
970 : TOT  ######.##   ######.##  ######.##   ######.##
980 DATA 12,4,1
990 DATA 2,10,100000,0,0,12,0
9999 END
```

The expressions for calculating the two interest components are:

```
550 FOR T=(J1+1) TO J2
560 IF C4=0 GOTO 600
570 LET Q2=H1*N(T+1)
580 LET Q2=INT(100*(Q2+.005))/100
590 LET L(T+1)=L(T+1)+Q2
600 LET Q1=H1*A1
610 LET Q1=INT(100*(Q1+.005))/100
620 IF C4<>0 GOTO 640
630 LET L(T+1)=L(T+1)+Q1

...

760 NEXT T

...

780 LET C4=0
```

The program tests C4 in line 560. For the varying interest rate case C4 will equal one, the test will be failed, and the program will calculate the interest Q2 using the interest rate N in line 570, round the result in line 580, and add Q2 to the period interest in line 590. For the constant interest rate case C4 will equal zero and the Q2 section will be bypassed.

For both cases the interest Q1 based on the initial interest rate A1 will be calculated and rounded in lines 600 and 610. But the interest Q1 will not be added to the period interest L in line 630 if the test in line 620 finds that the case is that of a varying interest rate.

The rest of the computation loop is the same as before so that the principal installment will be calculated in either case by subtracting the initial-interest-rate interest Q1 from the initial payment value U3. Thus the principal installment will be based on a constant interest rate while the interest component is free to float.

After leaving the loop line 780 resets C4 to zero in preparation for processing the next cash flow.

The flowchart for LOAN3 appears in Figure 2.12 and its listing in Figure 2.13.

LOAN3 can handle a variety of mortgage-type loans even though several options have not been incorporated. The loans can be defined by either payments or balances and the payments may be either in advance or arrears. The payments can be based on a remaining balance, in which case the balance will be paid off at the end of the term in the manner of a balloon payment. Changing amortization rates and stepped payments can be handled, as can floating interest rates. In the latter case the amortization rate can either float or be fixed. Multiple takedowns can be handled by treating each takedown as a separate loan, for there is no need for the loan term to begin at time zero. And any number of mixed loans can be combined into one amortization schedule, at least as long as the timing of their payments is the same.

It is now time to examine the subject of inputs in greater depth.

3

Inputs

The programs developed so far have relied entirely on READ / DATA statements to input data. There are several other methods for inputting, and, since each has its advantages and disadvantages, several or all may be used in any particular program.

SEMI-FIXED INPUTS

Constants should be defined in the program. The user should not have to constantly input a number that remains the same for every run.

But there are some constants that are subject to occasional change. The most obvious examples are tax rates, which are subject to legislative whims. A program can become obsolete overnight if the tax rate changes, its programmer has moved on to another position or another firm, and its documentation is incomplete.

Constants that might have to be changed in the future should be located in a prominent place in the program, such as the first several lines, and labeled with REMARK statements.

```
105 REM TAX RATE IS R1
115 LET R1=.48
125 REM COST OF CAPITAL IS R2
135 LET R2=.15
```

If all such semifixed values cannot be assembled at the beginning of the program, then insert a common identifying word in the REMARK statements.

. . .

```
975 REM R1 CONSTANT IS TAX RATE
985 LET R1=.48
```

. . .

```
2345 REM R2 CONSTANT IS COST OF CAPITAL
2355 LET R2=.15
```

All of the constants can now be readily found by using an editing command such as FIND ALL,"CONSTANT". Whatever identifying convention is used it should be mentioned in the program's documentation.

Of course one program's constant may be another program's variable. A lease program for example may be used to test the sensitivity of a lease's rate of return to changes in the tax rate. In that case the tax rate would be one of the input variables.

READ/DATA INPUT

READ and DATA statements have been the means of inputting data for the programs developed so far. But this approach has several major disadvantages.

First, the input data cannot be shared by other programs. The data must be typed separately into every program in which they will be used. This is a growing inconvenience because one program tends to multiply into a family of programs with the members differing in purpose or viewpoint.

Another disadvantage is that the data cannot be readily saved for use at a future time. True, the word DATA in the line can be replaced by the word REM and new data can then be added with new DATA statements. But this is a messy practice as the program becomes cluttered with inactive data. And additional REMARK statements must be added to point out which set of data goes with which case.

But the most serious disadvantage is that users untrained in programming are required to make changes directly to the program lines. If a typographical error causes a garbage symbol to be embedded in a line number it may be beyond the ability of the user to remove it. For a program to be long-lived it must be as foolproof as the programmer can make it. This requires as a minimum that the program be locked, or saved with a password, or otherwise protected so that it can be run but not changed. This precludes the use of the READ and DATA statements as an input method.

If the READ / DATA approach is used then all of the DATA statements should be placed in an isolated group at the end of the program. For example if the last non-DATA statement is numbered 6200 then the DATA statements can start at line 8000. This will help to keep the user away from the executable statements. The END statement can be numbered 9999, thus leaving sufficient unused line numbers that the number of DATA lines can vary without requiring a change in the END statement. The user can easily determine what data are saved by merely listing the program beginning with line number 8000 and letting it run out to the end.

The above does not mean that the READ / DATA approach is without use, for there are situations in which it is the most efficient means of accomplishing the desired result. If the program must print the names of the months in the output table for instance, then the months are constants and should be contained in the program rather than having the user input them. The direct approach would be to use LET statements. Assume the literal variable M$ is to be assigned the names of the months.

```
205 LET M$(1)="JAN"
215 LET M$(2)="FEB"
```

. . .

```
315 LET M$(12)="DEC"
```

This would require 12 lines. Alternatively a READ loop and a DATA statement would only require four lines.

```
205 FOR T=1 TO 12
215 READ M$(T)
225 NEXT T
235 DATA "JAN","FEB",. . ."DEC"
```

The READ / DATA approach is useful whenever a series of variables must be set to an initial series of values.

```
305 READ D1,K6,L3,X4
315 DATA .01,0,365,−2
```

TERMINAL INPUT

Placing an INPUT statement in the program will cause it to interrogate the terminal and wait for a response. This enables the user to input data and control the operation while the program is running. This facility is particularly valuable when several calculations are to be performed and the user needs the results of the first before he or she can decide on the second. Any other input method would require that the program be rerun for each calculation, thus increasing the total compilation time.

A disadvantage of this input method is that the run time of the program is increased because of the interruptions. Another is that if an error is made while typing the requested data and is not corrected before hitting the carriage return, then the run is ruined and the program must be rerun from scratch.

But these disadvantages are minor compared to the convenience of being able to control the program's operation during actual execution.

The increase in run time caused by interrupting the program repeatedly can be minimized by grouping all of the INPUT statements at the beginning of the program. That way once the question-and-answer session is out of the way the program can run through to the end without further interruptions. But as a practical matter any such increase in efficiency is too small to be evident to the user. It is preferable to let the INPUT statements occur naturally, thus making for a clean, straightforward logic flow. Aside from aesthetics, this enables other users to more readily understand the program from reading its documentation.

When writing INPUT statements, long and detailed instructions to the user should be avoided. Do not use the following.

```
205 PRINT "ENTER THE DESIRED PRESENT VALUE"
215 PRINT "OF THE DISCOUNTED CASH FLOWS,"
225 PRINT "SUCH AS THE AMOUNT OF THE INI-"
235 PRINT "TIAL INVESTMENT";
245 INPUT Z1
```

After running the program two or three times the user will have the questions memorized. If not, the user will have a copy of the Input Data Format sheet which the thoughtful programmer provided. The printing of overlong directions increases terminal time and bores the user. The programmer should strive for programs that execute in a lean and snappy fashion. Use the following.

```
205 PRINT "PV";
215 INPUT Z1
```

An exception to the above policy is when the program is intended for occasional use or by someone who is not an analyst. In that case the printing of explicit instructions for each question may bolster the user's self-confidence if nothing else.

When the terminal is used to solicit open-ended data terminal time can be minimized by not repeating the prompting instruction unnecessarily. LOAN3 in Chapter 2 contained an example of such open-ended data in the floating-interest-rate case. There the number of periods B3 and the secondary interest rates A2 were inputted repeatedly until B3 was read with a value of zero, which indicated the end of the data. For terminal input the statements would look like this.

```
205 PRINT "NO. OF PERIODS, INTEREST RATE";
215 INPUT B3,A2
225 IF B3=0 GOTO 325
235 FOR T=T+1 TO T+B3
245 LET N(T+1)=A2/(B1*100)
255 NEXT T
265 GOTO 215
```

Line 205 prints the prompting instruction while line 215 causes the printing of a question mark and the inputting of the two input data. After the data are processed line 265 causes the question to be repeated. Since the prompting instruction is printed the first time through it is available for reference by the user and there is no need to print it each time the data set is requested. For this reason line 265 tells the machine to go back to line 215 rather than 205.

This may seem like a minor point but there are professionally developed programs in which long prompting instructions are repeated over and over. The slowest part of any program is the printing. A little thought devoted to eliminating unnecessary printing does more than anything else to reduce terminal time so that the analysts can return to their desks quickly.

FILE INPUT

The use of data files to input data is the most flexible method of inputting. Several files can be used by one program. This is useful when some data are relatively permanent, such as a data base that is periodically updated, while other data are used only for the specific run.

Since one file can be used by several programs, a family of programs can be designed around a common input data format. The user then does not have to type the data separately for each program.

Data files permit the transfer of data from one program to another. The results of the computations of one program can be put into an output file that can then be used as the input file of another program.

Files also permit data to be readily saved for later use. Several alternative transactions may have to be evaluated or several variations of the same one, and any data set may have to be rerun before the analysis is complete. If the name of the input file is a program variable then the sets of data can be saved under different file names. When the program is run the user will specify the name of the file to be used. If the name of the input file is a program constant then each set of data can be entered under that name, the program run, and then the file renamed. Either way the parameters of each variation are available for future use without having to be retyped. Of course such files should be purged as soon as the likelihood of their reuse has passed. Otherwise the catalog quickly becomes cluttered with dead deals.

But, most important, the user can play with the inputs without fear of damaging the program. The user who makes a hopeless botch of the file can purge it and start over. The program itself is not touched.

There is a distinct disadvantage to file input on some systems. In CALL-OS BASIC, for instance, running the program file clears the data file from the work area. The data file must then be reloaded or called up again before the input data can be changed. This adds to the terminal time. With some systems the RUN command does not clear the data file from the work area. The program runs off-to-the-side. It is with these systems that the full potential of file input is enjoyed. Users play with the keyboard with the data file constantly before them and can make any number of runs, changing data each time, without having to call up the data file each time.

LOAN2 can be changed quite easily to file input. The name of the file will be INLOAN.

```
105 OPEN 1,'INLOAN',INPUT
115 GET 1:B2,B1,B
125 GET 1:K1,A1,H1,I2,J1,J2
135 LET T2=T2+1

. . .

375 IF T2<B GOTO 125
385 CLOSE 1

. . .
```

The only changes required are the addition of the OPEN and CLOSE statements, the replacement of the READ statements with GET statements, and the deletion of the DATA lines. The input data must now be typed into the INLOAN file instead of the program. Their format will be the same but without the word DATA. The opening of the file can be implied by the GET statement in many instances, so line 105 often is unnecessary. And the end of the program will automatically close the file, so line 385 is unnecessary unless subsequently opened files cause the system's limit on open files to be exceeded.

ACCORDION INPUT

The ability to handle a varying number of cash flows greatly increases the flexibility of a financial program. There are so many nonstandard and atypical financial transactions that a program rigidly structured to accept only one or two cash flows of a given type will have its use severely restricted. The program should be able to accept 20 cash flows as readily as one.

There are three ways to accomplish this flexibility. The first is to use a leading code to tell the program how many cash flows to expect. The program then counts each cash flow as it is inputted. When the count reaches the value of the leading code the program stops inputting and proceeds to the next stage. The input data in INLOAN for the leading code method looks like this.

```
10 24,4,2
20 4,8,100000,0,0,24
30 4,10,75000,0,0,24
```

This is the method used in the loan programs for which the corresponding program statements are those in the preceding section. The variable B specifies the number of cash flows, and T2 is the cash flow counter.

The disadvantage of the leading code is that it is necessary to manually count the number of cash flows and enter the total. This entails the risk that the user will miscount or will forget to change the value of B when he or she makes a change to the cash flows. If, as a result, the number of cash flows is overstated the program will run out of data, execution will stop, and the system will print an error message. If the number of cash flows is understated the program will not input one or more of the last cash flows. In a complex problem the omission of one of the cash flows might not be readily apparent from the output.

The second method uses a trailing code instead of a leading code. A specific number is entered after the last of the cash flow items to indicate the end of the data has been reached. The program will continue to input cash flows until it encounters this end-of-data code. Then it will stop inputting and proceed to the next stage.

```
105 OPEN 1,'INLOAN',INPUT
115 GET 1:B2,B1
125 GET 1:K1
135 IF K1=9 GOTO 385
145 GET 1:A1,H1,I2,J1,J2

. . .


375 GOTO 125
385 CLOSE 1
```

. . .

The number of cash flows B is no longer needed and has been deleted from line 115. This means there is no cash flow counter T2 either. There is now only one input variable K1 in line 125. The others have been moved to line 145 so that K1 can be inputted separately. This is so the program can test its value in line 135. If the program inputs nine as the value of K1 then it has reached the end of the data, stops inputting, and jumps to line 385 where the input file is closed. For any value for K1 other than nine the program will continue to input cash flow parameters.

Nine was chosen as the end-of-data code for this example. This is because the number of principal payments per year K1 would normally never equal nine. Zero could be used but one cannot because one is a possible normal value for K1. The end-of-data code should be easy to remember—thus eliminating, for example, 137—and easy to use—thus eliminating 999, which requires three finger strokes rather than one. The end-of-data code preferably should be the same for every program, or at least for every member of a family of programs, to ease the strain on the user's memory.

The input data in INLOAN for the trailing code method looks like this.

```
10 24,4
20 4,8,100000,0,0,24
30 4,10,75000,0,0,24
40 9
```

If the end-of-data trailing code is given a relatively high line number, such as 999 instead of 40 as above, and the cash flow lines are always assigned lower line numbers then the code can be left in the file permanently and the user does not have to input it for each run.

The number of cash flow lines picked up by the program can be controlled by moving the end-of-data code around. If the user must make two runs, one with both of the above loans and one with just the first, then the second loan can be dropped by inserting a nine before it between runs.

```
10 24,4
20 4,8,100000,0,0,24
25 9
30 4,10,75000,0,0,24
40 9
```

By properly planning the sequence of the cash flow lines a series of runs could be made with successively fewer cash flow lines by moving the nine up each time. Yet all of the data would still be saved in the file in case it were desired to repeat any run. This facility is more useful for a discounting or lease program than for a loan program.

The third method of providing accordion input is not available in CALL-OS BASIC, but is possible on some systems. These systems have an AT END or IF END statement that causes the machine to test the file for more data every time data is inputted. The machine looks ahead and if it finds that there is not enough data to enable it to input another line then it will continue on to the program line specified in the statement.

```
115 GET 1:B2,B1
125 GET 1:K1,A1,H1,I2,J1,J2
135 AT END 385


. . .


375 GOTO 125
385 REM NEXT STAGE IN PROGRAM
```

This is the simplest and easiest method because the user does not have to enter any variable related to the number of cash flows.

The input data in INLOAN for the AT END method looks like this.

```
10 24,4
20 4,8,100000,0,0,24
30 4,10,75000,0,0,24
```

PIGGYBACK INPUT

As a program grows its increasing number of options requires an increasing number of input variables. This makes the program more and more cumbersome to use. The programmer should therefore stay alert to opportunities to reduce the number of input variables.

It is often possible to use one input variable to carry two pieces of information. This is because one number can be considered to have three attributes: absolute value, position of the decimal point, and polarity.

Polarity can be used as the piggyback factor in those situations where both the following apply. The two variables must be mutually exclusive so that one or the other is required but not both. And the two variables must be unipolar; that is, each one must be of constant polarity and not sometimes positive and sometimes negative. In such situations the value of the relevant variable can be entered with its polarity indicating which variable it is.

This method was used in LOAN2 where I2 could be either the remaining balance or the balloon payment and in LOAN3 where it could be either the remaining balance or the payment amount. The advantage of this technique is that the user does not have to continually enter a variable that is not used.

The decimal point can be used as the piggyback factor when one of the variables must always be inputted and the other may or may not be needed. Each variable should have all of its significant digits either to the right or the left of the decimal point. That is each of the two variables should always either be an integer or have a value less than one. The latter point is not strictly required for the decimal point can always be shifted by multiplying or dividing, but then the input coding becomes involved and the advantage of piggybacking is lost.

LOAN3 has three variables related to the loan term. The variable J1 defines the beginning of the loan or loan segment term, J2 defines the end of the loan or segment, and J3 defines the end of the loan term. Variable J3 is required only for a mortgage-type loan which is broken into segments to accommodate a changing interest rate. Most of the loans that will be run will have a constant interest rate but the user still has to enter the then-unneeded J3. This can be avoided by piggybacking J3 onto J2.

Since J2 and J3 define number of periods they will both always be integers and always be of positive polarity. This means they can be combined into one number separated by a decimal point without losing any information.

For example if the end of the segment J2 is period eight and the end of the loan J3 is period twelve then J2 and J3 can be entered as 8.012. The digits to the left of the decimal point define J2 and those to the right define J3. The latter is entered as .012 rather than .12 because .12 is reserved to mean 120. Remember that the DIM statement specified that the number of periods could be as high as 365. This means that J3 may have as many as three digits and a distinction must therefore be maintained between 12 as .012 and 120 as .12.

```
125 GET 1:K1,A1,H1,I2,J1,J2
135 LET X2=J2
145 LET J2=INT(J2)
155 LET J3=1000*(X2–J2)
```

Line 125 inputs J2 as 8.012 and line 135 sets X2 to the same value. Line 145 takes the integer of J2, thus truncating it to 8. Line 155 subtracts 8 from 8.012, multiplies the difference of .012 by 1000 to give 12, and calls the result J3. Now J2 equals 8 and J3 equals 12 as desired.

For a simple loan in which J3 is not needed J2 would be entered simply as 8. Since the integer of 8 is still 8, the difference between X2 and J2 would be zero and J3 would be set to zero. From there the program proceeds as it did in Chapter 2.

The variable X2 is merely temporary and can be replaced in the expressions by J3. Its purpose above was to ensure the clarity of the logic.

```
125 GET 1:K1,A1,H1,I2,J1,J2
135 LET J3=J2
145 LET J2=INT(J2)
155 LET J3=1000*(J3-J2)
```

The same approach can be applied to the value of the number. This would enable entering J3 and J2 as 12008.

```
125 GET 1:K1,A1,H1,I2,J1,J2
135 LET J3=INT(J2/1000)
145 LET J2=J2-(J3*1000)
```

Line 135 divides 12008 by 1000 to give 12.008, truncates it to 12, and calls the result J3. Line 145 multiplies 12 by 1000 to give 12000, subtracts it from 12008 to give 8, and calls the result J2. For a simple loan J2 would be entered as 8 with the final result of J2 being 8 and J3 being 0.

In this approach the thousands position would be reserved for the seldom-used variable.

Although piggybacking is often useful it should not be carried to an extreme. Four variables with the values of 1, 2, 3, and 4 could be entered as one number with the value of 1002003.004 if the appropriate unscrambling statements are provided in the program. But the coding of the input data becomes confusing, and the practice increases the risk that the user will make an input error. As a practical matter the use of piggyback inputs should be confined to two simple cases. Polarity can be used to distinguish between two mutually exclusive variables with positive polarity being assigned to the variable that is used more often. The decimal point can be used to distinguish between two related variables when one of them is seldom used with that one being assigned to the right of the decimal point.

AVOIDING REDUNDANT INPUTS

The same information is sometimes inadvertently entered in more than one guise. A specific input variable may be added in an early stage of the program's development to serve a specific purpose. Then later another variable is added for a different purpose and the programmer fails to notice that one is redundant. All of the input variables should be examined in the context of the completed program in order to detect those that can be eliminated without loss of necessary information.

LOAN2 (and LOAN3) contains an example. The input variable B2 is defined as the total number of periods and J2 is defined as the end of the loan term. If there is only one cash flow line then B2 and J2 will have the same value. And if there are several loans or loan segments then B2 will equal the J2 with the highest value. Since the information contained by B2 can be derived from J2 then B2 is superfluous and can be eliminated as input.

```
115 GET 1:B1,B
125 GET 1:K1,A1,H1,I2,J1,J2
135 IF B2>=J2 GOTO 155
145 LET B2=J2
```

The first GET statement no longer inputs B2. This means that B2 will still have a value of zero when the first cash flow line is inputted with its J2. Since the value of B2 will be less than that of J2 the test in line 135 will be failed and B2 will be set equal to J2 by line 145. Each time a subsequent cash flow line is inputted B2 will be compared with the new J2. And each time B2 is found to be less than the new J2 it will be set to the higher value. After all of the cash flow lines have been inputted B2 will have a final value equal to the highest value of any J2 in the data set. Thus B2 is still available for use by subsequent statements in the program as before but the user no longer has to input it as a separate variable.

ERROR TESTING

If the user makes a mistake when entering the input data either a run will be wasted or, worse, the output will contain undetected erroneous data. The BASIC system itself will detect some types of errors such as insufficient data or the inputting of a letter when the program is expecting a number. But the system cannot detect errors that result in operable data but which violate the implicit assumptions built into the program. It is the programmer's responsibility to provide such testing. And neither the system nor the well-designed program can detect such typographical errors as transposing two digits.

Table 3.1 presents the characteristics of the input variables used in LOAN2 and LOAN3. These characteristics are categorized as polarity, absolute value, and special relationships.

It is a simple matter to test for polarity as it merely requires that the value of the input variable be compared with zero. A positive number will be

TABLE 3.1   CHARACTERISTICS OF THE LOAN INPUT VARIABLES

Variable	Polarity	Absolute Value		Special Relationship
A1 (LOAN 2)	+	>=1		None
A1 (LOAN 3)	+ or −			
B				
B1		Integer		<=Limit in
B2	+			DIM statement
H1 (LOAN 2)		>0		<=Field size in
H1 (LOAN 3)		>=0		IMAGE statement
I2	+or−			<=H1
J1		Integer or 0	<J2	<=Limit
J2		Integer	>J1	in DIM
J3	+	Integer or 0	>=J2	statement
K1 (LOAN 2)		Integer		B1/K1=+integer
K1 (LOAN 3)		1 or 2		None

greater than zero and a negative number will be less than zero. Variable H1, for example, should always be either positive or zero and can be tested as follows.

```
125 GET 1:K1,A1,H1,I2,J1,J2
135 IF H1>=0 GOTO 165
145 PRINT "INPUT ERROR: NEGATIVE LOAN AMOUNT."
155 STOP
```

Line 135 tests H1 for polarity and if H1 is not negative then the next two lines are bypassed. If H1 is negative then line 145 prints an error message and line 155 stops the program so that the user can examine and correct the input data.

An error message should always be printed when an error is detected so that the user knows a mistake was made. If the program just stops without comment the user may assume that there is a system malfunction. The message should state which test was failed but, as explained below, this does not necessarily identify the nature of the error.

Since the above test is designed to detect a negative number when the program expects a positive one it might be thought that the program could correct the error by reversing the polarity of the number instead of stopping execution. But the error actually might be unrelated to H1, in which case reversing polarity would merely perpetuate the error. Suppose for example that the intended loan data looked like this.

    20 2,10,100000,−9748.71,0,12

This is a 10% $100,000 loan with periodic payments of $9748.71. If the user inadvertently typed a period instead of a comma after the 10 then the program would input the interest rate A1 as 10.1% instead of 10%. It would then input the loan amount H1 as −9748.71. The error has caused two numbers to combine into one, thus moving all the subsequent numbers up one in sequence. What was intended to be I2 becomes H1 which fails the test.

The comma and the period are adjacent on the keyboard and it is a common error to type one for the other especially since the user is seldom a trained typist. Another common error is to omit a number entirely. Making either type of mistake will disturb the sequence of subsequent numbers. So when a test is failed and the tested variable appears to have been entered correctly the actual error may lie anywhere before, even on a preceding data line.

Since an error test may catch more errors than the one for which it was designed, it is important to test at least one variable. And the tested variable should be one that is so narrowly defined that it can be clearly distinguished from the two variables on either side of it.

None of the input variables in Table 3.1 are particularly suited for polarity testing. Variables A1 (LOAN3) and I2 can be either positive or negative, so they cannot be tested for wrong polarity. All of the other variables must be positive, but a positive number is seldom erroneously entered as a negative. It is much more likely for a negative number to be entered as positive for it is the negative number that requires an extra finger stroke in typing.

In the Absolute Value column of Table 3.1, K1 (LOAN3) stands out as a prime candidate for testing. This is because it is very narrowly defined, having only two acceptable values—one and two.

    135 IF K1=1 GOTO 175
    145 IF K1=2 GOTO 175
    155 PRINT "WRONG ADVANCE/ARREARS CODE."
    165 STOP

In this case if K1 has any value other than exactly one or exactly two then the error message is printed and the program stops.

Seven of the listed variables must be integers and cannot have a decimal component. Using B1 as an example, integers can be tested like this.

```
135 LET X2=INT(B1)
145 IF B1–X2=0 GOTO 175
155 PRINT "PERIODS/YEAR NOT AN INTEGER."
165 STOP
```

Line 135 truncates B1 to an integer and calls the result X2. If B1 is an integer to begin with then X2 will equal B1 exactly and their difference will be zero. In that event the test in line 145 will be passed and the error message bypassed.

The interest rate A1 is a preferred subject for testing because the program could have been written for either its percentage form or its decimal form. Since the decision was made to use the percentage form a test should be incorporated to ensure that the input variable as entered conforms to that assumption.

```
135 IF A1>=1 GOTO 175
145 IF A1<=−1 GOTO 175
155 PRINT "ENTER INTEREST RATE AS %."
165 STOP
```

Lines 135 and 145 are designed to trigger the error message if the value of A1 lies between (but not including) minus one and one, that is, for any decimal value whether negative or positive. This would be required for LOAN3 where A1 may be either polarity. Line 145 would not be required for LOAN2.

This is not a perfect test because it is based on likelihood rather than certainty as to the interest rate values. It implicitly assumes that the interest rate will not be less than 1%, for if it is then it cannot pass the test even if entered correctly in percentage form. It also assumes that the interest rate will not exceed 100%, for if it does then it will pass the test even if erroneously entered in decimal form. But the likelihood of a loan interest rate being less than 1% or greater than 100% is sufficiently remote that the test is justified.

The Special Relationship column in Table 3.1 indicates that B1, B2, J1, J2, and J3 cannot exceed the limit specified in the DIMENSION statement. This is because all five variables refer to number of periods. They do not have to be tested for this relationship because if they do exceed the limit the BASIC system will print an error message.

The loan amount H1 should not exceed the printout capacity of the program. If the IMAGE statements only have six digits to the left of the decimal point, then the loan amount must be less than $1,000,000. Actually it must be considerably less since the total payments will exceed the loan amount. But this is another relationship that does not have to be tested by the program for the BASIC system will print an overflow character if the capacity of any field is exceeded.

The variable K1 (LOAN2) should definitely be tested. The relationship between the frequency of the principal payments K1 and the frequency of the interest payments B1 is a critical assumption underlying the program structure.

```
150 LET K1=B1/K1
152 IF K1<1 GOTO 158
154 LET X2=INT(K1)
156 IF K1–X2=0 GOTO 160
158 PRINT "INT FREQ NOT MULTIPLE OF PRIN FREQ."
159 STOP
```

Line 150 is the conversion expression that appears in LOAN2. It is the converted K1 that must be a positive integer. Line 152 directs the program to the error message if K1 is negative or is a decimal. If K1 is a decimal less than one it indicates that the principal payments occur more frequently than the interest payments. This is contrary to the assumption upon which the skip-payment expressions were built. Lines 154 and 156 comprise the integer test that was discussed before. If K1 is not an integer it fails the test.

The test of whether the beginning loan period J1 is less than the ending loan period J2 is simple and straightforward.

```
135 IF J1<J2 GOTO 165
145 PRINT "LOAN ENDS BEFORE IT BEGINS."
155 STOP
```

It is neither practicable nor desirable to test every aspect of every variable tabled in Table 3.1. To do so would multiply the number of statements in the program out of all proportion to the benefits derived from such intensive testing. It is sufficient to restrain the testing to the most narrowly defined variables and the most critical underlying assumptions. For the two loan programs this means testing A1 and K1 and perhaps the relationship between J1 and J2.

One relationship that should be tested does not appear in the table. In LOAN3 any loan segments must be in the proper sequence so that one segment may pick up its beginning loan balance from the residual balance of the preceding segment. If the beginning balance H1 is entered as zero then the beginning period J1 must be the same as the ending period J2 of the prior segment. This requires an additional variable J4 to remember the value of J2.

```
115 LET J4=362
320 IF H1<>0 GOTO 360
322 IF J1=J4 GOTO 330
324 PRINT "LOAN SEGMENTS NOT IN SEQUENCE."
326 STOP

. . .

760 NEXT T
765 LET J4=J2
```

Line 115 sets J4 equal to one greater than the maximum number of periods permitted by the DIM statement to ensure that it will not equal J1 of the first cash flow. If J4 were not specifically set it would equal zero at the time of inputting the first cash flow whose J1 may also be zero. This would result in a false error response. After exit from the computation loop J4 is set equal to J2 in line 765. If the next cash flow line has an H1 of zero, indicating that the beginning balance is to be picked up, then line 322 compares the beginning period J1 with the ending period J4 of the prior segment. If they are not equal then the error message is printed.

4

Outputs

Outputs were discussed in Chapter 1 just enough to illustrate the printing of the output tables for the loan programs. This chapter explores some of the options associated with printing outputs. The examples will be based on LOAN2.

PRINTING INPUT PARAMETERS

LOAN1 provided for the printing of the interest rate as part of the loan amortization schedule's title. This provision was eliminated as soon as the program became capable of handling a package of loans with different interest rates. The lack of a printed heading that summarizes the parameters of the transactions is of no consequence to the analyst as long as he or she is the only one who uses the table. Presumably when the paper is removed from the terminal the input data is included with the table, so that the analyst then has a complete record for the files. However if the table, or its copy, is provided to others then they cannot be expected to interpret the input coding. In this case a printed summary of the parameters saves explanation and provides ready identification of the table.

Of the general input data only the frequency of payments B1 is of interest for printing. In this section the line numbers will be chosen to intermesh with those of LOAN2.

110 READ B2,B1,B

. . .

118 PRINT USING 494,B1

. . .

494 : FREQUENCY IS ### TIMES PER YEAR

Lines 118 and 494 are the PRINT and IMAGE statements respectively for the payment frequency B1. Using the phrase "times per year" permits printing B1 directly. An alternative approach would be to use the numerical value of B1 to define a literal variable with words such as "quarterly," "annual," and so on. But this would require a greater number of statements and would tend to lock the program into a rigid assumption regarding acceptable payment frequencies. On rare occasions an unusual payment pattern is encountered such as weekly or, for a firm with a four-week accounting cycle, thirteen times a year.

Since the program is structured to input the loans as individual cash flow lines the specific parameters can be printed as each line is inputted.

120 READ K1,A1,H1,I2,J1,J2

. . .

134 PRINT USING 496,T2,A1,H1,I2,(J2–J1)/B1

. . .

496 :##:##.###% $######.## TO $######.## OVER ##.## YEARS

The value of the cash flow counter T2 is printed in line 134 because this numbers the loans for easy reference. If the cash flow counter has been deleted because of changing to the trailing code input format then it can be reinstated. The interest rate A1, the beginning balance H1, and the ending balance I2 are then printed. Instead of printing the beginning and ending periods the term of the loan in years is printed by dividing the number of payments J2 − J1 by the payment frequency B1. The only significant information not printed by line 134 is the frequency of the principal payments K1 and the time the loan begins J1. But with 53 characters already in line 496 the printed line will slightly exceed the width of the table which is 48 characters. If the table columns were 12 characters wide rather than 9 then the printed line could be longer and another piece of information added. Alternatively two lines could be printed for each cash flow with the second line being suppressed if the loan neither begins later than zero nor has principal payments of a different frequency than the interest payments.

Using the cash flow counter T2 to number the loans as their parameters are printed means that each segment of a compound loan will be assigned its own number. But the reader will tend to think of all the segments together as a single loan. Therefore the only segment of a compound loan that should be numbered is the first one. This means that the counter should not be incremented nor its value printed for segments other than the first. If T2 is still being used to control the inputs then another counter T3 will have to be installed for the parameter printing.

To handle this refinement the program must be able to identify the segments of a compound loan other than the first. Such a segment will have two characteristics. Its beginning balance and its beginning period will be the same as the ending balance and ending period, respectively, of the prior segment. Testing for these characteristics requires a variable H2 to remember the ending balance and another variable J4 to remember the ending period. (LOAN3 already has these variables.)

```
119 LET J4=361
120 READ K1,A1,H1,I2,J1,J2

. . .

131 IF H1<>H2 GOTO 133
132 IF J1=J4 GOTO 138
133 LET T3=T3+1
134 PRINT USING 496,T3,A1,H1,I2,(J2–J1)/B1
136 GOTO 140
138 PRINT USING 498,A1,H1,I2,(J2–J1)/B1

. . .

362 LET H2=H1
364 LET J4=J2

. . .

498 :   ##.###% $######.## TO $######.## OVER ##.## YEARS
```

Line 119, by setting J4 equal to one greater than the number of periods permitted by the DIM statement, ensures that the initial value of J4 will not equal J1 of the first cash flow. If J4 were not set then it would have an initial value of zero which is a common value for J1. This could result in the first cash flow not being assigned a loan number. If the beginning balance H1 is not equal to the ending balance H2 of the prior cash flow then line 131 directs the program to line 133 where the cash flow counter T3 is incremented. Line 134 than prints the parameters including the loan number indicated by T3. If H1 does equal H2 then if the beginning period J1 equals the remembered ending period J4 of the prior cash flow then the counter is bypassed and the parameters are printed by line number 138 without a loan number. After the computation loop the ending balance H1 is remembered by H2 and the ending period J2 is remembered by J4 in lines 362 and 364.

The mechanics of printing the loan parameters are now complete. But the presentation looks bare. So some additional PRINT statements can be used to improve the overall appearance.

```
105 READ E$

. . .

112 PRINT
113 PRINT USING 492,E$
114 PRINT            "_____"
115 PRINT
116 PRINT "LOAN PARAMETERS:"
117 PRINT "_____"

. . .

375 PRINT "_____"

. . .

492 :            #################
```

The literal variable E$ can contain the name of the lender or borrower or some other designation that can be used as an identifying title for the table. Literals, also called string variables, are limited to 18 characters in CALL-OS BASIC although two or more can be used in succession if that is too short. Other systems permit other lengths and at least one system allows the length to be varied up to a maximum of 255 characters. Variable E$ is inputted in line 105, printed in line 113, and underlined in line 114. Line 116 prints a brief descriptive phrase and line 117 underlines it. Line 375 provides a corresponding underline after all of the cash flows have been inputted so that the parameter section is clearly distinguished from the table proper.

Figure 4.1 presents a sample run of LOAN2 with the parameter statements added, plus other features yet to be discussed.

PRINTING PAYMENT DATES

In tables so far payments are indicated only by period numbers. This is sufficient for analysis during negotiations but once the loan agreement is signed a complete run including the payment dates may be wanted for the file. This section develops the program statements for adding dates to the table.

```
LIST-N 1260
1260 DATA "  FIRST TRUST CO.",8,31,79
1270 DATA 12,4,5
1280 DATA 4,7.5,48000,0,0,12
1290 DATA 4,10,100000,100000,0,4
1300 DATA 4,10,100000,80000,4,8
1310 DATA 4,10,80000,0,8,12
1320 DATA 4,11.25,75000,0,0,8
1330 END
```

RUN

LOAN2   8:40   THURSDAY FEB.24,1977

FIRST TRUST CO.

LOAN PARAMETERS:

PAYMENTS ARE   4 TIMES PER YEAR

```
1: 7.500% $ 48000.00 TO $      0.00 OVER  3.00 YEARS
2:10.000% $100000.00 TO $100000.00 OVER  1.00 YEARS
   10.000% $100000.00 TO $ 80000.00 OVER  1.00 YEARS
   10.000% $ 80000.00 TO $      0.00 OVER  1.00 YEARS
3:11.250% $ 75000.00 TO $      0.00 OVER  2.00 YEARS
```

LOAN AMORTIZATION SCHEDULE

PER	DATE	PAYMENT	INTEREST	PRINCIPAL	BALANCE
0	1979 AUG 31	0.00	0.00	0.00	223000.00
1	NOV 30	18884.37	5509.37	13375.00	209625.00
	SUBTOTAL	18884.37	5509.37	13375.00	
2	1980 FEB 29	18545.70	5170.70	13375.00	196250.00
3	MAY 31	18207.03	4832.03	13375.00	182875.00
4	AUG 31	17868.36	4493.36	13375.00	169500.00
5	NOV 30	22529.69	4154.69	18375.00	151125.00
	SUBTOTAL	77150.78	18650.78	58500.00	
6	1981 FEB 28	22066.02	3691.02	18375.00	132750.00
7	MAY 31	21602.34	3227.34	18375.00	114375.00
8	AUG 31	21138.67	2763.67	18375.00	96000.00
9	NOV 30	26300.00	2300.00	24000.00	72000.00
	SUBTOTAL	91107.03	11982.03	79125.00	
10	1982 FEB 28	25725.00	1725.00	24000.00	48000.00
11	MAY 31	25150.00	1150.00	24000.00	24000.00
12	AUG 31	24575.00	575.00	24000.00	0.00
	SUBTOTAL	75450.00	3450.00	72000.00	
---	TOTAL	262592.19	39592.19	223000.00	0.00

TIME 1 SECS.

Figure 4.1   Run of LOAN2 with printout of input parameters and payment dates added.

The line numbers will be assigned as though this were a separate program for printing dates only, because the statements are too numerous to intermesh with LOAN2 without extensive line renumbering. When developing a new function to add to an existing program it is prudent to first develop the function as a separate program to test the concepts. Once the bugs have been found and eliminated then the statements for the new function can be inserted into the appropriate places of the old program.

The name of this temporary program will be DATES and its flowchart appears in Figure 4.2. It will have the same variables as LOAN2 for total number of periods B2 and period counter T. It will also need the following additional variables.

Day of payment is	D1
Month of payment is	D2
Year of payment is	D3
Name of month is	D$
Number of months between payments is	X3
Year print control is	X4

The period number will continue to be the first column in the table. Following that will be three narrow columns for the year, month, and day. So that the calendar years will stand out for better readability the year will be printed only for the first payment that occurs in any given calendar year. The payment months have to be calculated as numerals, that is, January is 1, February is 2, and so on. But they will be printed as three-letter abbreviations. In the final integrated program each print line would also include the payment components, but for simplicity they will be ignored in this temporary program. The underlying assumption used is that the payments occur on the anniversary dates of the loan. If a quarterly loan begins on February 10th, then each year payments will occur on February 10th, May 10th, August 10th, and November 10th.

```
100 DIM D$(12)
110 LET B2=24
120 FOR T=1 TO 12
130 READ D$(T)
140 NEXT T
150 DATA "JAN","FEB",. . .,"NOV","DEC"
160 INPUT D2,D1,D3,B1
170 IF D3>1900 GOTO 190
180 LET D3=D3+1900
. . .

200 LET X3=12/B1
210 LET X4=1
```

Whenever a subscripted variable has more than 10 subscripts it must be dimensioned. Since the month name D$ needs 12 subscripts, one for each month of the year, it is dimensioned in line 100. Line 110 sets the total periods B2 to a constant 24 for test purposes. When DATES is integrated with LOAN2 the latter program will supply B2 as a variable and this line will not be needed. Lines 120 to 150 comprise a READ / DATA loop that defines the 12 values of D$ as the names of the months. This is so that when later a payment month D2 is computed as month 3, for example, the PRINT statement can use D$(3) and "MAR" will be printed. Line 160 inputs the month D2, day D1, and year D3 of the beginning of the loan as numerals. For test purposes it also inputs the number of payments per year B1, but this variable would be supplied by LOAN2 after the programs are integrated. Lines 170 and 180 permit the year to be entered as either a four-digit or two-digit number. If the year is entered in the form of "1979" then line 180 is bypassed. If the year is entered in the form of "79" then line 180 will supply the missing 1900. This is merely an extra convenience to save the user two finger strokes in typing. Line 200 computes the number of months from one payment to the next as X3. Since there are 12 months in the year, dividing 12 by the number of payments per year B1 gives the increment in months between payments. Line 210 sets the year print control variable X4 to one to ensure that the first line in the table will include the year. If X4 = 1 the year is printed and if X4 = 0 the year is not printed.

```
220 FOR T=0 TO B2
230 IF X4=0 GOTO 270
240 PRINT USING 630,T,D3,D$(D2),D1
250 LET X4=0
260 GOTO 280
270 PRINT USING 640,T,D$(D2),D1
280 LET D2=D2+X3

. . .

300 IF D2<=12 GOTO 340
310 LET D2=D2-12
320 LET D3=D3+1
330 LET X4=1

. . .

620 NEXT T
630 : ## #### ### ##
640 : ##        ### ##
```

Lines 220 and 620 are for the FOR and NEXT statements for the print loop. After integration these lines will be supplied by the current lines 430 and

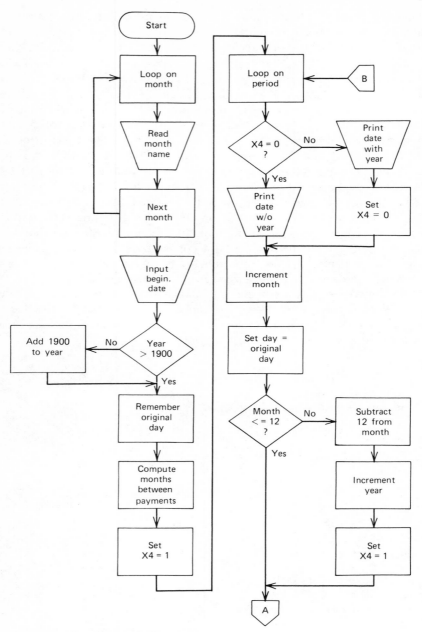

Figure 4.2   Flowchart of DATES.

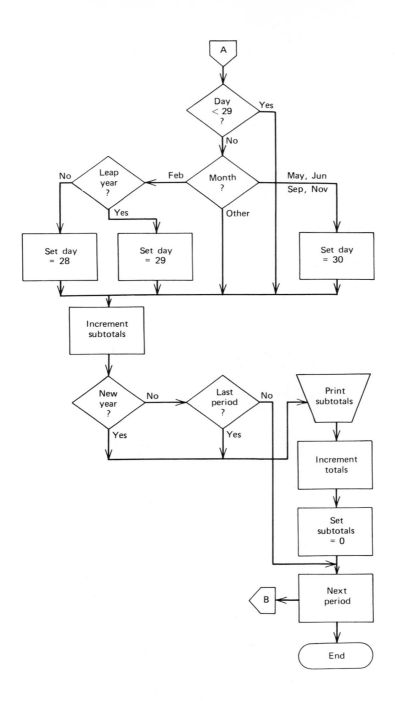

470 in LOAN2. Line 230 tests the year print control variable X4. If X4 = 1 the PRINT statement in line 240 is used which includes the year D3 in the printing. If X4 = 0 then the PRINT statement in line 270 is used which excludes the year D3. If line 240 is printed with the year D3 then X4 is set to zero in line 250 so that the year will not be printed again until a new calendar year is reached.

After printing, line 280 increments the month D2 by the number of months between payments X3. Thus for a quarterly loan if the initial month was 2 (February) then the next month becomes 2 + 3 or 5 (May). Line 300 tests to determine if the payment month D2 now exceeds 12. If it does this indicates that the payments are now into the next calendar year so line 310 subtracts 12 from the month number. Line 320 then adds one to the year D3 and line 330 sets X4 to one so that the new year will be printed the next time through the loop.

The above statements work well for most loans, but they will result in impossible payment dates if the loan begins on the last day of certain months. For example if a quarterly loan begins on January 31st its first quarterly anniversary date will be computed as April 31st. But April has only 30 days. Therefore the program must adjust the payment day D1 so that it does not exceed the number of days in the payment month. Since the payment day will be adjusted for some months, another variable is required to remember the original payment day.

Remember payment day is D4

The payment day adjustment can be done as follows.

```
190 LET D4=D1

. . .

290 LET D1=D4

. . .

340 IF D1<29 GOTO 500
350 IF D2<>2 GOTO 430

. . .

390 LET D1=28
```

. . .

```
420 GOTO 500
430 IF D1<31 GOTO 500
440 IF D2=4 GOTO 490
450 IF D2=6 GOTO 490
460 IF D2=9 GOTO 490
470 IF D2=11 GOTO 490
480 GOTO 500
490 LET D1=30
```

. . .

Line 190 remembers the payment day D1 by setting D4 equal to it before the print loop is entered. Once within the loop and after the new payment month is computed, line 340 causes the adjustment section to be bypassed entirely if the payment day D1 does not exceed 28, the number of days in the shortest month. Once that is done, the program tests to determine if the payment month D2 is February in line 350. If it is then the payment day D1 is set to 28. If it is not then the program tests to determine if the payment day D1 exceeds 30 in line 430. If it does then lines 440 to 470 test whether the payment month D2 is April, June, September, or November. If it is then the payment day D1 is set to 30. The next time through the loop and after the PRINT statement, D1 is reset to the original payment day D4 by line 290.

There is still one possible error in printing the payment dates. In a leap year February 29th becomes a feasible payment day. So if desired a leap-year adjustment can be incorporated.

```
360 LET D5=D3/4
370 LET X2=INT(D5)
380 IF D5–X2=0 GOTO 410
390 LET D1=28
400 GOTO 500
410 LET D1=29
420 GOTO 500
```

. . .

The leap-year test depends on the fact that a leap year, and only a leap year, is a multiple of four. That is, a leap year divided by four results in an integer. Line 360 divides the year D3 by four and lines 370 and 380 apply the integer test that was developed in Chapter 3. If the year is a leap year then line 410 sets the payment day D1 to 29. If the test is failed then line 390 sets the payment day D1 to 28 as before.

Now that the program is assigning dates to the periods the obvious next step is to print subtotals for the years. DATES has so far ignored the payment components but now they will have to be considered. Since DATES is basically merely an expanded print loop it is assumed that the interest payments L(T), the principal payments M(T), and the loan balances P(T) have already been calculated elsewhere. Two new cumulation variables that can be reset each year will be needed.

> Interest payments for the year is L2
> Principal payments for the year is M2

These are in addition to the LOAN2 cumulation variables L1 and M1 that will continue to be used for summing and printing the final totals.

```
500 LET L2=L2+L(T)
510 LET M2=M2+M(T)
520 IF X4=1 GOTO 550
530 IF T=B2 GOTO 550
540 GOTO 620
550 PRINT "          _____  _____  _____"
560 PRINT USING 650,L2+M2,L2,M2
570 LET L1=L1+L2
580 LET M1=M1+M2
590 LET L2,M2=0
600 IF T=B2 GOTO 620
610 PRINT
620 NEXT T
```

. . .

650 :   SUBTOTAL ######.## ######.## ######.##

Lines 500 and 510 add each period's interest and principal installments to L2 and M2, respectively. If X4 has been set to one, indicating that the next period will belong to the next calendar year, the program goes to the PRINT statements. Line 550 prints overlining for the subtotals and line 560 prints the values. Line 530 also directs the program to the PRINT statements if the period is the last period of the loan, even though it might occur before the end of the year. After the printing, the subtotals L2 and M2 are added to the cumulative total variables L1 and M1 in lines 570 and 580. Then L2 and M2 are set to zero in preparation for cumulating the values for the next year. Line 610 is a dummy print to provide spacing between the subtotal line and the next period line. This extra separation enhances the readability of the table. If the loop is in the last period of the loan this dummy PRINT is bypassed by line 600 as the table underlining will then provide the visual separation.

Figure 4.1 presents a run of LOAN2 after DATES has been merged with it.

CUMULATION CONTROL

The payment components for each payment are not always needed. And if only annual subtotals are needed then the time spent waiting for the full printout is wasted. This section develops a routine for the print loop that permits cumulating any number of periods and printing only the subtotals. Most of the variables will be the same as used in DATES but here is a new one.

Increment is C2

The increment is the number of periods cumulated between printout lines. Annual printouts of a quarterly transaction would require an increment of four, semiannual printouts of a monthly loan would require an increment of six, and so on. The program merely counts the number of passes through the loop until it reaches the specified increment and then the cumulative values are printed. Until that time the printing is suppressed.

```
105 PRINT "INCREMENT";
116 INPUT C2

. . .

185 FOR T=0 TO B2
195 LET L2=L2+L(T+1)
205 LET M2=M2+M(T+1)
215 IF T=0 GOTO 255

. . .

235 LET X4=X4+1
245 IF X4<C2 GOTO 295
```

```
255 PRINT USING . . .
265 LET L1=L1+L2
275 LET M1=M1+M2
285 LET L2,M2,X4=0
295 NEXT T
```

Line 105 asks the user for the desired increment and line 115 inputs it. Lines 185 and 295 are the FOR and NEXT statements for the print loop. Lines 195 and 205 cumulate the values of the interest and principal components in the same way as DATES. Line 215 directs the program to the PRINT statement at time zero to record the beginning balance. Line 235 increments the counter X4 which will count the periods between prints. As long as the count X4 is less than the desired increment C2 the PRINT statement is bypassed. When the count does reach the increment then line 255 prints the subtotal values of L2 and M2. These values are then added to the final totals L1 and M1 which will be printed after exit from the loop. Line 285 sets the counter X4 and the subtotals L2 and M2 to zero in preparation for cumulating for the next print line.

Thus if the increment were specified as four the program would print every fourth period and the values printed would be the sum of the values of four periods. If the loan is a 10-year loan with quarterly payments then the table will consist of only 10 lines instead of 40. Of course the entire 40 periods can be printed by specifying an increment of one.

But sometimes the user does not need the entire loan term but only a small part of it. To enable selecting only a portion of the term for printing requires a means of specifying exactly which periods are desired.

> *First period included in table is* C6
> *Last period included in table is* C7

Since this feature will only be used occasionally a code can be used so that the user does not have to enter C6 and C7 unnecessarily. The polarity of the answer C2 to the Increment question can be used to indicate whether the full term or a partial term is desired.

```
125 IF C2>0 GOTO 175
135 LET C2=-C2
145 PRINT "PRINT-CONTROL PERIODS: BEGIN, END";
155 INPUT C6, C7
165 GOTO 185
175 LET C7=B2
185 FOR T=C6 TO C7
```

Line 125 tests the polarity of the increment C2. If the polarity is negative it is reversed to positive polarity in line 135. Then line 145 asks for the first and last periods desired to be included in the table and line 155 inputs the data as C6 and C7. The program then goes to the beginning of the print loop at line 185. This line has been rewritten so that the limits of the period counter T are now C6 and C7 instead of zero and the end of the term B2. The print loop now steps from the first desired period C6 to the last desired period C7. Since the cumulation function is still active the first desired period C6 will not be printed unless the desired increment C2 is one. Otherwise it will be included in the subtotals of the first printed line.

If the increment C2 is entered with positive polarity the program will bypass the Print-Control question and go to line 175 where the last desired period C7 will be set to the total number of periods B2. Since the first desired period C6 is not entered it will retain its initial value of zero. Since the print loop limits in line 185 are defined as C6 and C7 the print loop will step from zero to the end of the term B2 as it did before the print-control statements were added.

The cumulation function is controlled by the increment C2 which does not vary once specified. If the increment is four then each printout line will represent four periods. It is often desired however to print the values on the basis of a calendar year instead of a loan year. If a quarterly loan begins in midyear then shifting to a calendar-year basis requires cumulating only two periods the first year and then cumulating four periods each year thereafter. To do this requires another input variable to specify when the first print occurs.

First period printed is C8

This change can be incorporated quite easily.

```
145 PRINT "PRINT-CONTROL PERIODS: BEGIN, END, FIRST PRINT";
155 INPUT C6,C7,C8
```

. . .

```
215 IF T=C8 GOTO 255
225 IF T=C7 GOTO 255
```

Lines 145 and 155 are rewritten to provide for specifying the first period printed C8. Line 215 is rewritten so that when the counter T equals the desired first print period C8 the program goes directly to the PRINT line number 255. If the print-control function is not used then the first print period C8 will retain its initial value of zero and line 215 will cause period zero to be printed as before. Line 225 directs the program to the PRINT statement when the loop counter has reached the last desired period C7. This is to prevent the printing from stopping with some still unprinted cumulative values. This would otherwise happen if, say, on a calendar-year basis the final year only had two payments but the specified increment C2 were four.

Assume a two-year quarterly loan that begins in June. If a full printout of every payment is desired then the Increment question is answered with 1. The program will then print period zero and every period thereafter through period eight. If an annual printout on a loan-year basis is desired then the Increment question is answered with 4. The program will then print period zero, period four with the cumulative values of the first four payments, and period eight with the cumulative values of the next four payments.

If only the final loan year is desired to be printed then the Increment question is answered with a negative value. To obtain every period answer with −1 and then answer the Print-Control question with 5,8,5. This will result in printing periods five, six, seven, and eight. To obtain the year's total answer the first question with −4 and the next question with 5,8,8. This will result in printing period eight with the cumulative values of the last four payments.

To obtain each year on a calendar-year basis answer with −4 and 0,8,2. This will result in printing period two with the cumulative values of periods one and two, period six with the cumulative values of periods three, four, five, and six, and period eight with the cumulative values of periods seven and eight.

By this means any number of contiguous periods can be selected from the loan term for printing, with any desired cumulative increment, and with any desired shift from the base period zero.

There is an implicit assumption in the program structure and that is that the first print period C8 will not exceed the beginning print period C6 by more than the increment C2. If it does the actual first print will be based on the increment and the desired first print will occur during some subsequent cumulation. To prevent this the relationship of the input variables can be tested as described in Chapter 3.

SELECTING COLUMNS

The prior section described how the printout of the table could be restricted to specified rows. This section will select columns for printing.

The user will not always need all four columns of the amortization schedule. He or she may need only the loan payments or perhaps just the interest payments to insert as one component of a broader analysis. Since it only takes one-fourth the time to print one column as to print four, it behooves the programmer to provide the means to so restrict the printout. The approach is to ask the user which column is desired and then provide the print loop with a choice of PRINT and IMAGE statements.

Select column for printing is C1

The code values for the selection C1 are as follows.

Value of C1	Column Printed
1	All
2	Payment
3	Interest
4	Principal
5	Balance

The selection and printing of the appropariate column headings must occur before entering the print loop.

```
105 PRINT "SELECT";
115 INPUT C1
125 PRINT
135 GOTO 145,175,195,215,235 ON C1
145 PRINT " PER    PAYMENT    INTEREST    PRINCIPAL    BALANCE"
155 PRINT USING 505
165 GOTO 245
175 PRINT " PER    PAYMENT"
185 GOTO 245
195 PRINT " PER    INTEREST"
205 GOTO 245
215 PRINT " PER    PRINCIPAL"
225 GOTO 245
235 PRINT " PER    BALANCE"
245 PRINT USING 515
```

. . .

```
505 : —- ————- ———— ———— - ————-
515 : —- ————-
```

Line 105 asks the user which printout is desired and line 115 inputs the selection C1. Line 135 is a GOTO . . . ON statement that causes the program to branch according to the selection made. If C1 has a value of one the program goes to the first specified line number 145, if C1 = 2 the program goes to the second specified line number 175, and so on. While a GOTO . . . ON statement may handle as many as nine values of the specified variable, from one through nine, only five are required here. If the program goes to line 145 then the headings for the full amortization schedule are printed as before. Line 155 provides the underlining. If the user answers the Select question with 2, 3, 4, or 5 the program goes to the appropriate line number to print the heading for the desired column. Since each of these selections is for only one column, other than the Period column, the same underlining statement can be used for all and this appears in line 245.

The program then enters the print loop where it again branches to the appropriate PRINT statement depending on the selection made.

```
255 FOR T=0 TO B2.
265 GOTO 275,295,315,335,355 ON C1
275 PRINT USING 525,T,L(T+1)+M(T+1),L(T+1),M(T+1),P(T+1)
285 GOTO 365
295 PRINT USING 535,T,L(T+1)+M(T+1)
305 GOTO 365
315 PRINT USING 535,T,L(T+1)
325 GOTO 365
335 PRINT USING 535,T,M(T+1)
345 GOTO 365
355 PRINT USING 535,T,P(T+1)
365 NEXT T
```

. . .

```
525 : ### ######.## ######.## ######.## ######.##
535 : ### ######.##
```

Lines 255 and 365 provide the FOR and NEXT statements for the print loop. Line 265 is another GOTO . . . ON statement that causes the program to branch according to the value of the selection C1. If C1 = 1 then all of the components are printed by line 275 and the program then jumps to line 365 and the NEXT statement. For any other allowable value of C1 the program goes to the appropriate PRINT line and prints only one component. The program then exits the print loop.

```
375 IF C1>1 GOTO 415
385 PRINT USING 505
395 PRINT USING 545,L1+M1,L1,M1,P(T+1)
405 STOP
415 IF C1=5 GOTO 495
425 PRINT USING 515
435 GOTO 495,445,465,485 ON C1
445 PRINT USING 555,L1+M1
555 STOP
565 PRINT USING 555,L1
575 STOP
485 PRINT USING 555,M1
495 STOP
```

. . .

```
545 : TOT ######.## ######.## ######.## ######.##
555 : TOT ######.##
```

Line 375 tests the value of the selection C1. If it is not greater than one then line 385 prints the table underlining and line 395 prints the totals of the components. These were presumably summed as before in the print loop although for simplicity the summing is not shown in this section. The program then stops execution. If the selection C1 is greater than one then the program jumps to line 415 where it is tested to determine if its value is five. If C1 does equal five this means that only the Balance column was printed and a total is not required. The program goes to line 495 and stops. If the selection C1 is not five then it must be either two, three, or four and line 425 prints the underlining for one column. The GOTO . . . ON statement then directs the program to the appropriate PRINT line for printing the column total. Note that even though the selection C1 cannot have a value of one at this point, because of the test in line 375, the GOTO . . . ON statement must still have a line number specified for a C1 value of one. This is because the machine must count through one before it can get to two. So a line number is specified in the one position even though it will not be used. After printing the column total the program stops execution.

FILE OUTPUT

It is sometimes useful to be able to transfer the results of one program's computations to another program. If the periodic loan components developed by the loan program are fed into an output file then another program can pick them up and there is no need for the second program to contain its own loan function. This can be done with a PUT loop.

```
105 OPEN 2,'LCF',OUTPUT
115 PUT 2:B2,B1
125 FOR T=0 TO B2
135 PUT 2:L(T+1),M(T+1),P(T+1)
145 NEXT T
155 CLOSE 2
165 PRINT
175 PRINT "LCF FILE FILLED"
```

Line 105 opens the file as file number two with the name LCF and specifies its use as output. Line 115 puts into the file the total number of periods B2 and the periods per year B1. This is so that when the next program inputs the data it can use the total number of periods B2 to set the limit for its GET loop. This also enables the next program to compare the periods per year B1 with its own B1 to ensure that both programs operate with the same frequency. Otherwise there is the possibility of mixing, say, monthly data with quarterly.

Lines 125 through 145 form a PUT loop that puts each period's interest, principal installment, and loan balance into the output file. When this is completed line 155 closes the file. Line 175 prints a message to inform the user that the transfer to the file has been completed. This line is not necessary but is used to reassure the user that something has been accomplished. Otherwise the program would merely stop or go on to something else with no external sign that anything has happened.

The advantage of file output is that it enables several programs to use the results of a given function without having to duplicate the function's statements in each program. Since each program is shorter than it would otherwise be storage space and thus storage charges are saved.

The disadvantage is that two programs have to be run instead of one and this increases run time and thus the computation charges.

A feasible compromise, one that will be used when the lease program is developed, is to incorporate a simple basic loan function in the lease program so that it can be run by itself in the majority of cases. When a complex loan is required then the loan program can be run first to develop the components which are transferred to the LCF file. Then the lease program is run which picks up the data from the file.

5

Developing the Compound Program

Two separate loan programs have been developed, one for sinking-fund loans and one for mortgage-type loans. Various input methods and outputs have also been discussed. This chapter combines them into a single compound program. The new program will be named LOAN.

It is assumed at this point that the loan programs have been converted to file input and the trailing code method of controlling input, and the total number of periods B2 is derived from the end-of-term variable J2 rather than being entered separately. Throughout the rest of the book the general rule is that cash flow parameters are entered with file input and execution instructions are entered with terminal input.

The master flowchart for LOAN appears in Figure 5.1. As a master flowchart it shows the logic, including the main decision points, connecting the various functions of the program. It does not show the logic within functions as this would be done with subsidiary flowcharts such as those in the prior chapters.

COMBINING THE LOAN FUNCTIONS

The first step is to combine the two loan programs into a single functioning entity. Combining them is done by renumbering one, say LOAN2, so that its lowest line number is higher than the highest line number of the other. Then both programs are merged with the appropriate editing command and the result is renamed LOAN.

Duplicated functions and expressions are removed. The print loop of the mortgage-type loan is now in the middle of the program and is deleted in its entirety. The print loop of the sinking-fund loan is at the end of the program and will perform the printing for both loan functions. The subscripted vari-

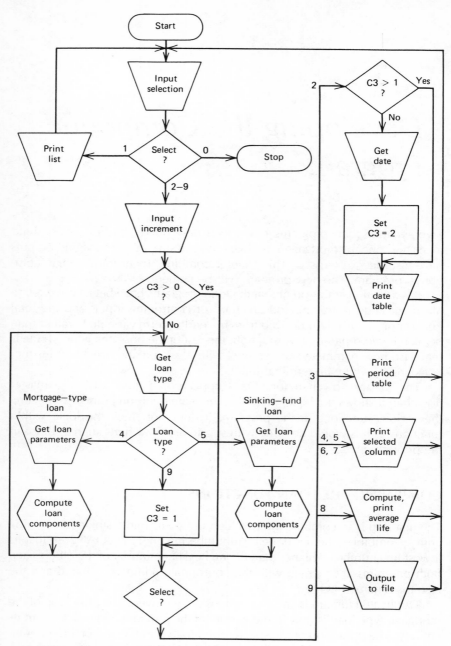

Figure 5.1   Master flowchart of LOAN.

ables L, M, and P in the print loop and in the sinking-fund loan function will have to have their subscripts changed from (T) to (T + 1) so that all functions will be on the same timing basis. Other duplicated expressions such as the DIM statement and the GET statement for the payment frequency B1 are deleted from the sinking-fund loan section.

An input variable is required to distinguish between the two loan types so that they can be directed to the proper section of the program.

Cash flow type is G1

The cash flow type G1 will be entered with a value of four for a mortgage-type loan and a value of five for a sinking-fund loan. These code numbers are used because the values one, two, and three are being reserved for other cash flow types that will be used in the discounting and lease programs to be developed later. Since the several programs will be related members of a family of programs they will share a common input coding nomenclautre.

The program inputs the cash flow type G1 and then immediately branches to the appropriate section where the loan parameters are inputted. Each loan type is thus processed independently of the other.

```
470 GET 1:G1
480 IF G1=4 GOTO 2000
490 IF G1=5 GOTO 4000
500 IF G1=9 GOTO 535
510 PRINT "ILLEGAL LOAN TYPE CODE."
520 STOP
535 CLOSE 1
545 GOTO 6000
. . .

2000 REM MORTGAGE-TYPE LOAN
2010 GET 1:K1,A1,H1,I2,J1,J2
. . .

2880 GOTO 470
4000 REM SINKING-FUND LOAN
4010 GET 1:K1,A1,H1,I2,J1,J2
. . .

4390 GOTO 470
```

Line 470 inputs the cash flow type G1 from the input file. Lines 480 and 490 direct the program to the appropriate section according to loan type. Line 500 tests for the end-of-data code. If it is the end of the data the program goes to line 535 where the input file is closed. Line 545 then directs the program to the print loop. If the cash flow type G1 is not one of the three acceptable values then an error message is printed and the program stops.

The two loan functions and the print loop have been renumbered to start at lines 2000, 4000, and 6000. This provides plenty of space for inserting additional lines or even additional functions if necessary. Each function section now begins with a REMARK statement which serves two purposes. First, it makes it easier to find a section when reading the program listing. Second, it provides a nonexecutable statement as the object of the GOTO statements. This permits inserting additional lines if necessary at the beginning of the sections without having to rewrite the GOTO statements. The last lines of the loan sections, lines 2880 and 4390, direct the program back to line 470 to input the next cash flow type.

From line 2010 it can be seen that J3 is no longer being inputted as a separate variable. This is because it is piggybacked upon J2 so that both loan types now have the same number of input variables. This presents the possibility of inputting the parameters of both loan types with the same statement at line 470 and then doing as much common processing as practicable before branching. As the program stands the number of lines saved by the latter approach would be negligible because the two loan types have little input processing in common. But if the floating interest rate technique developed for the mortgage-type loan were added to the sinking-fund loan then the open-ended loop for the interest rates could be shared.

The two loan functions have now been integrated. Before going any further the program would be run with a mixture of loans to ensure that it is operating properly.

FUNCTION SELECTION

LOAN is now an executable program that can process a wide variety of loans, either singly or in packages, but the only thing it can do with the results is print a full amortization schedule by period. To offer a choice of outputs requires an input variable by which the selection can be made known to the program.

Function selected is C1

The output functions made available should be determined by the needs of the specific user in the specific work environment. The indispensable function for one user may be an unnecessary appendage for another that merely increases the program size and thus its run time. To illustrate the method of controlling a variety of outputs all of those discussed in Chapter 4 will be incorporated, plus a new one. The numeric codes for the selection variable C1 follow.

Stop	0
List available selections	1
Full schedule with payment dates	2
Full schedule by period	3
Payments only by period	4
Interest only by period	5
Principal only by period	6
Balance outstanding only by period	7
Average loan life	8
File output	9

The value of C1 will be entered in response to a Select question. This follows from the book's policy of using file input for data concerning cash flows and terminal input for data that control the program's execution. So that the user can make a series of selections during one run, the program will return to the Select question after completing each task. This requires that the program be told when to stop and thus a Stop selection is provided. The List selection enables the user to obtain a printout of the available selections in case he or she has forgotten to bring the Input Data Format sheet to the terminal.

Only one selection is provided for the payment date schedule and that is the full schedule with all four amount columns. The assumption is that whenever the user needs dates he or she will also need all of the payment components. The period schedule however can be printed in full or any one of the columns can be selected. Selection eight results in the computation of average loan life, which will be discussed later. Selection nine results in the loan components being transferred to an output file, as discussed in Chapter 4.

The most obvious location of the select question is between the computation loops and the print loops. That way the program would input the loan parameters, process them, and then query the user as to what to do with the data. However, since the summary of the loan parameters is printed at the same time that the parameters are inputted, this location would result in the printing of the select question and its answer intruding between the parameter printout and the table printout. To improve the appearance of the presentation all of the control questions should be asked before any of the output-related printing takes place. But if the Select question occurs before inputting the cash flows, and the program returns to the Select question after completing each selected output, then some means must be employed to prevent the program from trying to input the cash flows again after the second and subsequent selections.

Status of input data is C3

If the input data status C3 has its initial value of zero then this indicates that the cash flows have not yet been inputted. When the end-of-data code indicates that all of the cash flows have been processed then the input status variable C3 will be set to a value of one. After the Select question is asked the program can test C3 and if it has a value greater than zero then the input section and computation loops will be bypassed.

```
130 PRINT
140 PRINT "SELECT";
150 INPUT C1
160 IF C1>0 GOTO 190
170 CLOSE 1
180 STOP
190 IF C1>9 GOTO 210
200 IF C1>1 GOTO 330
210 PRINT
220 PRINT " STOP         =0"
230 PRINT " LIST         =1"
240 PRINT " DATE SCHED   =2"

. . .

310 PRINT " FILE OUT     =9"
320 GOTO 130
330 IF C1>7 GOTO 400

. . .

400 IF C3>0 GOTO 550
```

. . .

530 LET C3=1

. . .

550 IF C1=2 GOTO 5000
560 IF C1=8 GOTO 7000
570 IF C1=9 GOTO 8000
580 GOTO 6000

. . .

5000 REM DATE SCHEDULE

. . .

5830 GOTO 130
6000 REM PERIOD SCHEDULE

. . .

6540 GOTO 130

. . .

7000 REM AVERAGE LIFE

. . .

7080 GOTO 130
8000 REM FILE OUTPUT

. . .

8090 GOTO 130

Line 140 asks the Select question and line 150 inputs the answer as C1. Lines 160, 190, and 200 test the value of the select variable C1. If it is equal to or less than zero the program stops. The CLOSE statement has been moved to line 170 so that the file will still be open to input the loan date in case the date schedule is selected. If C1 is one or greater than nine the program prints the list of available selections with lines 220 through 310 and then returns to the Select question. The greater-than-nine test is to provide the user with another chance should he or she inadvertently reply with an unacceptable value. If the user has planned his answers before sitting at the terminal he will respond with a selection from two through nine and the program will go to line 330. There C1 is again tested and if the selection is greater than seven the Increment question is bypassed, as it is not needed if a table is not to be printed.

The lines between 400 and 530 are those already described which input the cash flow type and branch to the loan functions. Line 400 tests the value of the input status C3 and if its value is greater than zero the cash flows have already been inputted and the input section is bypassed. Line 530 sets C3 to one after the cash flows have been inputted. Lines 550 through 580 direct the program to the appropriate output function depending on the selection made. The last lines of the output sections, lines 5830, 6540, 7080, and 8090, direct the program back to the Select question.

THE DATE SCHEDULE

The section for producing the period schedule needs no further discussion for it is the original print loop expanded for incrementing and column selection as discussed in Chapter 4.

The date schedule requires input data in addition to the loan parameters, namely the beginning date of the loan as represented by D1, D2, and D3. Since this data is needed only if the date schedule is selected then the user should only have to enter it in that event. This can be done by placing the date input data at the end of the input file after the cash flow end-of-data code. The data in the input file would look like this.

```
10 4
20 5,4,11,1000000,0,0,28
30 9
40 8,31,79
```

Since the date data in line 40 occur last, their absence would not be missed if the user does not select the date schedule.

The GET statement to input the date data is located near the beginning of the date schedule section of the program. Since the program will solicit successive selections and since the date data should be inputted only once, there must be a provision for bypassing the GET statement should the date schedule be selected more than once. This can be done by again using the input data status variable C3. This variable is set to one after the last cash flow is inputted. If the date data are inputted then C3 will be set to two. When the date schedule is selected C3 will be tested and if its value exceeds one then the GET statement for the date data will be bypassed.

```
5000 REM DATE SCHEDULE
5010 LET L1,L2,M1,M2=0
5020 IF C3>1 GOTO 5160
5030 GET 1:D2,D1,D3

. . .

5060 LET C3=2

. . .

5120 LET D5=D2
5130 LET D6=D3
5140 LET D4=D1

. . .

5720 LET D1=D4
5730 LET D2=D5
5740 LET D3=D6

. . .

5790 GOTO 130
```

There are two methods for presenting multiple selections to the user. One is a prestructured sequence in which the program asks whether the user wants a specific output, and then the program asks whether he or she wants the second output, and so on. If the user declines any option he does not get a second chance, at least not without rerunning the program. The structured multiple selection is used in those programs where the functions must be performed in a certain sequence as when the output of one is required as input for the next. The user is merely being asked whether a printed record of each processing stage is required.

The unstructured format, such as is being developed for LOAN, permits any function to be selected at any time and in any order. This is feasible when the output functions are autonomous or nearly so. But since any function can be selected more than once it is necessary that the function start with a clean slate each time. There must be no carryover values from a prior selection of that function.

This is why the first executable line in the date schedule section, line 5010 above, sets the cumulation variables to zero. Otherwise for any but the first selection of the schedule the cumulations would start with the final values of the preceding selection. The same statement is also used in the period schedule section and in any other section with cumulation variables.

The rule is that any variable that appears on both sides of the equals sign in an expression must be reset to its initial value. Thus the original values of the beginning date D1, D2, and D3 are remembered in lines 5120 through 5140. After exit from the print loop these variables are reset to their initial values by lines 5720 through 5740. Variables can be reset either at the beginning of the section before processing starts or at the end after processing is finished.

Line 5060 sets the input data status variable C3 to two after the beginning date is inputted. Should the date schedule be selected again line 5020 tests whether C3 is greater than one and if it is the input lines are bypassed.

If desired an increment option can be added to the date schedule section. This would use the increment variable C2 that is inputted after the Select question. Since the only increment normally of interest with a dated schedule is the annual subtotals, a line can be added to bypass the individual payment print line if C2 is greater than one. This would also require that the year number be added to the print line for the annual subtotals.

Line 5790 directs the program back to the Select question.

AVERAGE LIFE

For a complex loan or a package of loans it is sometimes difficult to visualize the impact of the repayment terms on the time and amount of the financing. One measure of this relationship is the average loan life. This measure is especially popular with banks who use it to determine whether a loan complies with bank policy concerning maximum term.

The average life refers to the average time that the loan amount is outstanding. It is the term of an equivalent loan that is repaid all at once at the end of the equivalent loan's term. It is calculated by finding the sum of the principal payments weighted by the time each is outstanding, and then dividing by the original amount of the loan. For example, assume a five-year $1000 loan repaid with five equal installments.

Year		Repayment Amount		Weighted Amount
1	×	$ 200	=	200
2	×	200	=	400
3	×	200	=	600
4	×	200	=	800
5	×	200	=	1000
		$1000		3000

The first $200 principal installment represents an amount that is outstanding for one year, the second installment is outstanding for two years, and so on. The sum of the products of the installment amounts times the length of time outstanding is 3000. Dividing this by the loan amount of $1000 results in an average life of three years. What this means is that the total payments of principal and interest for this five-year installment loan are the same as for a loan of the same size that is interest-only for three years and is then repaid with one principal payment.

This can be programmed as follows.

```
7000 REM AVERAGE LIFE
7010 LET Y1,Y2=0
7020 FOR T=0 TO B2
7030 LET Y1=Y1+M(T+1)
7040 LET Y2=Y2+(T*M(T+1))
7050 NEXT T
7060 PRINT
7070 PRINT USING 9200,Y2/(Y1*B1)
7080 GOTO 130
```

. . .

```
9200 : AVERAGE LIFE IS ###.## YEARS
```

Line 7010 sets the cumulating variables Y1 and Y2 to zero to eliminate carryover values in case the average life selection is made more than once. Lines 7020 and 7050 are the FOR and NEXT statements for a loop that steps through each period. Line 7030 uses Y1 to sum all the principal payments, thus deriving the total amount of the loan or loans. Line 7040 uses Y2 to take the sum of each principal installment times the number of periods it has been outstanding. The calculation of the average life is done by line 7070 which also prints the result. The number of periods per year B1 is included in the expression to convert the answer from periods to years. After the answer is printed line 7080 directs the program back to the Select question.

Other selections could have been added to the LOAN program, such as calculating the present value of the loan payments at various discount rates or calculating the weighted average interest rate of a package of loans. But the features incorporated are sufficient to illustrate the manner in which individual functions are combined to form a compound program.

6

Documentation

No program is complete until its documentation has been prepared. The documentation is a written record of the program. Its contents derive from its three purposes.

The first purpose of the documentation is to provide operating instructions for the user. These instructions should be written in a simple and straightforward style with the assumption that the user neither knows programming nor is concerned with the internal mechanics of the program. The contents should include the scope of the program so that the user knows to which situations the program is applicable, a description of the input data and the format in which they are entered, and general run instructions.

The second purpose is to provide to those making decisions based on the program's output an explanation of how that output was derived. This requires a description of the program's theory and methodology with particular emphasis on the critical assumptions used.

The third purpose is to provide an explanatory record of the program's mechanics to facilitate the future updating or revision of the program should that become necessary. This is useful not only to a successor programmer but also to the creator of the program whose memory of the program's specifics will fade with time.

The documentation should be prepared as soon as possible while the program is still fresh in the programmer's mind. The following are recommended as components of a complete and comprehensive documentation package.

PROGRAM SUMMARY

The Program Summary sheet is a one-page overview of the program. It enables the user to quickly determine whether the subject program is the appropriate one for the problem at hand. It also serves as an introduction to the more detailed information that follows. Copies of the Program Summary sheets for all programs can be bound together to provide a ready-reference booklet for the department's programs.

The name of the program should appear prominently at the top of the page. Following that should be a one- or two-line description of the program's purpose.

One or two paragraphs should describe the scope and functions of the program. This will often take the form of a list of the available outputs and options. Any particularly important assumptions of the program or any constraints upon its use should be noted.

The next item is one or two paragraphs concerning the operation of the program. This will briefly describe the nature of the inputs, whether file or terminal, and present a summary of the run instructions.

Additional information on the Program Summary sheet would be the language used, the length of the program, and the names of any input and output files. Cross-reference should be made to any related programs. If the department uses more than one system or user number then the one used for the subject program should be noted. If the program is infrequently used and thus stored on paper tape or magnetic cassette instead of in the computer, then the location of the storage medium should be stated.

INSTRUCTIONS FOR USE

The Instructions for Use section provides detailed instructions for using the program. It can be conveniently divided into inputs, outputs, and error messages.

The required input data should be discussed in detail. This is particularly important for file inputs as the program will not be providing any prompting instructions. Each datum should be discussed in the order in which it is entered. Any variations or options should be explained. Any constraints on the form of the datum, such as whether a rate is entered in decimal or percentage form, should be stated.

The programmer should write in a very simple style for the user will not have the programmer's advantage of being intimately familiar with the mechanics of the program. It is not necessary to mention the names of the variables in this section and doing so might merely confuse the user. Nor is it necessary to explain how the program works unless it is felt that an occasional explanatory phrase helps the user to understand the input format.

Examples of the input data in a wide variety of circumstances should be included.

The terminal input should be described next. Each terminal question should be stated, followed by a description of the required answer. Thoroughness here will enable the programmer to minimize the amount of prompting done by the program and thus reduce the amount of interactive time.

The nature of the outputs and the form they take should be described and illustrated. This lets the user know what to expect from the program. He is then better able to judge whether the program is functioning properly.

The error messages should be listed with a description of the nature of the test that was failed. A warning should be included that the specific error may be only symptomatic and the actual cause may lie elsewhere. The most probable causes should be described and corrective action recommended, even though it may be no more than an admonition to check the input data. Any troubleshooting hints that could be helpful should be included.

INPUT DATA FORMAT

The Input Data Format sheet should be a one-page summary of the required input data, its sequence, and the form in which it is entered. The Instructions for Use Section is a detailed narrative that serves as a lesson in how to run the program and would normally remain in the documentation book. The Input Data Format sheet, on the other hand, serves as a brief memory aid for the user whether he or she encodes the data at a desk or goes directly to the terminal. If desired, copies of the Input Data Format sheets for all the department's programs could be bound together and left permanently at the terminal.

There are several forms that the format sheet can take. The simplest is merely to list the input data with a short description of each. A variation is shown in Table 6.1 in which blank spaces are provided that the user can fill in with the values for the specific case. The form could be reproduced in quantity and the user would fill out a fresh one for each run. This approach is useful when the program requires much input data, or when the data is of a complex nature, or where the completed sheet is given to a secretary or clerk for entering and running.

If several related programs share a common input format then one format sheet can often be used for all. The items can be arranged in tabular form as in Table 6.2. Short explanatory comments or footnotes can point out the differences between programs.

SAMPLE RUNS

A generous range of sample runs should be provided. These are a great aid to the user as he or she can refer back and forth between the narrative of the instructions and the printouts of the examples.

TABLE 6.1   RATIOS INPUT DATA FORMAT

Input File: INRATIOS

Line No.	Description	Data
100	Cash & short-term investments	_____ ,
	Receivables, less reserve	_____ ,
	Flight equipment expendable parts	_____ ,
	Materials & supplies	_____ ,
	Other current assets	_____
110	Flight equipment, at cost	_____ ,
	Ground equipment & land, at cost	_____ ,
	Depreciation reserve—flight equip.	_____ ,
	Depreciation reserve—ground equip.	_____
. . .	. . .	. . .
140	Deferred income taxes	_____ ,
	Other deferred credits	_____ ,
	Stockholders' equity	_____

Terminal question:
  DATE OF REPORT? Month, Day, Year (two digits)

The examples should begin with the simplest or most common case and advance through every option and variation of which the program is capable. Since more than one point can be illustrated with a single run, a little planning can result in the program being well illustrated with relatively few runs. When the output consists of long tables space can be reduced by cutting out the middle of the tables and just showing the top and bottom sections.

The sample runs have an additional use that is appreciated only when it is needed. They provide a standard set of inputs and outputs for diagnostic purposes. If the program is revised or a bug develops these standard runs provide an easy way to determine whether the program is operating correctly again.

THEORY AND METHODOLOGY

The Theory and Methodology section is the one that explains how the program works. It serves as a guide for the programmer who might have to revise the program in the future and as a source for answering the questions of management and auditors.

The first section should discuss the overall organization of the program. It should briefly describe each function, how that function relates to the other functions, and the main logic and tests that determine the branching

TABLE 6.2   DISC, LEAS, LOAN INPUT DATA FORMAT

Input File Name: INDISC for DISC, LEAS; INLOAN for LOAN
Output File Name: NCF for LEAS, LCF for LOAN
FIRST LINE: Periods per year

Cash Flow Lines	CF Type Code	Tim-ing	Rate	CF Amount		Term	
				Beg.	End	Beg.	End
Single	1			d			m
Series of equal	2	a	.	d		l	n
Series of unequal	3	o		e			
Loan—mortgage type	4	a	b	f	h	l	q
Loan—sinking fund	5	p	b	f	i	l	n
Depreciation	6		c	g	j	l	n
Residual	7			d	k		m
ITC	8			d			m

END-OF-DATA CODE: 9
COMMENCEMENT DATE (LOAN only): Month, Day, Year (Optional)

a—Advance=1, Arrears=2
b—Interest rate as %, e.g., 8½%=8.5
c—Straight line=1, 150% DB=1.5, 200% DB=2, SYD=3, ADR=4
d—Dollar amount of cash flow
e—Dollar amount cash flow each period in sequence, then 1
f—Dollar amount of loan
g—Equipment cost
h—Ending balance *or* dollar payment as negative amount
i—Ending balance *or* balloon payment as negative amount
j—Amount to which depreciated (final tax book value)
k—Final tax book value (amount of tax shield)
l—Period at end of which term begins
m—Period at end of which cash flow occurs
n—Period at end of which term ends
o—Period of first cash flow
p—Number of principal payments per year
q—Period of term end (float int.—segment end left of decimal point, loan end right
   of decimal point)

between the functions. A master flowchart at this point is an aid to understanding how the parts of the program fit into the whole.

Next each function or section of the program is explained. It is not
necessary to give a line-by-line description of the program for most of the
statements are readily understood by reading the program listing. But the
general sequence of the logic and critical equations such as present value

formulas should be explained and the variables described. Critical assumptions that underlie the function's structure should be pointed out and explained.

FLOWCHARTS

The need for flowcharts is directly related to the amount and complexity of branching within the program. For a compound program with many functions and decision points a flowchart is almost indispensable as an aid to understanding the program's structure. It serves the same purpose as a roadmap by visually stating which logic paths lead to which results.

In its most basic form a flowchart is merely a collection of roughly drawn rectangles connected by lines with arrows. The rectangles represent operations performed by the program and the arrowed lines indicate the sequence in which they are performed. The scope of the operation represented by a single rectangle can vary from a single program statement to an entire block of logic. This scope is determined by the need to facilitate understanding while avoiding unnecessary and confusing clutter.

A number of specialized symbols can be used in addition to the basic rectangle as shown in Figure 6.1. For the progammer-analyst a reasonable degree of specialization can be obtained by using trapezoids for inputs and ouputs, diamond shapes for decision points, and rectangles for all other operations.

While the production of neat, professional-looking flowcharts should not be discouraged, the programmer should realize that even a hasty pencil draft can save the future reader many hours of study in attempting to decipher the program listing.

VARIABLES LIST

A list of the program's variables with their definitions is an indispensable part of the documentation. This is the key that unlocks the hieroglyphics of the program listing. An otherwise incomprehensible program statement can become almost self-evident if the definitions of the variables are at hand.

The variables list presents each variable used in the program in alphabetical order with its definition. The definition is a short description and seldom needs to be more than one sentence. If the variable is coded, that is, if specific values have specific meanings such as for a selection variable, then the code should be listed.

Ideally the list will be compiled while the program is being developed.

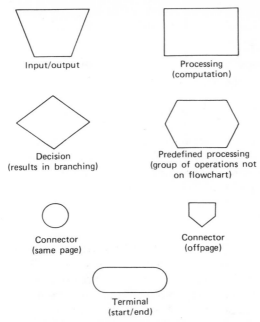

Figure 6.1   Flowchart symbols.

Every time a new variable is used it should be jotted down on the list. This not only serves as a reference for the programmer while writing the program but also ensures that the same name will not be given to two different variables by mistake. When the program is completed it is necessary only to arrange the list of variables into alphabetical order.

PROGRAM LISTING

When the program is in final form a listing of it should be placed with the documentation. This is so that all material necessary for a study of the program is in one convenient package.

The program would normally be stored in the computer, unless it is infrequently used, and would therefore be available for listing upon demand. But the program listing is the easiest item of documentation to produce and the hard copy provides insurance against the day the machine and its archive tapes are swallowed by an earthquake.

The program listing is particularly important if the program is saved in object code. There is a mysterious "computer drift" that can cause a program to begin producing run errors if it is saved in object code for a few years. Since it cannot be listed for debugging purposes in this form the only cure is to purge the program and enter it again.

REMARK STATEMENTS

The REM statement is nonexecutable and provides a means for the programmer to insert parenthetical and explanatory comments in the program itself. Such statements can be of considerable help to the reader of the program. REM statements should be used to identify the main sections and critical expressions of the program. To increase their utility a line can be drawn across the page above each REM statement with a felt-point pen. This makes each section stand out and the reader can more quickly find what he or she is looking for in the listing.

To some extent REM statements can compensate for incomplete documentation. It is a time-consuming task to prepare thorough documentation. Until it is completed a generous use of REM statements can serve as a temporary guide to the mechanics of the program. The programmer can insert them as he or she develops the program, use them as a guide to writing documentation, and progressively delete them. In case the documentation is never completed the REM statements can prove invaluable.

However the REM statements add to the number of characters in the program and thus increase the storage charges. They should therefore be used judiciously and the more thorough the formal documentation the fewer REM statements need to be used.

Following is an example of the documentation for a short, special-purpose program.

DAILY—PROGRAM SUMMARY

Purpose: DAILY calculates interest on a loan on the basis of the actual number of days between two dates.

Functions: Given the loan balance, the annual interest rate, and two calendar dates the program will print the interest amount, the number of days, and the amount of interest per day. The daily interest rate is based on a 365-day year with the option of a 366-day year for leap years.

Operation: When run the program will ask separate questions for the loan balance, interest rate, beginning date, and ending date. Then the answer will be printed.

Files: None.

Language: BASIC.

Length: 1760 characters, 78 lines.

Related Program: None.

DAILY—INSTRUCTIONS FOR USE

All input data for DAILY are entered in response to four terminal questions. After the loan balance, interest rate, beginning date, and ending date are entered the program will print the total interest, the number of days for which interest was calculated, and the daily interest amount.

The total interest is the product of the number of days and the daily interest amount. For the number of days count the program will automatically increase February from 28 to 29 days during a leap year. The daily interest rate is based on a 365-day year. As an option the daily interest rate can be automatically adjusted to a 366-day basis for leap years.

Input

When run the program will ask the following questions.

LOAN BALANCE?   Answer with the dollar amount of principal upon which interest is to be calculated.

INTEREST RATE?   Answer with the annual interest rate in percentage form rather than decimal form. For example 9½% would be entered as 9.5 and not as .095.

The polarity of the interest rate is used to indicate whether the daily interest rate for leap years is to be based on a 365 or 366-day year. If the interest rate is entered with positive polarity then the 365-day basis is used for all years. If the interest rate is entered with negative polarity, for example as −9.5, then the daily interest rate for leap years only will be based on a 366-day year.

BEGINNING DATE?   Answer with the month, day, and year from which interest is to be calculated. The month must be in numerical form, that is January is 1, February is 2, and so on. The year may be entered as either a four-digit or two-digit number. For example April 12, 1978 can be entered either as 4,12,1978 or as 4,12,78. The three date components must be separated by commas.

Interest will be calculated *from* the beginning date but not *on* it.

ENDING DATE?   Answer with the month, day, and year to which interest is to be calculated. Use the the same format as above. Interest will be calculated *to* and *including* this date.

The questions and their answers will appear as follows.

```
LOAN BALANCE?135000
INTEREST RATE?9.5

BEGINNING DATE?4,12,78
ENDING DATE?4,27,78
```

The program will then calculate the interest for 15 days and print the results.

Output

The program calculates the total interest amount by counting the days between the two dates and multiplying by the amount of interest per day. All three items—total interest, number of days, and daily interest—are printed at the terminal as output. There are two output formats and which one is used depends on whether the two given dates lie in the same or different calendar years.

If both dates occur in the same calendar year then a one-line printout is used.

TOTAL $ 222.12 FOR 47 DAYS AT $ 4.726027 PER DAY

If the beginning and ending dates occur in different calendar years then the amounts for each year are printed on separate lines as subtotals followed by the totals line.

1979- $ 7006.85 FOR 31 DAYS AT $ 226.027397 PER DAY
1980- $ 21698.63 FOR 96 DAYS AT $ 226.027397 PER DAY
TOTAL $ 28705.48 FOR 127 DAYS

Error Messages

Two tests have been incorporated in the program and a failure of one will result in the printing of an error message.

ENTER RATE AS %, NOT DECIMAL.   This error message is triggered when the entered interest rate has an absolute value, without regard to polarity, of less than one. After printing the message the program will repeat the interest rate question which the user should answer with a number equal to or greater than one.

ENDS BEFORE IT BEGINS. TRY AGAIN.   This message results when the entered ending date occurs before the entered beginning date. The program will return to the beginning date question and the user can try again.

DAILY—INPUT DATA FORMAT

All input is entered in response to terminal questions.

LOAN BALANCE?   Dollar amount of loan.

INTEREST RATE?   Interest rate as %, e.g., 5% is entered as 5 and not as .05. Enter as negative if leap year daily rate based on 366-day year.

BEGINNING DATE?   Month, day, year as numbers. Year may be four or two digits.

ENDING DATE?   Month, day, year as above.

DAILY—SAMPLE RUNS

The following three sample runs (Figure 6.2) illustrate (1) a term entirely within one calendar year, (2) a term straddling two years, one of which is a leap year, both of which use 365 days for determining the daily rate, and (3) same as (2) except the leap year uses a 366-day basis.

DAILY—THEORY AND METHODOLOGY

DAILY is divided into two functional areas: input and computation. The input section requests the required input data, tests it, and then defines the number of days in each month. The computation section tests for leap years, calculates the daily interest amount, and then counts the number of days between the beginning and ending dates. When the ending date is reached the program multiplies the cumulative number of days by the daily interest amount and prints the result. Whenever the end of a calendar year is reached the program will print the results for the year as a separate subtotal.

Input

Figure 6.3 presents the flowchart for the input section. The program asks for the loan balance and the interest rate. If the interest rate is negative the program reverses it to positive and sets C5 equal to one. C5 "remembers" that the 366-day option was selected and will be used later when calculating the daily rate. If the value of the interest rate is less than one the program assumes that it was entered incorrectly in decimal form and prints an error message. It then returns to the interest rate question to give the user another chance. Once past the test the interest rate is converted from the percentage form in which it was entered to the decimal form for calculations.

The program asks for the beginning and ending dates. The two specified years are tested to determine whether they are greater than 1900. If they are not the program assumes they were entered in the two-digit form and adds 1900 to them. The two dates are then compared and if the ending date does not occur later than the beginning date the program prints an error message and returns to the beginning date question. This is a particularly important test as it prevents the program from running forever in a vain attempt to reach a nonexistent cutoff date.

As part of the date comparison the ending year is tested to determine whether it is greater than the beginning year. If it is then C4 is set to one. Variable C4 "remembers" that there is more than one calendar year and will be used later to control the print format.

The subscripted variable M is assigned the values of 28, 30, and 31 by

```
RUN

DAILY          8:31    THURSDAY, MARCH 31, 1977

LOAN BALANCE?15000
INTEREST RATE?11.5

BEGINNING DATE?3,25,77
ENDING DATE?5,11,77

  TOTAL $        222.12 FOR  47 DAYS AT $     4.726027 PER DAY

TIME 0 SECS.

RUN

DAILY          8:32    THURSDAY, MARCH 31, 1977

LOAN BALANCE?1000000
INTEREST RATE?8.25

BEGINNING DATE?11,30,79
ENDING DATE?4,5,80

  1979- $      7006.85 FOR  31 DAYS AT $   226.027397 PER DAY
  1980- $     21698.63 FOR  96 DAYS AT $   226.027397 PER DAY
  TOTAL $     28705.48 FOR 127 DAYS

TIME 0 SECS.

RUN

DAILY          8:33    THURSDAY, MARCH 31, 1977

LOAN BALANCE?1000000
INTEREST RATE?-8.25

BEGINNING DATE?11,30,79
ENDING DATE?4,5,80

  1979- $      7006.85 FOR  31 DAYS AT $   226.027397 PER DAY
  1980- $     21639.34 FOR  96 DAYS AT $   225.409836 PER DAY
  TOTAL $     28646.19 FOR 127 DAYS

TIME 0 SECS.
```

Figure 6.2   DAILY sample runs.

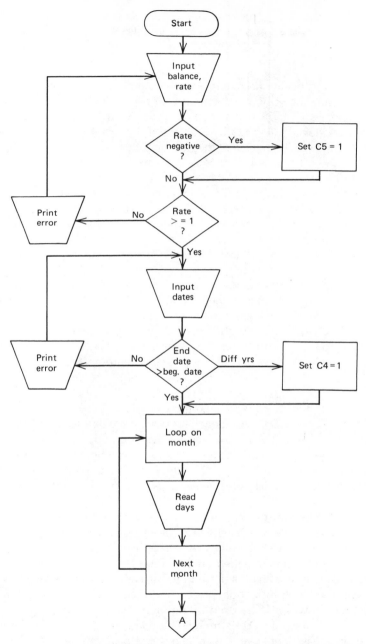

Figure 6.3   DAILY input flowchart.

means of a short loop. This defines the number of days in each month. For example January is represented as M(1) which will have the value of 31.

Computation

Figure 6.4 presents the flowchart for the computation section. The first step in the computation section is the leap-year test. This test is based on the fact that a leap year, and only a leap year, is evenly divisible by four. The program divides the year D3 by four and if the result is an integer then the year is a leap year. In that event the number of days in February M(2) is set to 29. If it is not a leap year then M(2) is set to 28.

The program then calculates the amount of daily interest R2. This is equal to the loan balance P1 times the annual interest rate B1 divided by the number of days in a year. Normally the days in a year will be 365, even for a leap year, as most loan agreements do not provide for adjusting the divisor during leap years. If however the user has chosen the adjustment option (C5 = 1) then the program will base the daily interest calculation on 366 days for leap years.

The program then begins counting days. It starts with the beginning day D1, beginning month D2, and beginning year D3 as entered by the user. The day D1 is successively incremented by one until it equals the last day of the month M(D2). Then the month D2 is incremented by one and the day D1 is reset to zero. The day D1 continues through its monthly cycles until the month D2 equals 12. Then the year D3 is incremented by one and the month D2 is reset to one. The program continues to progress through the dates.

Each time the day D1 is incremented the day counter S1 is also incremented. The day D1 is reset each month but the day counter S1 is not and so it equals the cumulative number of days counted.

Before the counting begins the program tests whether the starting day is the last day of the month. If it is then the initial incrementing of the day D1 and the day counter S1 are bypassed as it is not desired to count, say, January 32.

When the end of the calendar year is reached the program prints the cumulative results for the year. The value of the day counter S1 is added to the total days S2 and S1 is reset to zero. The distinction between S1 and S2 is that S1 is used to cumulate the number of days for the calendar year printout and S2 is used for the final total printout. Also at year-end the total interest S3 is increased by the product of the number of counted days S1 and the daily interest R2. S3 will also be used in the final total printout.

Each time the day D1 is incremented the program tests whether the ending date has been reached. If it has the program stops counting and

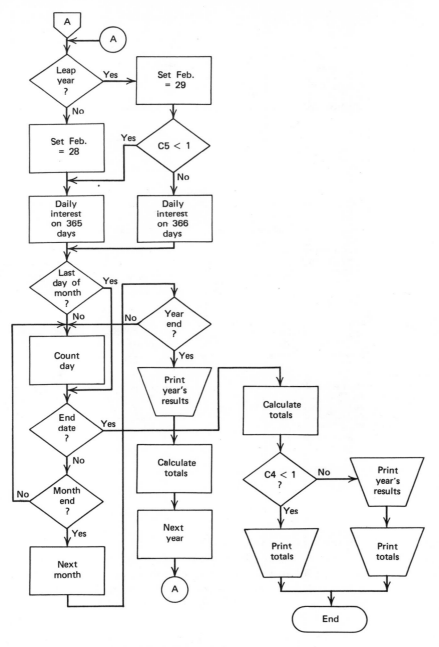

Figure 6.4   DAILY computation flowchart.

```
LIST

DAILY          8:35    THURSDAY, MARCH 31, 1977

100 DIM M(12)
110 REM***DATA INPUT
120 PRINT
130 PRINT "LOAN BALANCE";
140 INPUT P1
150 PRINT "INTEREST RATE";
160 INPUT R1
170 IF R1>0 GOTO 200
180 LET R1=-R1
190 LET C5=1
200 IF R1>=1 GOTO 230
210 PRINT "  ENTER RATE AS %, NOT DECIMAL."
220 GOTO 150
230 LET R1=R1/100
240 PRINT
250 PRINT "BEGINNING DATE";
260 INPUT D2,D1,D3
270 IF D3>1900 GOTO 290
280 LET D3=D3+1900
290 PRINT "ENDING DATE";
300 INPUT E2,E1,E3
310 IF E3>1900 GOTO 330
320 LET E3=E3+1900
330 IF E3>D3 GOTO 380
340 IF E2>D2 GOTO 390
350 IF E1>D1 GOTO 390
360 PRINT "  ENDS BEFORE IT BEGINS.  TRY AGAIN."
370 GOTO 250
380 LET C4=1
390 PRINT
400 REM***DAYS IN MONTH
410 FOR T=1 TO 12
420 READ M(T)
430 NEXT T
440 DATA 31,28,31,30,31,30,31,31,30,31,30,31
450 REM***LEAP YEAR TEST
460 LET X2=INT(D3/4)
```

Figure 6.5   DAILY program listing.

jumps to the output section. Here the day counter S1 value is added to the total days S2 and the product of the day counter S1 and the daily interest R2 is added to the total interest S3. The program then tests C4 to determine whether only one calendar year is involved. If so then the total interest, number of days, and daily interest are printed on one line. If it is a multiple-year case then the results of the current calendar year are printed using S1. Then the total results are printed on a separate line using S2 and S3.

```
470 IF (D3/4)-X2=0 GOTO 520
480 REM***CALC DAILY RATE
490 LET M(2)=28
500 LET R2=P1*R1/365
510 GOTO 550
520 LET M(2)=29
530 IF C5<1 GOTO 500
540 LET R2=P1*R1/366
550 REM***COUNT DAYS
560 IF D1>=M(D2) GOTO 590
570 LET D1=D1+1
580 LET S1=S1+1
590 IF D3<E3 GOTO 630
600 IF D2<E2 GOTO 630
610 IF D1<E1 GOTO 630
620 GOTO 760
630 IF D1<M(D2) GOTO 570
640 REM***NEXT MONTH
650 LET D2=D2+1
660 LET D1=0
670 IF D2<=12 GOTO 570
680 REM***NEXT YEAR
690 PRINT USING 840,D3,S1*R2,S1,R2
700 LET S2=S2+S1
710 LET S3=S3+(S1*R2)
720 LET S1=0
730 LET D3=D3+1
740 LET D2=1
750 GOTO 450
760 REM***OUTPUT
770 LET S2=S2+S1
780 LET S3=S3+(S1*R2)
790 IF C4<1 GOTO 830
800 PRINT USING 840,D3,S1*R2,S1,R2
810 PRINT USING 860,S3,S2
820 STOP
830 PRINT USING 850,S3,S2,R2
840 : ####- $########.## FOR ### DAYS AT $#####.###### PER DAY
850 : TOTAL $########.## FOR ### DAYS AT $#####.###### PER DAY
860 : TOTAL $########.## FOR ### DAYS
870 END
```

DAILY—VARIABLES LIST

C4–Remember multiple-year case
C5–Remember leap-year case
D1–Day ⎫
D2–Month ⎬ Entered as beginning date, then incremented as date
D3–Year ⎭ counter
E1–Day ⎫
E2–Month ⎬ Ending date
E3–Year ⎭
M(T)–Number of days in month T
P1–Loan balance
R1–Interest rate
R2–Daily interest as dollars per day
S1–Count number of days in calendar year
S2–Total number of days
S3–Total interest amount
T –Counter for month loop
X2–Intermediate step in leap-year test

7

Compounding and Discounting

The analysis of cash flows eventually and inevitably leads to the discounting of those cash flows. Since discounting is the reciprocal of compounding, both are discussed in this chapter.

A program named TABLE will be used to produce interest rate factors similar to those found in the "Blue Book" (*Financial Compound Interest and Annuity Tables,* Financial Publishing Company, Boston, 1968). This will permit checking the accuracy of the equations against a readily available standard.

COMPOUNDING

Compound interest refers to the reinvesting of interest or earnings on a loan or investment as it is earned so that the interest also earns interest. This is in contrast to simple interest which is withdrawn or paid as it is earned. The loan programs developed before were all based on simple interest.

Assume a $1000 loan earning interest at 10% per annum compounded annually for five years. The use of the word "compounded" implies that the interest will accumulate and be added to the principal balance rather than being paid.

During the first year the $1000 loan will accrue $100 of interest at 10% which will be added to the balance. The year-end balance will then be $1100. During the second year the $1100 balance will accrue $110 interest which will be added to the balance making it $1210. The balance will grow throughout the term in this fashion.

COMPOUND GROWTH OF $1000 AT 10%

Year	Beginning Balance	Interest	Ending Balance	Factor
1	$1000	$100	$1100	1.100
2	1100	110	1210	1.210
3	1210	121	1331	1.331
4	1331	133	1464	1.464
5	1464	146	1610	1.610

The factor column is derived by dividing the balance at the end of the year by the original investment. The purpose of the factors is to provide a set of multipliers that can be used to determine the amount to which any investment will grow. For example $1500 will grow to 1500 × 1.610 or $2415 at the end of the fifth year.

The factor for the first year equals one plus the interest rate or 1 + .1 = 1.1. The factor for the second year equals the factor for the first year times itself or 1.1 × 1.1 = 1.21. The factor for the third year equals the first year's factor raised to the third power or 1.1 × 1.1 × 1.1 = 1.331. This relationship holds true throughout so that the general expression is one plus the interest rate raised to the power of the number of periods compounded. The equation is

$$E1 = (1 + R1) \uparrow T$$

where E1 is the factor, R1 is the periodic interest rate, and T is the number of periods.

Figure 7.1 presents a run of TABLE in which the first column contains the compound growth factors at 10% for an initial investment (or loan or deposit) of 1 dollar. The column is entitled "Single" because its factors are based on a single or one-shot investment.

Going further, if $1000 is invested at 10% each and every year then each year's investment will grow as in the table above and the total investment will grow as in the table below.

COMPOUND GROWTH OF $1000 PER YEAR AT 10%

Year	Individual Investments 1	2	3	4	5	Total	Factor
1	$1000	$ —	$ —	$ —	$ —	$1000	1.000
2	1100	1000	—	—	—	2100	2.100
3	1210	1100	1000	—	—	3310	3.310
4	1331	1210	1100	1000	—	4641	4.641
5	1464	1331	1210	1100	1000	6105	6.105

```
RUN

TABLE          8:38    TUESDAY MAY 10 ,1977


DISCOUNT=1, COMPOUND=2?2
ANNUAL RATE, PERIODS/YEAR?10,1
FIRST PERIOD, LAST PERIOD?1,10

              COMPOUND FACTORS AT   10.000000 %
                     1 PERIODS PER YEAR

   PER-                        SERIES OF
   IODS        SINGLE           EQUAL          SINKING FUND
   ----     ---------------  ---------------  ---------------
     1       1.1000000000     1.0000000000     1.0000000000
     2       1.2100000000     2.1000000000     0.4761904762
     3       1.3310000000     3.3100000000     0.3021148036
     4       1.4641000000     4.6410000000     0.2154708037
     5       1.6105100000     6.1051000000     0.1637974808
     6       1.7715610000     7.7156100000     0.1296073804
     7       1.9487171000     9.4871710000     0.1054054997
     8       2.1435888100    11.4358881000     0.0874440176
     9       2.3579476910    13.5794769100     0.0736405391
    10       2.5937424601    15.9374246010     0.0627453949

TIME 0 SECS.
```

Figure 7.1   Run of TABLE. Compound factors.

The factor column is derived by dividing the total amount outstanding at the end of the specific period by the amount of the periodic investment. By convention the table assumes that the first investment is made at the end of the first period rather than the beginning.

A comparison of the factors in the two tables reveals that the factors for the periodic investment case can be derived from those of the single investment case by subtracting one and dividing by the interest rate.

$$E2 = \frac{E1 - 1}{R1}$$

Substituting for E1 results in the following.

$$E2 = (((1 + R1) \uparrow T) - 1) / R1$$

The factors produced by TABLE for this equation appear in the second column of Figure 7.1. The "Series of Equal" heading refers to the recurring and periodic nature of the investments on which the factors are based.

The "Sinking Fund" column in Figure 7.1 contains the factors for determining what periodic amount must be invested to yield a given amount at the end of the term. This column is the reciprocal of the "Series of Equal" column next to it. That is, if multiplying a periodic investment of $1000 by a factor of 6.105 gives a future value of $6105 then dividing the $6105 by the same factor will give the amount of the periodic investment $1000. But dividing by 6.105 is the same as multiplying by 1/6.105 or .1638. The latter value is the one used as the table's format is designed so that all of the factors are multipliers.

$$E3 = \frac{1}{E2}$$

By substitution then

$$E3 = R1 \; / \; (((1 + R1) \uparrow T) - 1)$$

The three sets of factors in Figure 7.1 provide the means of calculating the following.

1. The future value of a given present investment.
2. The future value of a series of given equal investments.
3. The series of equal investments to produce a given future value.

All three depend on the basic expression $(1 + R1) \uparrow T$.

DISCOUNTING

The first compounding example showed how to derive factors for determining the future value of a single initial investment. The same example can be restated to show how to derive the factors for determining the amount of investment required to obtain a given future value. If $1000 grows to $1100 after one year at 10% then the investment is 1000/1100 or .909 of the future amount. Doing this for each of five years gives the following set of discount or present value factors.

SINGLE DISCOUNT FACTORS AT 10%

Year	Initial Investment	Future Value	Factor
1	$1000	$1100	.909
2	1000	1210	.826
3	1000	1331	.751
4	1000	1464	.683
5	1000	1610	.621

Compounding adds interest to an initial investment to determine its value in the future. Discounting subtracts interest from the future value to determine the initial investment. This is a simple reciprocal relationship.

$$E4 = \frac{1}{E1}$$

Since the compound factor is $(1 + R1) \uparrow T$ then the discount factor is

$$E4 = 1 / (1 + R1) \uparrow T$$

Figure 7.2 presents a run of TABLE in which the results of this equation appear in the "Single" column.

This equation is used often in financial programs because it provides the means for evaluating future cash flows using a quantitative standard. It directly answers the question of how much must be invested today at a given interest rate to realize a specific sum in the future. But this relationship is also used to answer such questions as how much to pay for the right to receive a certain amount in the future in order to earn the same rate as on an alternative investment. A very important application of the equation is to solve for the rate when both the present and future values are given, for example to calculate the rate of return on a proposed investment.

If the future value is not a single, one-shot receipt or payment but is a recurring, periodic amount then the present value factor of the cash flow stream is the sum of the factors for the individual components. The present value factor for an amount one year in the future is .909. The factor for an amount two years in the future is .826. The total present value factor for receiving an amount for each of two years is .909 + .826 or 1.735. The factors for five years follow.

```
RUN

TABLE          8:39   TUESDAY MAY 10 ,1977

DISCOUNT=1, COMPOUND=2?1
ANNUAL RATE, PERIODS/YEAR?10,1
FIRST PERIOD, LAST PERIOD?1,10

              DISCOUNT FACTORS AT 10.000000 %
                   1 PERIODS PER YEAR

  PER-                        SERIES OF      PARTIAL
  IODS       SINGLE            EQUAL         PAYMENT
  ----    -------------    -------------   -------------
     1    0.9090909091     0.9090909091    1.1000000000
     2    0.8264462810     1.7355371901    0.5761904762
     3    0.7513148009     2.4868519910    0.4021148036
     4    0.6830134554     3.1698654463    0.3154708037
     5    0.6209213231     3.7907867694    0.2637974808
     6    0.5644739301     4.3552606995    0.2296073804
     7    0.5131581182     4.8684188177    0.2054054997
     8    0.4665073802     5.3349261979    0.1874440176
     9    0.4240976184     5.7590238163    0.1736405391
    10    0.3855432894     6.1445671057    0.1627453949

TIME 0 SECS.
```

Figure 7.2   Run of TABLE. Discount factors.

SERIES OF EQUAL DISCOUNT FACTORS AT 10%

| | *Single Factor* | | | | | |
Year	1	2	3	4	5	Total
1	.909	—	—	—	—	.909
2	.909	.826	—	—	—	1.735
3	.909	.826	.751	—	—	2.486
4	.909	.826	.751	.683	—	3.169
5	.909	.826	.751	.683	.621	3.790

What this table says is that investing $3790 now at 10% will return $5000 in the form of $1000 per year for five years. This can be demonstrated with an amortization table.

AMORTIZATION OF $3790 INVESTMENT

Year	Beginning Balance	Earnings at 10%	With- drawal	Ending Balance
1	$3790	$ 379	$(1000)	$3169
2	3169	317	(1000)	2486
3	2486	249	(1000)	1735
4	1735	174	(1000)	909
5	909	91	(1000)	0
Total		$1210	$(5000)	

The $5000 withdrawn consists of the original investment of $3790 plus total earnings of $1210.

The series of equal discount factor E5 is equal to one minus the single discount factor E4 divided by the interest (discount) rate.

$$E5 = \frac{1 - E4}{R1}$$

By substitution this becomes

$$E5 = (1 - (1 / (1 + R1) \uparrow T)) / R1$$

The "Series of Equal" column in Figure 7.2 presents the results of this equation for annual periods at 10%.

The "Partial Payment" column of Figure 7.2 is the reciprocal of the "Series of Equal" column.

$$E6 = \frac{1}{E5}$$

$$E6 = R1 / (1 - (1 / (1 + R1) \uparrow T))$$

These factors produce the amount of the periodic payment if the initial investment is known. The most common application is to calculate the payment for a mortgage-type loan. Another application is annuity problems to determine the amount of periodic withdrawals that could be made from a given investment earning at a given rate.

The factors in Figure 7.2 provide the means of calculating the following.

1. The present value of a given future amount.
2. The present value of a series of given equal amounts.
3. The series of equal future amounts required to amortize a given present value.

A summary of the compounding and discounting equations with their derivations is presented in Figure 7.3. The root for all of the equations is the basic expression $(1 + R1) \uparrow T$.

TABLE

The listing of TABLE appears in Figure 7.4. While TABLE is useful for producing factors at interest rates not appearing in the "Blue Book" its primary

---

Compound Factors

Single   E1 = $(1 + R1) \uparrow T$

Series of Equal   E2 = $\dfrac{E1 - 1}{R1}$ $= (((1 + R1) \uparrow T) - 1) / R1$

Sinking Fund   E3 = $\dfrac{1}{E2}$ $= \dfrac{R1}{E1 - 1}$ $= R1 / (((1 + R1) \uparrow T) - 1)$

Discount Factors

Single   E4 = $\dfrac{1}{E1}$ $= 1 / (1 + R1) \uparrow T$

Series of Equal   E5 = $\dfrac{1 - E4}{R1}$ $= \dfrac{1 - \dfrac{1}{E1}}{R1}$ $= (1 - (1 / (1 + R1) \uparrow T)) / R1$

Partial Payment E6 = $\dfrac{1}{E5}$ $= \dfrac{R1}{1 - \dfrac{1}{E1}}$ $= R1 / (1 / (1 + R1) \uparrow T))$

Figure 7.3   Equations for compound and discount multiplier factors. R1 is periodic rate. T is number of periods.

TABLE   8:45   TUESDAY MAY 31,1977

```
100 PRINT
110 PRINT "DISCOUNT=1, COMPOUND=2";
120 INPUT C1
130 PRINT "ANNUAL RATE, PERIODS/YEAR";
140 INPUT R1,B1
150 LET R1=R1/(B1*100)
160 PRINT "FIRST PERIOD, LAST PERIOD";
170 INPUT B3,B2
180 IF C1=2 GOTO 210
190 LET F$="DISCOUNT"
200 GOTO 220
210 LET F$="COMPOUND"
220 PRINT
230 PRINT USING 440,F$,R1*B1*100
240 PRINT USING 450,B1
250 PRINT
260 IF C1=2 GOTO 300
270 PRINT USING 460
280 PRINT USING 470
290 GOTO 320
300 PRINT USING 480
310 PRINT USING 490
320 PRINT USING 500
330 FOR T=B3 TO B2
340 IF C1=2 GOTO 390
350 LET E1=1/(1+R1)↑T
360 LET E2=(1-(1/(1+R1)↑T))/R1
370 LET E3=R1/(1-(1/(1+R1)↑T))
380 GOTO 420
390 LET E1=(1+R1)↑T
400 LET E2=(((1+R1)↑T)-1)/R1
410 LET E3=R1/(((1+R1)↑T)-1)
420 PRINT USING 510,T,E1,E2,E3
430 NEXT T
440 :              ######## FACTORS AT ###.###### %
450 :                 ### PERIODS PER YEAR
460 : PER-                    SERIES OF        PARTIAL
470 : IODS       SINGLE        EQUAL          PAYMENT
480 : PER-                    SERIES OF
490 : IODS       SINGLE        EQUAL       SINKING FUND
500 : ----     --------------  --------------  --------------
510 : ####     ###.##########  ###.##########  ###.##########
520 END
```

Figure 7.4   List of TABLE.

purpose here is to provide a vehicle for testing the equations developed above. Its structure is simple and straightforward.

Terminal questions are used to solicit the input data. A choice is presented between discount and compound factors and the answer sets the value of C1 which is used throughout the program to distinguish between the two cases. Then the program asks for the rate and frequency of the computations and the range of periods desired.

The computations are performed within a period loop that contains the six equations in two groups of three. The discount equations are at lines 350, 360, and 370, while the compound equations are at lines 390, 400, and 410. The two groups of factors share the names E1, E2, and E3 so that the same print line 420 can print either group.

The rest of the program consists of PRINT and IMAGE statements to determine the format of the table.

PRESENT VALUE AS A FUNCTION OF RATE

If $10,000 is invested at 10% compound interest for five years it will grow to $10,000 × 1.6105 or $16,105. Interest of $6105 will be earned over the term and added to the original investment. If the future value of $16,105 is discounted at 10% the present value is found to be $16,105 × .6209 or $10,000. The discounting process will subtract the interest component of $6105 from the future value in order to determine the original investment. If the rate used for discounting is the same as that used for compounding then the calculated present value will equal the investment.

However if the future value of $16,105 is discounted at 12% the present value is only $9138 which is less than the investment. The reason for this is that at the higher interest rate more interest is subtracted through discounting than was added through compounding. Similarly if a discount rate is used that is lower than the compound earnings rate then the calculated present value will be higher than the investment. In this case less interest is subtracted through discounting than was added through compounding.

The graph in Figure 7.5 shows the present value of $16,105 received after five years at discount rates from 0% to 200%. At a discount rate of 0% the future amount is not being discounted, no interest is being extracted, so the present value is the same as the future value or $16,105. As the discount rate increases the present value decreases so that at 200% it is only $66.

Figure 7.5 also shows the present value at various rates of $2638 received annually for five years. This series of equal amounts is based on a $10,000 investment earning at a 10% rate. At a 0% discount rate the present

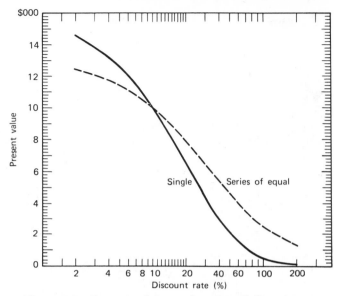

Figure 7.5   Present value as a function of discount rate.

value is equal to the total gross amounts of $2638 × 5 or $13,190. At a 200% discount rate the present value has fallen to $132.

In both cases the present value equals the initial investment of $10,000 when the discount rate equals the compound or earnings rate of 10%. This relationship is a general one and forms the basis for calculating the rate of return on an investment. Various discount rates are applied to the future cash flows until one is found at which the present value equals the investment. That discount rate is then also the rate of return.

The two curves in Figure 7.5 are both negative, that is, they slope downward to the right. Present value is inversely related to the discount rate. This is the normal relationship and these curves can be called "normal" PV/Rate curves.

Unfortunately the normal relationship does not always hold. If there is a stream of cash flows in which some are of positive polarity and some are negative then the PV/Rate curve may reverse its slope and become U-shaped.

In Table 7.1 there are three sets of cash flows with 16-year terms. Each set starts with a relatively high positive value, decreases, turns negative, and then becomes increasingly negative. They are derived from the net after-tax cash flows of a leveraged lease. All assume an initial equity investment of

TABLE 7.1 POLARITY REVERSAL CASES

	Cash Flow		
Year	"−200" Case	"Null" Case	"+200" Case
1	$4,351	$ 4,551	$ 4,751
2	3,661	3,861	4,061
3	2,996	3,196	3,396
4	2,467	2,667	2,867
5	1,930	2,130	2,330
6	1,387	1,587	1,787
7	835	1,035	1,235
8	273	473	673
9	−299	−99	101
10	−882	−682	−482
11	−1,243	−1,043	−843
12	−1,383	−1,183	−983
13	−1,538	−1,338	−1,138
14	−1,712	−1,512	−1,312
15	−1,905	−1,705	−1,505
16	−2,138	−1,938	−1,738
Total	$6,800	$10,000	$13,200

$10,000. The "null" case has a total cash flow that is just equal to the investment or $10,000. The "−200" case was derived by subtracting $200 from each year's cash flow of the "null" case. This results in a total cash flow of $6800 which is $3200 less than the investment. The "+200" case was derived by adding $200 to each year's cash flow of the "null" case. This results in a total cash flow of $13,200 which is greater than the investment. The graph in Figure 7.6 shows the present values of these three sets of cash flows at discount rates from 0 to 30%.

At a 0% discount rate the present value of the "−200" case is equal to its total cash flow of $6800. As the discount rate increases the present value also increases. This relationship is opposite to the normal situation. At 11% the present value reaches its maximum of $10,303 and then declines as the rate continues to increase. Now the curve has a normal slope. At 30% the present value is down to $8330.

Remember that the rate of return of an investment is equal to that discount rate at which the present value of its cash flows equals the investment. This means that the "−200" case has two rates of return. A line drawn horizontally across the graph from the $10,000 mark, which is the amount of the investment, crosses the curve at two points. This indicates two rates of

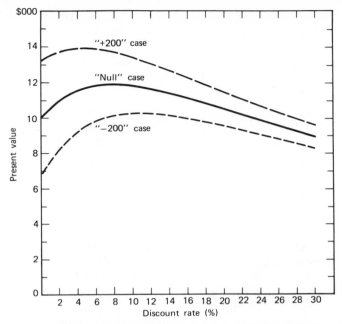

Figure 7.6   Present value as a function of discount rate. Polarity reversal cases.

return, one on the "abnormal" slope of the curve and the other on the "normal." The two rates are 6.8% and 16.3%. If an amortization schedule for the investment is prepared for each of the two rates it is found that both rates will exactly amortize the investment to zero. Actually the positive cash flows overamortize the investment and then the negative cash flows bring the balance back up to zero.

Not only does the "−200" case offer two rates of return but it does so without giving an investor all of the investment back. The investor had to invest $10,000 in order to receive $6800.

The present value of the "null" case cash flows starts at $10,000 at 0%, rises until it peaks at about $11,938 at 8%, and then declines to $8986 at 30%. This case also has two rates of return, 0% and 23.3%, and returns to the investor the exact amount of the investment.

The present value of the "+200" case cash flows starts at $13,200 at 0%, rises to a peak of $13,939 at 4.5%, and then declines to $9643 at 30%. This curve looks almost normal as it intersects the $10,000 investment line at only one point, which is at 27.9%. However the curve looks as though it would intersect the $10,000 line again if it were extended to the left by applying negative discount rates. In fact, doing this results in a second rate of return being found at −4.4%.

The three cases of cash flow streams reversing polarity are summarized below. The rates of return are categorized as normal or abnormal depending on which slope of the PV/Rate curve they lie.

POLARITY REVERSAL CASES

	"−200"	"Null"	"+200"
Gross Cash Flow	$ 6,800	$ 10,000	$ 13,200
Investment	(10,000)	(10,000)	(10,000)
Net Cash Flow	$ (3,200)	$ —	$ 3,200
Normal ROR	16.252%	23.344%	27.887%
Abnormal ROR	6.764%	0%	−4.352%

Each of the cases has two rates of return which are mathematically correct. In some of the cases it is possible to identify one return that appears to be financially correct by examining the cash flows. The "+200" case has a positive net cash flow; that is, the investor receives more than his or her investment. This would imply that the rate of return is positive and that therefore the −4.4% return is not a valid answer. The financially correct rate of 27.9% lies on the normal slope of the curve.

The "null" case has a zero net cash flow. If the investor only gets the investment back with nothing in addition then one is strongly tempted to say that the return on investment is zero and to reject the calculated 23.3% return as invalid. The zero rate lies on the abnormal slope of the curve.

The "−200" case has a negative net cash flow. The investor receives less than was invested. Financial logic would indicate that the investor realizes a negative return on the investment. But both calculated rates are positive. A choice cannot be made between the two rates by looking at the slope of the curve because the two prior cases had apparently valid answers that lay on opposite slopes.

Return to the "+200" case. An investment of $10,000 returns to the investor the initial investment plus $3200, for a calculated rate of return of 27.9%. But if the investor had instead purchased a 16-year annuity at 10% he or she would receive $1278 a year for a total of $20,448, which is $10,448 more than was invested. How can a 28% investment result in net earnings of only $3200 when a 10% investment earns over $10,000?

The solution to the paradox lies in the reinvestment assumption implicit to the rate calculation process. The "+200" case has high cash inflows during the first few years of the term. This initial positive cash flow is assumed to be reinvested to produce further earnings. These additional earnings are more than enough to compensate for the negative cash flows when they occur toward the end of the term.

It is beyond the scope of this book to explore the conceptual problem of multiple rates when a stream of cash flows reverses polarity. But the programmer must be aware of the problem when developing a program that solves for a rate of return. Such a program is the subject of the next chapter.

8

The Discounting Program

A general-purpose discounting program rivals and even exceeds the loan program in usefulness. If the user understands that discounting and compounding are reciprocal processes and that both are based on loan concepts then the discounting program can be used in many more applications than implied by its name. In addition to calculating present values it can be used to find rates of return, the payments of mortgage-type loans, the weighted average interest rate on packages of loans, and annuity investments and payments.

The discounting process involves three components: future cash flows, the present value of those flows, and the discount rate. The discounting program should be able to solve for any one of these components if the other two are given. Further, it should have the flexibility to handle any number of individual cash flows of varying types and combine them into a net cash flow stream for discounting.

DEFINING THE PROGRAM

The program developed here will be named DISC. Its primary function will be to apply a discount rate to future cash flows so as to calculate their present value. The basic structure then will be to input the discount rate and the cash flow parameters, solve for the present value, and print the answer.

Once the mechanics of discounting are in place a second function can be added to solve for the rate if the present value is given. Then a third function can be added to solve for the amount of a future payment or recipt if the rate and present value are given.

Since the program will have three functions a means for selecting the one desired will be needed. And since the user's problem may require finding the present value or future payment at several different discount rates the selection should be repetitive.

The output for each function will be a single number, either the present value, the discount rate, or the payment amount. This means that the print format can be simple and straightforward. In addition provision will be made for printing the net cash flows and their present values period-by-period. This will enable the user to analyze the components of the total present value.

The discount rate and present value as inputs will be single numbers and can be inputted quite simply through terminal questions. The future payments or receipts, that is, the cash flow inputs, will require more complicated handling. Since a discounting problem may involve from one cash flow to a dozen or more accordion input will be required. And each cash flow must have its timing specified as well as its amount, so simple single-number input will not suffice. Therefore the program will use the same input format for the cash flow parameters as was used for LOAN. The master flowchart for DISC appears in Figure 8.1.

CASH FLOW INPUTS

The simplest way to structure the input format would be to have the user input the net cash flows period-by-period. This however is a tedious procedure for even a five-year transaction will have 60 periods if the payment frequency is monthly. This chore can be avoided in most cases by providing two features. One is to enter the individual cash flow components and have the program take their algebraic sum to derive each period's net cash flow. The other is to categorize the cash flows by type and specify their timing parameters. Then the program can allocate the amounts by period. DISC will be developed to handle three types of cash flows—single, series of equal, and series of unequal. This requres a variable to distinguish between the cash flow types. This variable will be named G1, the same as for LOAN. Figure 8.2 presents the flowchart of the input section.

The single or one-shot cash flow is the simplest of the cash flow types. It consists of a single payment or receipt that occurs at a specific time. It requires only three input data—the code number to indicate cash flow type, the amount of the cash flow, and the period at which the cash flow occurs. The value one will be used as the code for the single type. Then the input file data for $1500 received at the end of six months would look like this, assuming the line number is 20.

20 1,1500,6

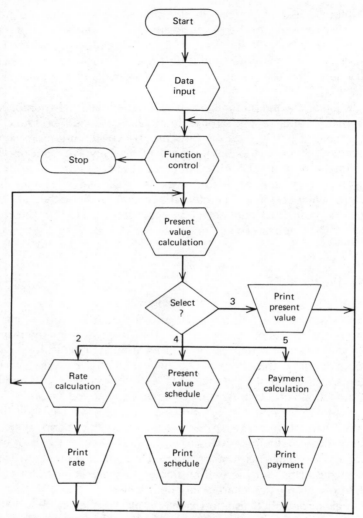

Figure 8.1   Master flowchart of DISC.

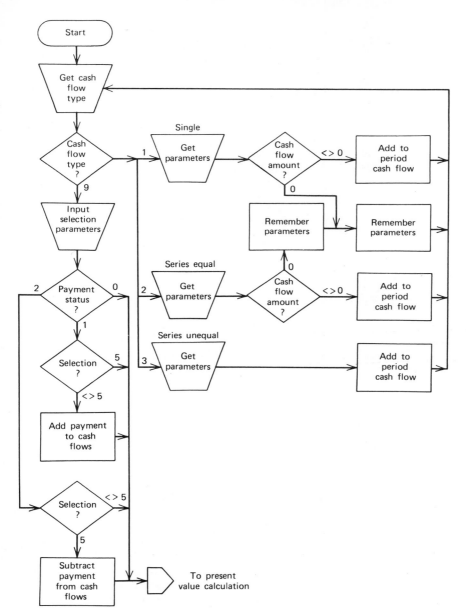

Figure 8.2   Input section flowchart of DISC.

Using the same nomenclature that was developed for the loan cash flows, the amount will be named H1 and the period of occurrence J2. The front end of the program begins developing like this.

```
100 DIM N(366),V(366)
110 REM INPUT
120 OPEN 1,'INDISC',INPUT
130 GET 1:B1
140 GET 1:G1
150 IF G1=9 GOTO 190
160 GOTO 210,310,490 ON G1
170 PRINT "ILLEGAL CASH FLOW TYPE."
180 STOP
190 CLOSE 1
200 GOTO 590
210 REM SINGLE CF
220 GET 1:H1,J2
230 IF B2>=J2 GOTO 250
240 LET B2=J2
```

. . .

```
260 LET N(J2+1)=N(J2+1)+H1
270 GOTO 140
```

Line 100 sets the maximum number of periods the program will accept by dimensioning the variables that will contain the net cash flow and present value for each period.

Net cash flow for period is   N
Present value of net cash flow for period is   V

Line 120 opens the input file which is named INDISC. Line 130 inputs the number of periods per year B1 which will determine the frequency of discounting. Line 140 inputs the cash flow type G1 which must be on a line by itself because it must be tested for its value before the program knows what to do next. If G1 equals the end-of-data code of nine then the program goes to line 190 and closes the input file before moving on to the next stage. If G1 equals one, indicating a single-payment cash flow, then line 160 directs the program to line 210 after which the cash flow amount and its period are inputted by line 220. Lines 230 and 240 compare the total number of periods B2 with the cash flow period J2 to ensure that B2 is no less than J2. This is necessary because B2 will be used later as the limit for period loops.

The object of all the foregoing is to build up to line 260. Here the cash flow amount H1 is added to the net cash flow N for the period J2. Then the program returns to line 140 to input the next cash flow.

The series of equal cash flow consists of a series of discrete payments, each of the same amount, and occurring in each period of the specififed term. This cash flow type requires five input data—the type code, which will be two, the advance or arrears code K1, the periodic cash flow amount H1, the period marking the beginning of the term J1, and the period marking the end of the term J2. The specification of the timing is exactly the same as for the loan programs. If $350 will be monthly in arrears throughout the second year then the input file data would look like this.

```
30 2,2,350,12,24
```

When the program inputs a cash flow type G1 with a value of two it jumps to line 310 to process the series of equal type.

```
310 REM SERIES EQUAL CF
320 GET 1:K1,H1,J1,J2
330 IF B2>=J2 GOTO 350
340 LET B2=J2

. . .

360 IF K1>1 GOTO 410
370 FOR T=J1 TO (J2−1)
380 LET N(T+1)=N(T+1)+H1
390 NEXT T
405 GOTO 140
410 FOR T=(J1+1) TO J2
420 LET N(T+1)=N(T+1)+H1
430 NEXT T
445 GOTO 140
```

Line 320 inputs the cash flow parameters and lines 330 and 340 ensure that the total number of periods B2 is no less than the highest period of the cash flow. Line 360 tests the advance/arrears code K1 which determines the loop by which the cash flow will be processed. Lines 370 to 390 comprise the loop for advance payments which steps through each period from J1 to J2 − 1. Lines 410 to 430 comprise the loop for arrears payments which steps through every period from J1 + 1 to J2. Thus a stream of advance payments is shifted forward one period in time compared to a stream of arrears payments. Within each loop the cash flow amount H1 is added to the net cash flow N for the appropriate periods. After leaving either loop the program returns to line 140 to input the next cash flow.

In some problems the cash flow may vary from period to period so that the series of equal type cannot be used. And using the single type would require typing three numbers for each and every period. The series of unequal cash flow type is designed to handle this situation. After entering the type code of three, the period of the first cash flow is entered, and then each cash flow amount is entered in sequence. After all the amounts are entered an end-of-data code of one is entered. For example if $300 is received at period five, $725 at period six, nothing is received at period seven, $205 at period eight, $470 at period nine, and a payment of $517 is made at period ten, the input data would look like this.

40 3,5,300,725,0,205,470,−517,1

Zero is not used as the end-of-data code so that periods of zero cash flow can be incorporated in the data line without having to start a new type three data line. One is a convenient value for the end-of-data code because a cash flow of exactly $1 is seldom encountered in financial problems. On those rare occasions in which there is a cash flow of $1 the program can be tricked by entering 1.001 or 1.0001 to signify $1. The difference from one prevents the cash flow amount from being interpreted as the end-of-data code yet the difference is too small to affect the output which is rounded to the nearest cent.

```
490 REM SERIES UNEQUAL
500 GET 1:J1
510 GET 1:H1
520 IF H1=1 GOTO 560
530 LET N(J1+1)=N(J1+1)+H1
540 LET J1=J1+1
550 GOTO 510
560 IF B2>=J1−1 GOTO 140
570 LET B2=J1−1
580 GOTO 140
```

If the program encounters a value of three for the cash flow type G1 it goes to line 490. From there the program inputs the period of the first cash flow J1 with line 500 and the first cash flow amount H1 with line 510. The cash flow amount H1 is added to the net cash flow N for the period J1 in line 530. Then J1 is incremented by one in line 540 and line 550 directs the program back to line 510 to input the cash flow amount for the next period. Thus J1 is used as a period counter, being stepped one after each cash flow amount is processed so that J1 defines the period of each cash flow. When the program encounters a value for H1 equal to one this indicates the end of the type three cash flow amounts. The program then goes to line 560 where the total number of periods B2 is compared with the period of the last cash flow. The comparison is to one less than J1 because J1 was incremented after the last cash flow was processed so it now overstates the cash flow period. Then the program returns to line 140 to input the next cash flow.

Putting the three numerical examples together results in input data like this.

```
10 12
20 1,1500,6
30 2,2,350,12,24
40 3,5,300,725,0,205,470,−517,1
50 9
```

The first line in the data file specifies the number of periods per year which determines the discounting frequency, which is monthly in the example. Then come the cash flow lines with each one beginning with its type code of one, two, or three. There may be any number of cash flow lines, in any order, and the types can be freely intermixed. The last datum in the data file is nine to indicate the end of the data. This input data format is the same as shown in Figure 6.2.

FUNCTION SELECTION

Once the cash flows have been inputted and allocated to the appropriate time periods the program can query the user as to what to do with them. The program has been defined to have four functions, namely, calculate the present value, print a schedule of net cash flows and present values, calculate the discount rate (rate of return), and calculate the future payment or payments. In addition to selections for the four functions there must be a selection to stop the program, since the select question will be repetitive, and one to list the selections. The function select variable will again be named C1.

```
590 REM FUNCTION SELECT

. . .

610 PRINT
620 PRINT "SELECT";
630 INPUT C1
640 IF C1>0 GOTO 660
650 STOP
660 GOTO 670,750,830,860,890 ON C1
670 PRINT
680 PRINT " STOP      = 0"
690 PRINT " LIST      = 1"
700 PRINT " RATE CALC = 2"
710 PRINT " PV TOTAL  = 3"
720 PRINT " PV SCHED  = 4"
730 PRINT " PMT CALC  = 5"
740 GOTO 610
```

Lines 620 and 630 ask the select question and input the answer. An answer of zero or less will fail the test at line 640 and stop the program. For any answer from one to five line 660 will direct the program to branch appropriately. If the answer is greater than five then the program will proceed to line 670 by default and print the list of selections. A selection of one will also cause the list to be printed.

The Stop and List selections have been given the code values of zero and one respectively the same as LOAN. The various members of a family of programs should share the same code values for the same selections as much as practicable. This lessens the strain on the user's memory and enables him or her to work at the terminal more effectively.

With the selection made the program can now solicit the input data unrelated to cash flow parameters.

Desired present value is	Z1
Discount rate is	R1
Increment is	C2
Precision of rate calculation is	D1

The desired present value Z1 is the amount that the cash flows should equal after discounting. This input is required when either the rate or the payment is to be calculated. It is the amount of the initial investment that produces the future cash flows. The discount rate R1 is the rate at which it is desired to discount the cash flows and is required if either the present value or the payment is to be calculated. The increment C2 is the number of periods to be cumulated for each printout line if the present value schedule is selected. The precision of the rate calculation D1 will be discussed below.

Line 660 above directed the program to various lines depending on the function selected as indicated by the value of C1. If the rate calculation was selected the program goes to line 750.

```
750 PRINT "PV";
760 INPUT Z1
770 IF Z1=0 GOTO 800
780 LET D1=.000000001*Z1
790 GOTO 810
800 LET D1=.001
810 LET R1=10
820 GOTO 910
```

Line 750 asks for the desired present value or investment and it is inputted as Z1 at line 760. Now two assumptions are made. One concerns the precision with which the rate calculation is made and the other is the initial trial discount rate. Since the program will seek that rate at which the calculated present value equals the desired present value Z1, and since the machine works with a finite number of digits and would seldom, if ever, be able to produce a difference exactly equal to zero, a decision must be made as to how close is close enough. This is done in line 780 where the level of precision D1 is set to .0000001% of the desired present value Z1. This is equivalent to an accuracy of 1 cent per $10 million. If the desired present value is specififed as zero then lines 770 and 800 act to set the precision to .001 or a flat one-tenth of a cent.

Since the program solves for the rate by trying various rates until the correct one is found an initial trial discount rate must be assumed to get things started. This is done in line 810 where the discount rate R1 is set to 10%. The program then goes to line 910.

```
830 PRINT "RATE";
840 INPUT R1
850 GOTO 910
860 PRINT "RATE, INCREMENT";
870 INPUT R1,C2
880 GOTO 910
890 PRINT "RATE, PV";
```

```
900 INPUT R1,Z1
910 IF R1>=1 GOTO 940
920 PRINT "ENTER RATE AS %, NOT DECIMAL."
930 GOTO 660
940 LET R1=R1/(B1*100)
```

If the selected function was the present value calculation, the present value schedule, or the payment calculation then line 660 sends the program to line 830, 860, or 890 respectively. The required input data of rate, rate and increment, or rate and present value are inputted and all branches reconverge at line 910. Here the discount rate R1 is tested and if it is not in percentage form an error message is printed. Then the program returns to line 660 where it can be redirected to the proper input question. The user can thus try again. Once the discount rate R1 is in percentage form the program goes to line 940 and converts it to a periodic decimal. If this seems like a pointless runaround remember that the reason for inputting a rate in the percentage form is to conform to the way in which the user normally thinks of a rate.

PRESENT VALUE CALCULATION

Regardless of the function selected the present value of the net cash flows has to be calculated.

Total present value is X1

The total present value can be derived by placing the present value equation within a loop that steps through each period and cumulating the results.

```
1170 REM PV CALC
1180 LET X1=0
1190 FOR T=0 TO B2
1200 LET V(T+1)=N(T+1)/(1+R1)↑T
1210 LET X1=X1+V(T+1)
1220 NEXT T
1230 IF C1<>3 GOTO 1250
1240 PRINT USING 1970,(R1*B1*100),X1
1250 GOTO 590,1260,590,1490,1670 ON C1
```

. . .

```
1970 : TOTAL PV AT ###.###### % IS $############.##
```

Since the program may go through the present value calculations several times in the course of a single run the total present value X1 must be reset to its initial value of zero each time. This is done in line 1180. Lines 1190 and 1220 form the loop with the former setting the limits from period zero to the total number of periods B2. Within the loop line 1200 calculates each period's present value V(T). The equation uses the single discount factor formula from Figure 7.3. Line 1210 adds each period's present value V(T) to the total present value X1.

After leaving the loop the program tests the function select variable C1 and if the present value selection is the one made (C1 = 3) then the discount rate R1 and present value X1 are printed by line 1240. The rate is converted to the annual percentage form for printing. If some other selection is the one desired than the print line is bypassed.

Line 1250 causes the program to branch according to which selection C1 is desired. If it is the present value calculation then the program returns to the select question at line 590 for the answer will have just been printed. The user may then stop the program, ask for a present value calculation at a different discount rate, or choose an alternative calculation.

RATE CALCULATION

The method of calculating the rate is the same as the manual approach used by an analyst armed only with the "Blue Book." A reasonable discount rate is chosen and the present value of the cash flows calculated. The calculated present value is compared with the desired present value and if it is too high then a higher discount rate is chosen for the second trial. If it is too low then a lower discount rate is chosen. The analyst continues to adjust the discount rate after each trial until the problem's rate is bracketed as closely as possible given the rates available in the "Blue Book." The analyst then interpolates to obtain an approximation of the final answer.

The program will use exactly the same method except that an inter/extrapolation formula will be used for all but the first two trials. The flow-chart for the rate calculation appears in Figure 8.3. New variables are required.

Number of trials (iterations) is	T2
Prior trial discount rate is	R2
New trial discount rate is	R3
Prior trial present value is	X3

The iteration counter T2 is set to an initial value of zero in line 600 just before the select question is asked. This is to prevent any carryover value

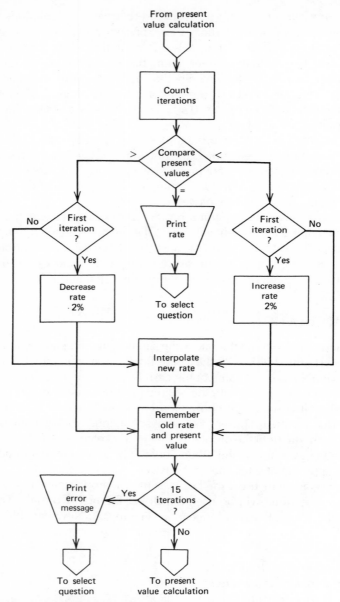

Figure 8.3   Rate calculation flowchart.

from a prior selection. As already discussed if the rate calculation is selected the program asks for the desired present value Z1, sets the calculation precision D1, and sets the discount rate R1 to 10%. The program then calculates the present value of the cash flows at the assumed rate of 10% and is directed by line 1250 to line 1260 for calculating the rate.

. . .

600 LET T2=0

. . .

1260 REM RATE CALC
1270 LET T2=T2+1

. . .

1310 IF Z1−X1>D1 GOTO 1350
1320 IF Z1−X1<−D1 GOTO 1380
1330 PRINT USING 1960, (R1*B1*100),T2
1340 GOTO 590
1350 IF T2>1 GOTO 1410
1360 LET R3=R1−(.02/B1)
1370 GOTO 1420
1380 IF T2>1 GOTO 1410
1390 LET R3=R1+(.02/B1)
1400 GOTO 1420
1410 LET R3=R2+((Z1−X3)/(X1−X3))*(R1−R2)
1420 LET R2=R1
1430 LET R1=R3
1440 LET X3=X1
1450 IF T2<15 GOTO 1170

. . .

1960 : RATE IS ###.###### % T2=##

The iteration counter T2 is increased by one in line 1270. Every time a new rate is tried a new present value is calculated and T2 keeps track of how many times this has been done. Lines 1310 and 1320 compare the desired present value Z1 with the calculated present value X1. If they are within the precision limit D1, plus or minus, then the answer has been found and line 1330 prints the calculated rate in annual percentage form. It also prints the number of tries T2 it took. Line 1340 then directs the program back to the select question at line 590 and the user can make another selection.

If the calculated present value is not within the acceptable limit of the desired present value then the program branches according to whether it is too low or too high. In either case the iteration counter T2 is tested in lines 1350 and 1380 as the inter/extrapolation formula cannot be used until at least two trial passes have been made. If only one has been made then the next trial rate R3 will be two percentage points lower or higher than the current discount rate R1. This is done in lines 1360 and 1390. If at least two iterations have been made then the program is directed to line 1410 which calculates the new trial rate R3 by means of a straightline interpolation formula. The formula takes the difference between the last two discount rates R1 and R2, divides it by the difference between the last two present values X1 and X3, and multiplies the result by the difference between the desired present value Z1 and the prior calculated present value X3. The product is added to the prior discount rate R2 to derive the next trial discount rate R3. This is the same process used manually by the analyst with the "Blue Book."

Once the new trial rate R3 is decided upon the current rate R1 becomes the prior rate R2 in line 1420, the new trial rate R3 becomes the current trial rate R1 in line 1430, and the current present value X1 becomes the prior present value X3 in line 1440. The program then returns to line 1170 and calculates the present value at the new rate.

To summarize the rate calculation process, an initial discount rate of 10% is assumed and the present value of the cash flows is calculated at that rate. Then the trial rate is changed by two percentage points and the present value calculated again. After that the program always has two rates and two present values with which to work and computes new trial rates based on the two sets of differences. It continues to calculate new rates, each one based on the results of the last two, until the present value lies within the precision level defined by D1. The number of iterations required to find the rate is generally in the range of five to eight.

If the program were given an insolvable prolem it would run forever seeking a rate that did not exist. To prevent this the rate search is stopped after the fifteenth iteration.

```
1450 IF T2<15 GOTO 1170
1460 PRINT "NO ANSWER BY 15 ITERATIONS."
1470 PRINT USING 2000,X3,(R2*B1*100)
1480 GOTO 590
```

. . .

```
2000 : LATEST CALCULATED PV IS ###########.## AT
###.###### %
```

Line 1450 tests the iteration counter T2 and if it is less than 15 the program continues the search. Otherwise the program prints an error message and reports the results of the last calculation. This serves both as a trouble-shooting aid and as a pacifier for the user who in some exasperation is wondering how close the program came to finding an answer. The program then returns to the select question. The user can either stop the program or calculate the present values at various given rates in an attempt to identify the nature of the trouble. Experience indicates that failure to find the rate within 15 iterations is due to (1) an error in the input data, (2) an inherently insolvable problem such as trying to discount an all-positive stream of cash flows to zero, or (3) a polarity-reversal case in which the present value/discount rate curve is U-shaped.

The program's response to a U-shaped curve varies. Instead of the iteration error above, it may merely find one of the possible rates and print it as the answer. Or the interpolation formula may cause the program to swing wildly back and forth between the two slopes of the curve. Such wild swings may result in the BASIC system printing an overflow error message. On occasion the result may be that two successive calculated present values are the same so that their difference is zero. An attempt to divide by zero in the interpolation formula causes the BASIC system to print a division-by-zero error message. The latter problem can be avoided as follows.

```
1280 IF X1−X3<>0 GOTO 1310
1290 LET R3=.4/B1
1300 GOTO 1420
```

If the difference between the current present value X1 and the prior present value X3 is determined by line 1280 to be zero then the new trial rate R3 is set to 40% by line 1290. The purpose of this is to dislodge the program from the pattern that evolved from the initial trial discount rate of 10%.

PRESENT VALUE SCHEDULE

Producing a schedule of net cash flows and their present values is relatively simple as both the period cash flows N and period present values V are already known. The only complicating factor is the need to cumulate the values if an increment greater than one is specified. For this purpose cumu-lation variables are needed.

Period counter for increment comparison is	X2
Cumulative period cash flow for increment is	X4
Total net cash flow is	X5
Cumulative period present value for increment is	X6

The basic structure is a period print loop with heading and totals lines.

```
1490 REM PV SCHED
1500 LET X2,X4,X5,X6=0
1510 PRINT USING 1910,(R1*B1*100)
1520 PRINT USING 1920
...

1910 : PER   NET CASH FLOW   PV AT ###.######%
1920 : ——    ——————————      ——————————————
```

Line 1500 sets the cumulation variables to zero to avoid carryover values. Lines 1510 and 1520 print the heading.

```
1530 FOR T=0 TO B2
1540 LET X4=X4+N (T+1)
1550 LET X6=X6+V(T+1)
1560 IF T=0 GOTO 1590
1570 LET X2=X2+1
1580 IF X2<C2 GOTO 1620
1590 PRINT USING 1930,T,X4,X6
1600 LET X5=X5+X4
1610 LET X2,X4,X6=0
1620 NEXT T
...

1930 : ### ############.## ############.##
```

Lines 1530 and 1620 form the loop that steps through all periods from zero to the last period B2. Lines 1540 and 1550 cumulate the period cash flow N and present value V in the cumulation variables X4 and X6. Line 1570 increments the period counter X2 until it equals the desired increment C2. As long as X2 is less than the increment C2 line 1580 causes the print line to be bypassed. Once the number of passes through the loop equals the increment then line 1590 prints the cumulated values X4 and X6. Then the total net cash flow X5 is increased by the cumulated net cash flow X4 in line 1600 and all three cumulation variables used for the increment are reset to zero.

Line 1560 bypasses the cumulation at time zero and causes the period zero values to be printed by line 1590. If it is desired to include period zero in the first cumulation yet not disturb the timing of subsequent cumulations then line 1560 can be eliminated and X2 set to −1 instead of 0 before entering the loop.

```
1630 PRINT USING 1920
1640 PRINT USING 1940,X5,X1
1650 PRINT USING 1950
1660 GOTO 590
```

. . .

```
1940  TOT  $############.##    ############.##
1950  ===  ================  ===============
```

Lines 1630 and 1650 print the underlinings and line 1640 prints the totals. Then line 1660 directs the program back to the select question at line 590 to request the next selection.

PAYMENT CALCULATION

The final selection is to calculate a future payment. This is a useful feature for not only can it be used to determine the payment amount required to realize a given rate of return on a given investment, but it can also calculate the increment to a given set of cash flows to obtain the desired rate.

The calculated payment may be either of two types, the single cash flow or the series of equal. That is, it can be either one payment or a stream of level payments. In either case the timing of the payment or payments must be specified. In short the input for a calculated payment must have all the parameters of a given cash flow except the amount. This suggests that a payment to be calculated can be entered into the input file INDISC exactly like any other cash flow but with an amount of zero. For example to solve for the amount of a payment to be made the end of the second year of a monthly transaction would require INDISC input data like this.

```
50 1,0,24
```

Zero as the cash flow amount is thus used as the code to tell the program that a payment amount is to be calculated. But since the calculation cannot be done until after all of the cash flows have been inputted some variables are needed to remember the parameters of the unknown cash flow.

Remember cash flow type (G1) is   G2
Remember cash flow timing (J2) is   J4

Provision for handling this situation can be inserted into the input section at the beginning of the program.

```
210 REM SINGLE CF
220 GET 1: H1,J2

. . .

250 IF H1=0 GOTO 280

. . .

280 LET J4=J2
290 LET G2=G1
300 GOTO 140
```

The new lines are 250 and 280 through 300. If in the course of inputting the cash flow data the program encounters a cash flow amount H1 of zero line 250 will direct it to line 280 where the timing specification J2 will be remembered by J4. Then in line 290 the cash flow type G1 will be remembered by G2. Then line 300 directs the program back to line 140 to input the next cash flow.

The advantages of this approach are two. It uses the same format for the unknown cash flow parameters as for the known and is therefore easy to remember. And it maintains the program's ability to handle cash flows in any order. The unknown cash flow can be the first cash flow line, the last, or inserted anywhere among the other cash flow lines. The user does not have to worry about maintaining any predetermined order.

The series of equal unknown payment can be handled in the same way except that two more "remember" variables are needed.

> Remember advance/arrears code (K1) is   K2
> Remember beginning of term (J1) is   J3

The input data for 12 unknown monthly payments to be made in arrears during the second year would look like the line below. The only difference from a known type two cash flow is that the amount is entered as zero.

```
50 2,2,0,12,24
```

Statements are added to the input section of the program to handle the unknown amount case.

```
210 REM SINGLE CF

. . .

280 LET J4=J2
290 LET G2=G1
300 GOTO 140
310 REM SERIES EQUAL
320 GET 1:K1,H1,J1,J2

. . .

350 IF H1=0 GOTO 460

. . .

460 LET K2=K1
470 LET J3=J1
480 GOTO 280
```

The new lines are 350 and 460 through 480. If after inputting the cash flow parameters at line 320 the program finds in line 350 that the cash flow amount H1 is zero it proceeds to line 460. There the advance/arrears code K1 is remembered by K2. In line 470 the term beginning J1 is remembered by J3. Then line 480 directs the program to line 280. The term ending J2 and cash flow type G1 have to be remembered and statements for doing this have already been added to the single cash flow section. So rather than repeat the statements in the series of equal section the program merely hops up to the prior section. There J2 and G1 are remembered and the program goes to line 140 to input the next cash flow.

Calculating a payment thus takes two steps. A zero amount cash flow line is placed in the input file and, when running, the select question is answered with a code value of five. If any other selection is made the program will effectively ignore any zero amount cash flow for nothing will have been added to the period cash flow N. If there is more than one zero amount cash flow line in the input file the program will only remember the last one by the time the select question is reached.

If the payment calculation is selected the program will solicit and input the desired rate and present value at lines 890 and 900 as discussed before. It will then calculate the present value of any known cash flows and then go to line 1670, the beginning of the payment calculation section.

To calculate a future payment the program solves for that amount whose present value equals the difference between the desired present value Z1 and the present value X1 of the known cash flows, if any. Some more variables are used.

Present value factors are E1,E2,E3,E4

```
1670 REM PMT CALC
1680 IF G2=1 GOTO 1720
1690 IF G2=2 GOTO 1750
1700 PRINT "PAYMENT NOT DEFINED."
1710 GOTO 590
1720 LET H1=(Z1−X1)*(1+R1)↑J4
1730 PRINT USING 1980,H1
1740 GOTO 1870
. . .
1870 LET H1=INT(100*(H1+.005))/100
. . .
1890 GOTO 590
. . .
1980 : SINGLE PAYMENT IS $#############.##
```

Lines 1680 and 1690 cause the program to branch according to the remembered cash flow type G2. If the user has selected the payment calculation without putting a zero amount cash flow in the input file then G2 will still have its initial value of zero. This will cause the tests to be failed and the program prints the error message at line 1700. It then returns to the select question at line 590.

If the cash flow type is single (G2 = 1) then the program goes to line 1720 where the payment amount is calculated. This is done by multiplying the difference between the desired present value Z1 and the calculated present value X1 by the compound factor for a single cash flow. The formula for the factor is taken from Figure 7.3. If there are no known amount cash flows in the input file then X1 will equal zero and the payment will be calculated on the entire desired present value Z1. The calculated payment amount is named H1 the same as an inputted cash flow amount and is printed by line 1730. The program then goes to line 1870 where the calculated payment is rounded to the nearest cent. The reason for this is so that it will be to the same number of decimal places as an actual payment in case the user should make another selection.

```
1750 IF K2>1 GOTO 1830
. . .
1830 LET E1=(1−(1/(1+R1)↑J4))/R1
1840 LET E2=(1−(1/(1+R1)↑J3))/R1
1850 LET H1=(Z1−X1)/(E1−E2)
1860 PRINT USING 1990,H1
. . .
1990 : PERIODIC PAYMENT IS $#########.##
```

If the payment is to be the series of equal type then the program goes to line 1750 where the remembered advance/arrears code K2 is tested. For payments in arrears the program goes to line 1830 and calculates the first payment factor E1. The formula used is that for series of equal discount factors in Figure 7.3. Note that the single type calculation used a compound factor while the series of equal calculation uses a discount factor. This is not contradictory for the former used its factor as a multiplier while the latter uses its factor as a divisor. In either case the result will be a future value of a present amount.

If the stream of payments starts at time zero ($J3 = J1 = 0$) then the factor E1 is sufficient for calculating an answer as it will produce the amount of each payment from the present to the end of the term J4. But the program must also handle the situation where the payments do not start until some time in the future, in which case J3 is greater than zero. This can be done by calculating a second factor covering the time from the present to the beginning of the term J3 and subtracting it from the first factor. That is, if the first factor E1 covers the time from the present to period J4 and the second factor E2 covers the time from the present to period J3, then E1 minus E2 will apply to the time from period J3 to period J4. The second factor E2 is calculated in line 1840. The payment itself is calculated in line 1850 by dividing the difference between the two factors into the difference between the desired present value Z1 and the present value of known cash flows X1.

Line 1860 prints the answer which is rounded to the nearest cent by the IMAGE statement at line 1990. Then the calculated amount is formally rounded by the same statement that rounded the single payment and the program returns to the select question.

If the payments are in advance then the program goes to line 1760 instead of 1830.

```
1760 LET E3=(1−(1/(1+R1)↑ (J4−1)))/R1
1770 IF J3=0 GOTO 1810
1780 LET E4=(1−(1/(1+R1)↑(J3−1)))/R1
1790 LET H1=(Z1−X1)/E3−E4)
1800 GOTO 1860
1810 LET H1=(Z1−X1)/(1+E3)
1820 GOTO 1860
```

If payments are in advance then the last payment occurs at period J4 minus one. The present value factor for this stream is produced by line 1760. If the term begins at time zero then line 1770 sends the program to line 1810 where the payment is calculated. The payment calculation is based on one plus the factor E3 because the first payment occurs at period zero, is undiscounted, and so has a factor of one.

If the payment term begins in the future, and thus J3 is greater than zero, then the present value factor E4 is calculated in line 1780. This factor covers the time before the first payment is made and is subtracted from E3 when calculating the payment in line 1790.

The list below summarizes the specific periods covered by the four present value factors and their combinations.

Factor	Periods Included
E1	1 through J4
E2	1 through J3
E3	1 through J4−1
E4	1 through J3−1
E1−E2	J3+1 through J4
E3−E4	J3 through J4−1
1+E3	0 through J4−1

After calculating the payment the program goes to line 1860 where the answer is printed. Then the answer is rounded and the program returns to the select question.

CONTROL OF THE CALCULATED PAYMENT

The program is now complete except for one remaining item. A future cash flow or payment can be calculated but it is not yet added to the net cash flows. The answer is printed but the user cannot make another selection whose result will include the payment. He or she cannot check whether the printed answer actually gives the desired rate of return or calculate the present value with the payment included. To do so requires that the user stop the program, type the payment amount into the input file, and then rerun the program.

A just-calculated payment amount should therefore be added to the period cash flows so that it is included in subsequent selections. But then if the user should wish to make another payment calculation, perhaps at a different rate, the old calculated payment will distort the calculation of the new payment. Unless, of course, each new payment is recognized as being incremental to the last one.

The solution to the problem of being able to make successive selections when one or more of them is a payment calculation is to add a bit of logic that will either add or subtract a calculated payment from the period cash flows. This will require another variable.

Status of payment calculation is C3

The payment status variable C3 will have three code values. If no payment has been calculated its value will be zero. If a payment has been calculated but not added to the cash flows then C3 will equal one. And if the calculated payment has been added to the cash flows then C3 will equal two.

The logic that controls the treatment of the calculated payment must be inserted after the select question, so that the selection is known, but before the present value calculation begins.

```
950 REM CONTROL OF CALC PMT
960 PRINT
970 IF C3=0 GOTO 1170
980 LET K1=K2
990 LET J1=J3
1000 LET J2=J4
1010 IF C3=1 GOTO 1110
. . .

1110 IF C1=5 GOTO 1170
1120 LET C3=2
. . .

1670 REM PMT CALC
. . .

1880 LET C3=1
```

Taking the last line first, line 1880 is added to the payment calculation section. This line sets the payment status C3 to one to indicate that a payment has been calculated.

For the sake of appearance a space should be inserted between the printing of the conversation at the select question and the printing of any answer. Instead of adding a dummy PRINT statement before each of the possible answer PRINT statements it is inserted at line 960 where it may serve for all.

Line 970 tests the calculated payment status C3 and if it equals zero the program bypasses the control section to go directly to the present value calculation at line 1170. If no payment has been calculated then there is nothing to add to or subtract from the cash flows. Lines 980 through 1000 rename the payment parameters K2, J3, and J4 with their original input designations of K1, J1, and J2. This will facilitate the control process below.

Line 1010 again tests C3 and if its value is one, indicating a payment has been calculated but not added to the cash flows, then the program goes to line 1110. If the selection C1 equals five, meaning that another payment calculation has been chosen, then the remainder of the control section is bypassed as the new calculated payment should not be based on cash flows that include the old calculated payment. For any other selection the status variable C3 is set to two for the payment is about to be added to the cash flows.

```
1130 IF G2<>2 GOTO 1160
1140 GOSUB 360
1150 GOTO 1170
1160 LET N(J4+1)=N(J4+1)+H1
```

If the calculated payment is a type one or single then line 1130 directs the program to line 1160 where the payment H1 is added to the period cash flow N at period J4.

If the calculated payment is a series of equal type (G2 = 2) then the payment amount must be added to periods J1 to J2 − 1 or J1 + 1 to J2 depending on whether it is in advance or arrears. This requires a test of the advance/arrears code K1 and a loop to step through the periods. Such a set of statements already exist in the input section. So line 1140 sends the program to line 360 and the series of equal loops in the input section by means of a GOSUB statement. GOSUB is a convenient means of using the same set of statements as a subroutine to serve several sections of the program. A RETURN statement at the end of the subroutine sends the program back to the line following the one with the GOSUB statement. Here it is line 1150 which in turn sends the program to the present value calculation.

In the present situation a few changes in the series of equal input section converts it into a subroutine that can be used to add or subtract a calculated series of payments from the period cash flows. This is in addition to its original and primary function of allocating series of equal cash flows from the input file to the period cash flows.

```
310 REM SERIES EQUAL

. . .

360 IF K1>1 GOTO 410
370 FOR T=J1 TO (J2−1)
380 LET N(T+1)=N(T+1)+H1
390 NEXT T
400 GOTO 440
410 FOR T=(J1+1) TO J2
420 LET N(T+1)=N(T+1)+H1
430 NEXT T
440 IF C3=0 GOTO 140
450 RETURN TO 1070 OR 1150
```

Almost the entire section is repeated here to provide context but only two statements have been changed and one has been added. After exit from the advance loop, line 400 now sends the program to line 440 which is also the exit line for the arrears loop. There the payment status C3 is tested and if it is equal to zero then no payment has been calculated, which means the subroutine must be performing its input function. So the program is directed to line 140 to input the next cash flow. For any other value of C3 the subroutine must be performing its payment control function and line 450 sends the program back to the originating GOSUB statement. Only the first word of line 450 is executable as the program remembers where it came from. Anything after RETURN will be ignored. The line numbers are specified merely for the convenience of the reader of the program listing.

```
1020 IF C1<5 GOTO 1170
1030 LET C3=1
1040 IF G2=1 GOTO 1090
1050 LET H1=−H1
1060 GOSUB 360
1070 LET H1=−H1
1080 GOTO 1170
1090 LET N(J4+1)=N(J4+1)−H1
1100 GOTO 1170
```

Back at the payment control section if the payment status C3 equals two, indicating that a calculated payment has already been added to the cash flows, then the program goes to line 1020 by default. There the selection C1 is tested and if the payment calculation has not been chosen then the program bypasses the rest of the section and goes to the present value calculation. For anything other than another payment calculation the cash flows should include the prior calculated payment. If the payment calculation has been chosen then line 1030 sets the payment status C3 to one for the payment is about to be subtracted from the cash flows.

If the payment type is single (G2 = 1) then line 1040 sends the program to line 1090 where the payment amount H1 is subtracted from the period cash flow N at period J4. Then the program continues on to line 1170 and the present value calculation.

If the payment type is series of equal line 1050 reverses the polarity of the payment amount H1. Then line 1060 sends the program to the subroutine at line 360 in the input section. There the period loops add the reversed polarity amount to the appropriate period cash flows, thus effectively subtracting them. Upon its return to line 1070 the program reverses the payment amount H1 back to its original polarity and then goes to line 1170 and the present value calculation.

In summary, as long as no payment has been calculated the payment status C3 is zero and the payment control section is bypassed. When a payment is calculated C3 is set to one. If a subsequent selection is anything other than a payment calculation and C3 is one then C3 is set to two and the payment amount is added to the cash flows. If a subsequent selection is the payment calculation and C3 equals two then C3 is reset to one and the prior payment amount is subtracted from the cash flows.

A run of the completed DISC program is presented in Figure 8.4. Using three cash flow inputs, one of each type, the run illustrates the rate, present value, and payment calculations.

ALTERNATIVE RATE CALCULATION

Another method of calculating the discount rate or rate of return may be called the fixed increment approach.

The inter/extrapolation method is based on a formula that uses the results of two previous trials to predict the rate that will produce the desired present value. Essentially a straight-line formula is used to solve for a curvilinear function. But the overshoot of each trial rapidly decreases until the calculated rate gives a result that is within the specified limit of precision.

The fixed increment method also starts with a predetermined initial rate but this rate is varied by a fixed increment for each trial until the desired present value is overshot. Then the size of the increment is decreased and the trials continue until the desired present value is again overshot. The program oscillates around the unknown rate with smaller and smaller trial rate increments until the specified number of increments has been reached. Then the answer is printed.

Rate increment is R2

The fixed increment method requires fewer program statements than the inter/extrapolation method.

```
1260 REM RATE CALC
1275 FOR T1=1 TO 6
1285 LET R2=.1↑T1
1295 LET R1=R1+R2
1305 LET X1=0
1315 FOR T=0 TO B2
1325 LET X1=X1+(N(T+1)/(1+R1)↑T)
```

```
LIST

INDISC          8:52    MONDAY MAY 23,1977

10 12
20 2,2,333.33,0,24
30 1,2657.32,24
40 3,5,-100,-200,0,300,1
50 2,2,0,12,24
999 9


RUN DISC

DISC            8:52    MONDAY MAY 23,1977

SELECT?2
PV?10000

  RATE IS   5.000021 %  T2= 6

SELECT?3
RATE?5.000021

  TOTAL PV AT   5.000021 % IS $        10000.00

SELECT?5
RATE, PV?10,10000

  PERIODIC PAYMENT IS $      58.71

SELECT?5
RATE, PV?15,10000

  PERIODIC PAYMENT IS $     121.64

SELECT?3
RATE?15

  TOTAL PV AT  15.000000 % IS $       9999.98

SELECT?0

TIME 1 SECS.
```

Figure 8.4   Run of DISC. Line 20 of the input file specifies 24 monthly receipts in arrears of $333.33 each. Line 30 specifies a receipt of $2,657.32 after the twenty-fourth month. Line 40 specifies payments of $100 and $200 at months five and six, respectively, and a receipt of $300 at the end of the eighth month. Line 50 contains the timing parameters for calculating 12 monthly in arrears payments or receipts during the second year.

```
1335 NEXT T
1345 IF X1>0 GOTO 1295
1355 LET R1=R1-R2
1365 NEXT T1
1375 PRINT USING 1965,R1*B1*100
```

. . .

1965 : RATE IS ###.###### %

The basic structure consists of a period loop nested within an increment loop. Lines 1315 and 1335 form the period loop whose counter T steps through all periods from zero to the total number of periods B2. Line 1325 within the loop calculates the present value X1 in the same manner as before except that the period calculation and the cumulation are combined in the same statement.

Lines 1275 and 1365 are the FOR and NEXT statements for the increment loop. The counter T1 steps from one to six which is the number of times the increment is reduced. This determines the precision of the answer because the upper limit of T1 is the number of decimal places to which the rate will be calculated. Line 1285 sets the rate increment R2 to .1 raised to the power T1 which is the value of the loop counter. For the first pass through the loop the increment will be .1, for the second pass it will be .01, for the third pass, .001, and so on. Each time the loop counter is stepped the increment becomes one-tenth of its prior value. Line 1295 sets the trial discount rate R1 to itself plus the rate increment R2. The first trial rate will thus be 10% per period, which is equivalent to an annual rate of 40% for a quarterly transaction, 120% for a monthly transaction, and so on. Line 1305 sets the present value X1 to zero to eliminate the carryover value and the program then enters the period loop where the present value X1 is calculated at the trial rate R1.

After exit from the period loop line 1345 compares the calculated present value to zero. Solving for a net present value of zero implies that the investment amount or desired present value is included in the net cash flow at period zero instead of keeping it separate as Z1. Either approach can be used with either method of rate calculation. If the net present value X1 is greater than zero the program goes back to line 1295 where the increment R2 is added to the trial rate R1 for decreasing the present value requires a higher discount rate. If the net present value R1 is not greater than zero then the increment R2 is substracted from the trial rate R1 in line 1355 for the desired rate has been overshot. In this event the loop is stepped by line 1365, the increment is reduced by line 1285, and the new increment added to the trial rate by line 1295.

For example, if the initial trial rate of 10% per period is too low the next trial rate will be .1 + .1 or 20%, and if that is too high the third trial rate will be .2 − .1 + .01 or 10.1% per period. The result is that the program swings back and forth around the unknown rate with a decreasing rate increment. This is done until the last increment is .1↑6 or .000001. Then the final trial rate is printed as the answer by line 1375.

Table 8.1 compares the results of the rate calculation methods for three cases—a single cash flow of $12,820.37 at the end of 20 months, a series of equal cash flow of $719.62 monthly in arrears for 20 months, and the "null" case from Chapter 7. The investment in all three cases is $10,000. The fixed increment method is shown in two variations—with a limit on the number of increments T1 of six and also of twelve.

All three approaches produce basically the same rate, especially when it is considered that the rate would be rounded before being presented to anyone. As expected doubling the number of increments for the fixed increment method increases its precision by doubling the number of decimal places to which it calculates the answer. (Although presented here in percentage form the rates are calculated in decimal form.)

The net present value, which is the present value of the future cash flows minus the investment, is the measure of the routines' accuracy. Finding the exact rate would result in a net present value of zero. None reached this perfect state but both the interpolation and the fixed increment—12 methods

TABLE 8.1   COMPARISON OF RATE CALCULATION METHODS

Case/Method	Calculated Rate	Net Present Value	Number of Trials
Single			
Fixed increment— 6	4.999600000000%	−.001807346745	31
Fixed increment—12	4.999996340000	−.000000136983	43
Inter/extrapolation	4.999996340125	−.000000001351	7
Series of equal			
Fixed increment— 6	14.999600000000%	−.013525098130	38
Fixed increment—12	14.999939560400	−.000000002037	42
Inter/extrapolation	14.999939551289	+.000002126370	6
"Null" case			
Fixed increment— 6	23.344200000000%	−.010508337929	24
Fixed increment—12	23.344233857300	−.000000013727	22
Inter/extrapolation	23.344233857284	+.000000004755	7

produce more than sufficient accuracy for any financial application and could be made more precise if desired.

It is in the number of trials or iterations that a significant difference becomes apparent between the two rate calculation methods. The number of trials is the number of times that the program calculates the present value by stepping through each period. It is an indication of how quickly the program finds the rate. The fixed increment method required from 22 to 43 trials. The interpolation method took only six or seven trials. The latter is more efficient in terms of computation time because of its feedback formula in which each trial rate is determined by the results of the prior trial. Of course this is also the source of its greater instability. The fixed increment method is less prone to overflows and divisions by zero.

SOLVING FOR TWO RATES

DISC will solve for a rate and in most cases that rate will be a unique rate. But as discussed in Chapter 7 it is possible to derive a set of cash flows for which two rates are mathematically correct. In its present form DISC will merely print the first rate it finds without giving any indication whether another rate is possible. It would be useful if the program could solve for both rates, one for the positive slope of the present value curve and the other for the negative.

Only two characteristics distinguish the two rates. One rate will be higher than the other. And one rate will be on the positive (or abnormal) slope of the present value curve and the other will be on the negative (or normal) slope. It cannot be assumed that either rate will always lie on a specific slope for the entire curve can be flipped over by reversing the polarity of all the cash flows. That is, the U-shaped curve may be either right-side-up or upside down without affecting the values of the two rates.

The interpolation method is the one that should be used for dual-rate calculations for, unlike the fixed increment method, it does not have a built-in assumption regarding the slope of the curve. By choosing a very low discount rate for the first trial the program will be operating on the initial slope of the curve, whether upsweeping or downsweeping, and the interpolation formula will follow the slope to find the lower of the two possible rates. The process can then be repeated in its entirety. The second time a relatively high discount rate can be chosen for the first trial so that the program will be operating on the second slope of the curve. Again the interpolation formula will follow the slope to find the higher of the two possible rates.

The rate calculation section in DISC can be expanded quite easily to incorporate the second rate solution. The initial trial discount rate will be set to 1% rather than 10% and the program will then solve for the rate as before. After the answer is printed various variables will be reset to their initial values, a new initial trial rate of 40% will be set, and the program will again solve for a rate. If the present value curve does not have two slopes then the program will find the same rate both times. In that event, which is the normal case, the printing of the second solution will be suppressed. Two new variables are required.

> *Remember that one rate has been found is* C4
> *Remember the value of the found rate is* R4

The following line numbers have been assigned to lie within the range of the rate calculation section already developed. If the line number ends in zero then the statement is unchanged from before.

```
815 LET R1=1
```

```
. . .
940 LET R1=R1/(B1*100)
. . .
1260 REM RATE CALCULATION
1270 LET T2=T2+1
1280 IF X1−X3<>0 GOTO 1310
1283 IF C4>0 GOTO 1297
1287 LET R3=.02/B1
1293 GOTO 1420
1297 LET R3=.3/B1
1300 GOTO 1420
```

Line 815 replaces line 810 and sets the first trial rate to 1% rather than 10% after the rate calculation function is selected. Line 940 is unchanged and converts the rate R1 to the periodic decimal form. The only change to the beginning of the rate calculation section is the alternative rate used in the event that the program calculated a present value X1 that is the same as the prior calculated present value X3. Remember that the test at line 1280 is designed to avoid dividing by zero in the interpolation formula. Now two alternative rates are offered instead of one. If the program is solving for the lower rate then the remember variable C4, which will be used to control branching throughout the section, will have its initial value of zero. The test at line 1283 will be failed and line 1287 will set the alternative rate for the next trial to 2%. If the lower rate has already been found then C4 will equal one and line 1297 will set the alternative rate to 30%. In either case the program then goes to line 1420 and proceeds with the next trial. If the test at line 1280 is passed the program goes to line 1310 to test whether the answer has been found.

```
1310 IF Z1−X1>D1 GOTO 1350
1320 IF Z1−X1<−D1 GOTO 1380
1323 IF C4=0 GOTO 1330
1327 IF INT(R1*10↑8)=INT(R4*10↑8) GOTO 1477
1330 PRINT USING 1960, (R1*B1*100),T2
1332 IF C4>0 GOTO 1477
1334 LET C4=1
1336 LET R4=R1
1338 LET R1=.4/B1
1342 LET R2,R3,T2,X3=0
1344 GOTO 1170
```

If lines 1310 and 1320 determine that the difference between the calculated present value X1 and the desired present value Z1 is within the level of precision specified by D1 then the answer has been found. If this is the first answer then C4 will equal zero and the program goes to line 1330 to print the answer. If this is the second answer then line 1327 tests whether the current answer's value R1 is equal to that of the first answer R4. The test statement truncates the two answers to eight decimal places for comparison because the two rates will not be equal to 15 decimal places. The first answer was found by working up from 1% and the second answer by working down from 40%. The slight difference allowed by the precision level D1 also contributes to the lack of absolute equality. The comparison is made to eight decimal places in the decimal form because the answer is only printed to six decimal places in the percentage form. If the two answers are substantially the same then the print statement is bypassed and the program returns to the select question via line 1477. Otherwise the second answer is printed by line 1330. After the answer is printed line 1332 tests whether it was the first or the second one. If C4 is greater than zero then it was the second answer and the program goes to line 1477 and from there to the select question.

If C4 is zero then the second rate must still be found. Line 1334 sets C4 to one to indicate that the first answer has been found. Then line 1336 sets R4 to the just-found answer R1 so that it can be used later in the comparison and then R1 is set to 40% by line 1338 to serve as the initial trial rate for the second solution. Line 1342 sets the old trial rates R2 and R3, the iteration counter T2, and the old present value X3 to zero in preparation for the second solution. Then line 1344 directs the program back to line 1170 in the present value calculation section to calculate the new present value X1.

```
1350 IF T2>1 GOTO 1410
1365 LET R3=.75*R1
1370 GOTO 1420
1380 IF T2>1 GOTO 1410
1395 LET R3=1.25*R1
1400 GOTO 1420
1410 LET R3=R2+((Z1−X3)/(X1−X3))*(R1−R2)
1420 LET R2=R1
1430 LET R1=R3
1440 LET X3=X1
1450 IF T2<15 GOTO 1170
1460 PRINT "NO ANSWER BY 15 ITERATIONS."
1470 PRINT USING 2000,X3,R2*B1*100
1473 IF C4=0 GOTO 1334
1477 LET C4,R4=0
1480 GOTO 590
```

If the rate has not been found the program goes to either line 1350 or 1380. If it is the first trial for either solution the next trial rate is no longer determined by a fixed increment of two percentage points. The next rate R3 is set to either 75% or 125% of the current rate R1 by line 1365 or 1395. This is intended to avoid a negative rate since the initial trial rate is now only 1%. Both methods—fixed increment and proportion—work equally well. If T2 is greater than one then more than one trial has been made and the program goes directly to the interpolation formula at line 1410 as before. The remembering of the variables and the interation limit test are also the same. If the error message should be triggered then C4 is tested at line 1473. If the second solution has not yet been sought then the program goes to line 1334. The initial trial rate for the second solution is set to 40% and the program proceeds. Otherwise the remember variables C4 and R4 are reset to zero and the program returns to the select question at line 590.

Figure 8.5 presents a run of the modified DISC to find the two rates for each of the "−200," "null," and "+200" cases described in Chapter 7.

The initial trial rates used in this chapter have been selected empirically and work well with the general range of financial problems. Their values are not critical however and they can be adjusted if desired to fit unusual circumstances.

Since DISC has the basic structure for discounting, finding rates, and calculating payments, it can be used as the nucleus for a lease evaluation program. This is done in the next chapter.

```
LIST

INDISC          8:49    WEDNESDAY JUN1,1977

10 1
30 3,1,4551,3861,3196,2667,2130,1587,1035,473
40 -99,-682,-1043,-1183,-1338,-1512,-1705,-1938,1
50 2,2,-200,0,16
999 9


RUN DISC2

DISC2           8:49    WEDNESDAY JUN1,1977

SELECT?2
PV?10000

  RATE IS   6.763725 %   T2=10
  RATE IS  16.251519 %   T2= 7

SELECT?0

TIME 1 SECS.

CLE
READY

LOA INDISC
READY

50
SAVE
READY

RUN DISC2
```

Figure 8.5   Run of DISC to solve for dual rates.

```
DISC2            8:50    WEDNESDAY JUN1,1977


SELECT?2
PV?10000

 RATE IS    0.000000 %   T2= 7
 RATE IS   23.344234 %   T2= 6

SELECT?0

TIME 1 SECS.

CLE
READY

LOA INDISC
READY

50 2,2,200,0,16
SAVE
READY

RUN DISC2


DISC2            8:51    WEDNESDAY JUN1,1977


SELECT?2
PV?10000

 RATE IS   -4.351851 %   T2=12
 RATE IS   27.887430 %   T2= 6

SELECT?0

TIME 1 SECS.
```

9

The Lease Program

The lease program to be developed in this chapter is designed for the evaluation and/or structuring of financing leases as opposed to operating leases. These are leases in which the lessor purchases the asset and leases it to the lessee for a substantial portion of its useful life. The cash flows are sufficient for the lessor to recover the investment and realize a profit; that is, they are full-payout leases.

In return for the investment in the cost of the equipment the lessor receives the periodic rental payments, the investment tax credit if applicable, and the tax deferral benefits of accelerated depreciation on the equipment. In addition he or she regains possession of the equipment at the end of the lease term and may either sell it or re-lease it. The cash flows from these components are discounted to calculate the lessor's rate of return.

These same components—rent, investment tax credit, depreciation, and residual value—are also what the lessee gives up in order to avoid paying the purchase price of the equipment. They thus provide the measure of the cost of the lease. Although specific parameters, such as depreciation policy and expected residual value, may differ between lessor and lessee, still the components are the same. This means that the same program can be used to calculate both the lessor's return and the lessee's cost.

DISC may be expanded into such a program by making provisions for income taxes and the additional cash flow types. The new program will be named LEAS.

LEASE STRUCTURE

The lease provides the lessor with a stream of rentals over its term. As owner of the equipment the lessor is entitled to deduct depreciation expense from the rental income in order to determine taxable income. Depreciation is the allocation of the equipment cost over some period of time and is the mechanism by which the lessor's return *of* investment is relieved of taxation, leaving only the return *on* investment to be taxed.

Assume an eight-year lease of equipment costing $1,000,000. Rentals are quarterly in arrears in the amount of $37,161.98. The equipment qualifies for the 10% investment tax credit (ITC) and is expected to have a fair market value (residual value) of 20% of cost at the end of the term. The lessor will depreciate the equipment over seven years to 10% below the expected residual value using the asset depreciation range (ADR) method.

The net cash flow from the rental payments can be determined like this.

Rental income	$1,189,183
Less: Depreciation	(900,000)
Taxable income	$ 289,183
Income tax at 48%	(138,808)
Net income	$ 150,375
Plus: Depreciation	900,000
Net cash flow	$1,050,375

The total depreciation of $900,000 is the difference between the equipment cost of $1,000,000 and the final book value of $100,000. It is deducted from the rentals to determine taxable income, but is added back to net income to determine net cash flow because depreciation is not a cash expenditure. The only two cash items above are the rentals and the taxes as can be seen by subtracting the latter from the former.

At the end of the lease the lessor still owns the equipment and can either sell it (even if only for scrap) or re-lease it (either to the original lessee or a successor). If the lessor sells it and realizes a price equal to the expected residual value the cash flow from this terminal transaction is derived like this.

Residual value	$200,000
Less: Book value	(100,000)
Taxable income	$100,000
Income tax at 48%	48,000
Net income	$ 52,000
Plus: Book value	100,000
Net cash flow	$152,000

The book value is that portion of the $1,000,000 original cost that was not allocated as depreciation expense during the term. It is in fact the tag-end of the depreciation and is treated the same way. It is deducted from the sale price of the equipment to determine the amount of taxable gain upon disposition. Being a noncash charge it is added back to net income after tax to determine the net cash flow.

The investment tax credit is a credit that the purchaser of qualifying equipment can apply against federal income taxes. The lessor in the example can directly reduce the tax bill by 10% of the equipment cost or $100,000.

The total net cash flow from the lease is the sum of the above components.

Net cash flow from:	
Rentals	$1,050,375
Residual	152,000
ITC	100,000
Total net cash flow	$1,302,375
Less: Investment	(1,000,000)
Gain from transaction	$ 302,375

The cash flows in the aggregate are not sufficient information to permit calculating the lessor's rate of return. To do this requires knowing the cash flows on a period-by-period basis so that each may be discounted for the appropriate length of time. Figure 9.1 presents the cash flows for the example lease on a quarterly basis which is the same frequency as the rental payments.

Despite the level rentals the net cash flows are skewed to the front end. It is an eight-year lease yet the lessor recovers 30% of the investment during the first year. This effect is caused by the quick realization of the investment tax credit and the use of accelerated depreciation. During the first three and one-half years depreciation exceeds rental income so that taxable income is negative. This provides a book loss that can be used to offset income from other sources, thus reducing taxes on the other income. These reduced taxes constitute, in effect, a cash inflow for the account of the lease. As depreciation declines below rental income the lessor shows increasing taxable income and pays increasing amounts of tax. After five and a quarter years depreciation has run out and taxes are applied to the full amount of the rental income.

The effect of such accelerated depreciation is not to reduce taxes but instead to shift them from the early years of the lease to the later years. This gives the lessor the opportunity to invest them in the interim and earn a return. This is the time value of money, which the discounting process seeks to measure.

The net cash flows of $1,302,375 in the last column of Figure 9.1 equal the $1,000,000 investment at a discount rate of 8%. The lessor's after-tax rate of return is thus 8%. Further, if the lessee also expects a 20% residual value (which he or she is giving up by not owning the equipment), uses the same depreciation method, and has sufficient taxable income to benefit from accelerated depreciation and the investment tax credit, then 8% is also the after-tax cost of leasing to the lessee.

It should be emphasized that the critical assumption of the above analysis is the lessor's having income from other sources, and thus taxable income, to which the investment tax credit and book losses from the lease can be applied. If the losses must be carried forward to future years and not used immediately then the lessor's rate of return drops. If lessors attempt to compensate for this by raising rental rates then they price themselves out of the market. This explains why lessors sometimes place a moratorium on booking new lease transactions until their tax position justifies it.

DEFINING THE LEASE PROGRAM

The primary function of a lease program is to calculate the after-tax rate of return (lessor's viewpoint) or cost (lessee's viewpoint) of a lease. This enables the lessor to compare the return of a proposed lease with a target rate of return and with the return of other lease investment opportunities. It enables the lessee to compare the cost of a lease proposal with that of competitive proposals and with the cost of debt financing.

A second important function is to calculate the rentals when given the rate. The lessor, when solicited for a lease bid, will first determine the structural parameters—term, investment tax credit, depreciation, residual, frequency and timing of rentals. He or she will then solve for the rental amount that will give the desired (target) rate of return in light of the perceived risks. The lessor may then change some of the parameters and recalculate the rentals in order to offer the lessee a choice of terms—quarterly versus monthly rentals, with or without investment tax credit, and so forth.

The lessee also finds the rent calculation useful. Having received a lease proposal, the lessee can determine—or rather estimate, as he or she will not know all of the lessor's rate-determining assumptions—the lessor's rate of

INCREMENT?1
TAX RATE?48

LEASE PARAMETERS:

TERM:	8.00 YEARS	FREQUENCY:	4 TIMES PER YEAR
RENT:	$ 37161.98	IN ARREARS FOR	8.00 YEARS
ITC:	$ 100000.00	AT PERIOD 0	
ADR DEPR:	$ 1000000.00	COST TO $ 100000.00	OVER 7.00 YRS
RESIDUAL:	$ 200000.00	(BOOK $ 100000.00)	AT PERIOD 32

CASH FLOW ANALYSIS

PER	RENTALS	DEPRE-CIATION	INTEREST	OTHER	TAXABLE INCOME
0	0.00	0.00	0.00	0.00	0.00
1	37161.98	-71428.57	0.00	0.00	-34266.59
2	37161.98	-71428.57	0.00	0.00	-34266.59
3	37161.98	-61224.49	0.00	0.00	-24062.51
4	37161.98	-61224.49	0.00	0.00	-24062.51
5	37161.98	-61224.49	0.00	0.00	-24062.51
6	37161.98	-61224.49	0.00	0.00	-24062.51
7	37161.98	-46768.71	0.00	0.00	-9606.73
8	37161.98	-46768.71	0.00	0.00	-9606.73
9	37161.98	-46768.71	0.00	0.00	-9606.73
10	37161.98	-46768.71	0.00	0.00	-9606.73
11	37161.98	-38265.31	0.00	0.00	-1103.33
12	37161.98	-38265.31	0.00	0.00	-1103.33
13	37161.98	-38265.31	0.00	0.00	-1103.33
14	37161.98	-38265.31	0.00	0.00	-1103.33
15	37161.98	-29761.90	0.00	0.00	7400.08
16	37161.98	-29761.90	0.00	0.00	7400.08
17	37161.98	-29761.90	0.00	0.00	7400.08
18	37161.98	-29761.90	0.00	0.00	7400.08
19	37161.98	-21258.50	0.00	0.00	15903.48
20	37161.98	-21258.50	0.00	0.00	15903.48
21	37161.98	-10544.22	0.00	0.00	26617.76
22	37161.98	0.00	0.00	0.00	37161.98
23	37161.98	0.00	0.00	0.00	37161.98
24	37161.98	0.00	0.00	0.00	37161.98
25	37161.98	0.00	0.00	0.00	37161.98
26	37161.98	0.00	0.00	0.00	37161.98
27	37161.98	0.00	0.00	0.00	37161.98
28	37161.98	0.00	0.00	0.00	37161.98
29	37161.98	0.00	0.00	0.00	37161.98
30	37161.98	0.00	0.00	0.00	37161.98
31	37161.98	0.00	0.00	0.00	37161.98
32	37161.98	0.00	0.00	0.00	37161.98
TOT	1189183.36	-900000.00	0.00	0.00	289183.36
RES	200000.00	-100000.00	0.00	0.00	100000.00
TOT	1389183.36	-1000000.00	0.00	0.00	389183.36

PER	TAX AT 48.00 %	NET INCOME	ITC	PRINCIPAL REPAYMENTS	NET CASH FLOW
0	0.00	0.00	100000.00	0.00	100000.00
1	16447.96	-17818.63	0.00	0.00	53609.94
2	16447.96	-17818.63	0.00	0.00	53609.94
3	11550.00	-12512.51	0.00	0.00	48711.98
4	11550.00	-12512.51	0.00	0.00	48711.98
5	11550.00	-12512.51	0.00	0.00	48711.98
6	11550.00	-12512.51	0.00	0.00	48711.98
7	4611.23	-4995.50	0.00	0.00	41773.21
8	4611.23	-4995.50	0.00	0.00	41773.21
9	4611.23	-4995.50	0.00	0.00	41773.21
10	4611.23	-4995.50	0.00	0.00	41773.21
11	529.60	-573.73	0.00	0.00	37691.58
12	529.60	-573.73	0.00	0.00	37691.58
13	529.60	-573.73	0.00	0.00	37691.58
14	529.60	-573.73	0.00	0.00	37691.58
15	-3552.04	3848.04	0.00	0.00	33609.94
16	-3552.04	3848.04	0.00	0.00	33609.94
17	-3552.04	3848.04	0.00	0.00	33609.94
18	-3552.04	3848.04	0.00	0.00	33609.94
19	-7633.67	8269.81	0.00	0.00	29528.31
20	-7633.67	8269.81	0.00	0.00	29528.31
21	-12776.53	13841.24	0.00	0.00	24385.45
22	-17837.75	19324.23	0.00	0.00	19324.23
23	-17837.75	19324.23	0.00	0.00	19324.23
24	-17837.75	19324.23	0.00	0.00	19324.23
25	-17837.75	19324.23	0.00	0.00	19324.23
26	-17837.75	19324.23	0.00	0.00	19324.23
27	-17837.75	19324.23	0.00	0.00	19324.23
28	-17837.75	19324.23	0.00	0.00	19324.23
29	-17837.75	19324.23	0.00	0.00	19324.23
30	-17837.75	19324.23	0.00	0.00	19324.23
31	-17837.75	19324.23	0.00	0.00	19324.23
32	-17837.75	19324.23	0.00	0.00	19324.23
TOT	-138808.01	150375.35	100000.00	0.00	1150375.35
RES	-48000.00	52000.00	0.00	0.00	152000.00
TOT	-186808.01	202375.35	100000.00	0.00	1302375.35

TIME 3 SECS.

Figure 9.1   Period cash flows of a lease.

return. The lessee can then predict the effect on rentals of any contemplated variations or counterproposals.

A third function is to calculate the present value of the after-tax cash flows of the lease. Some companies prefer to evaluate transactions on the basis of present value or net present value so the lease program should be able to accommodate this approach.

The lease program should be made as flexible as possible. The structure of individual leases vary so widely that developing the program around a "typical" lease will result in its being inapplicable to many cases. The programmer should resist the temptation to simplify the input format and the program structure by taking advantage of seemingly obvious relationships.

For example, the investment tax credit is 10% of equipment cost, depreciation is based on equipment cost, and lessor's cost is the measure of the lessor's investment. Also the equipment cost is the amount that is depreciated to a book value of 10 percentage points (of equipment cost) below the expected residual value. If these relationships are built into the program then the investment amount, the investment tax credit, the depreciation schedule, and the residual net cash flow can all be determined with relatively little required input. But the investment tax credit has an off-again, on-again history, has not always been 10%, and is subject to future change. Lessor's cost may include items other than equipment cost. And tying the book value to the expected residual value means that the user cannot test the sensitivity of the rate of return to various residual values. The book value is set up on the company's books at the beginning of the term on the basis of the expected residual, but the amount actually realized will not be known until the end of the lease when the equipment is sold. The residual value is a speculative component of the return as opposed to the rentals which are a contractual component. Several runs may be made to test the rate's sensitivity to the residual and this requires that the residual be independent of the book value in the program.

The more a program is prestructured the less able it is to cope with leases that deviate from the "typical" lease model. For a practical example an aircraft lease may involve a new airframe with used engines. Together they comprise the fly-away configuration being leased. The airframe, being new in the lessor's hands, is eligible for the investment tax credit and ADR depreciation. The engines, being used, are not eligible for the investment tax credit and the only accelerated depreciation method allowed is 150% declining balance. The depreciable lives may also differ. Further the lessor may pay a broker's fee and/or a finder's fee at the front-end which will be capitalized as part of the investment and amortized straight-line over the lease term.

The flexibility to handle such cases can be obtained by using accordion input, categorizing the cash flow components by type, and maintaining the independence of the individual cash flows.

DISC is already structured in this manner and can perform the three desired functions. The first step is thus to save a copy of DISC under the name LEAS and build from there. The line numbers in this chapter will be those resulting after completing LEAS and renumbering.

TAX ASSUMPTIONS

The cash flows of a financial transaction are normally discounted at the same frequency as the periodic payments. That is, if a loan has semiannual payments then those payments would be discounted on a semiannual basis. Monthly payments are discounted on a monthly basis. For a lease the frequency of discounting would be the same as the frequency of the rental payments.

Income taxes are, however, calculated annually but with quarterly declarations of estimated taxes and payments. And the payment dates do not fall within the accounting periods to which the payments apply. Further, some firms with a strong seasonal pattern to their profits may pay all of the year's taxes in one season and none in another.

Thus there is no simple, general relationship between the frequency and timing of the cash flows of a financial transaction and that of the tax impact of those flows. It would be possible to design a program around the tax profile of the individual firm but the program would then lack general applicability. Short of that the problem could be handled by discounting all cash flows on a continuous basis and not at discrete intervals, or by using a common frequency, say, monthly, for all, or by discounting taxes on a quarterly basis and all other cash flows at their primary frequency.

The assumption used here will be the simplest of all, namely that the tax impact of any cash flow, with one exception, occurs simultaneously with that cash flow. The exception is that rents payable in advance will be taxed in arrears.

The assumption that tax flows occur simultaneously with their causative cash flows is not an uncommon one. For example the after-tax cost of a loan is usually considered to be the interest rate times one minus the tax rate. Strictly speaking this relationship is true only if the loan payment dates coincide with the tax payment dates. The time lag between the closing of an accounting period and the payment of taxes related to that period prevent this but that does not invalidate the usefulness of the expression. The purpose of calculating after-tax rates is to permit comparisons between alternatives and a simplifying assumption is acceptable if it is consistently applied.

ENTERING THE TAX RATE

If the tax rate used in the calculations does not change from run to run then it can be part of the program as a constant. If so then it should be located in a prominent spot where it can be easily changed as discussed in Chapter 3. If the tax rate is subject to change with different runs, say to determine the tax sensitivity of the results, then it should be an input variable.

Tax rate is R5

Since the tax rate must be known before any of the cash flow inputs can be processed it must be the first input datum. For LEAS it will be inputted in response to a terminal question.

```
130 PRINT "TAX RATE";
140 INPUT R5
150 IF R5=0 GOTO 200
160 IF R5>1 GOTO 190
170 PRINT USING 4590
180 GOTO 130
190 LET R5=R5/100
200 GET 1:B1
```

. . .

```
4590 : ENTER RATE AS %, NOT DECIMAL.
```

Line 130 asks the question and line 140 inputs the answer. Line 150 tests to see whether the tax rate is zero and if it is the program proceeds to line 200 and begins to input the data from the input file. This simple acceptance of a zero tax rate permits LEAS to be used as a general-purpose discounting program since LEAS can do everything that DISC can. Lines 160 to 180 test that the entered rate is in percentage form and line 190 converts it to decimal form. The program then proceeds to input the data from the input file.

Occasionally it is desired to evaluate a lease under the assumption that the tax rate will change during the term. This can be accomplished by incorporating an open-ended input loop for the tax rate in the same manner that floating interest rates were handled in Chapter 2. This loop could be bypassed unless the tax rate is coded with a negative sign.

TAXING THE RENTS

The lease rentals are usually periodic equal amounts. These would be entered in the input data file as series of equal (type 2) cash flows. For some leases the rental amount may change one or more times during the lease term ("stepped rents"), and these cases would be handled by including an additional type 2 cash flow line for each step. Renewal rentals would be handled the same way if the renewal term is being evaluated.

On rare occasions the rental amount may change with each payment. The author has encountered one such case in which the rentals followed the declining pattern of a sinking-fund loan. This would require the series of unequal (type 3) cash flow input with the entering of each individual amount.

LEAS is thus already prepared to process rental payments. It is merely necessary to tax them.

What is really wanted is not the taxes per se but the after-tax cash flow to be added to the total period cash flow N. Its derivation in the aggregate was discussed above. Applying that approach to one period would result in this.

	Period 16
Rental income	$37,161.98
Less: Depreciation	(29,761.90)
Taxable income	$ 7,400.08
Income tax (48%)	(3,552.04)
Net income	$ 3,848.04
Plus: Depreciation	29,761.90
Net cash flow	$ 33,609.94

The net cash flow is basically rental income minus income tax. But the determination of the tax requires knowledge of both the rental and the depreciation amounts. Applying this approach to the program would destroy the independence of the input cash flow lines since the rental and the depreciation could not be treated separately. The rental cash flow line could not be processed until the depreciation line is inputted and vice versa. Fortunately the integrity of the input format can be maintained by abandoning the accounting approach now that it has served its explanatory purpose. The after-tax cash flow can be derived by taxing the rental fully and then separately calculating the amount of tax shelter provided by the depreciation.

	Period 16	
Rental income	$37,161.98	
Income tax (48%)	(17,837.75)	
Rental cash flow		$19,324.23
Depreciation	$29,761.90	
Tax shelter (48%)		14,285.71
Net cash flow		$33,609.94

The after-tax or net cash flow is equal to the sum of (1) the rental times one minus the tax rate, plus (2) the depreciation times the tax rate. The result is the same as that produced by the accounting method and has the advantage of permitting the rentals and depreciation to be processed separately.

Rentals in arrears can be taxed quite simply in the program by inserting one minus the tax rate in the expression that adds the cash flow to the total period net cash flow N.

```
400 REM SERIES EQUAL

. . .

450 IF K1>1 GOTO 510

. . .

510 FOR T=(J1+1) TO J2
520 LET N(T+1)=N(T+1)+(H1*(1−R5))
530 NEXT T
```

Within the series of equal section line 450 tests for arrears payments and lines 510 and 530 establish the arrears period loop. The only change from DISC is at line 520 where taxes are extracted from the rental H1 before it is added to the period net cash flow N. This expression is equally valid for problems requiring analysis on a pretax basis for if the tax rate R5 is zero then one minus the tax rate is one and the full amount of the cash flow H1 will be added to the period cash flow.

If rentals are payable in advance they will be taxed in arrears. This is consistent with the real world in which income taxes are payable after the period to which they apply rather than before.

```
460 FOR T=J1 TO (J2−1)
470 LET N(T+1)=N(T+1)+H1
480 LET N(T+2)=N(T+2)−(H1*R5)
490 NEXT T
```

Lines 460 and 490 define the advance period loop. Line 470 adds the full amount of the rental H1 to the period cash flow N at the time of payment T (T+1 with the subscript adjustment). Then line 480 subtracts the taxes on that rental from the period cash flow N at a time one period later T+1 (T+2 with the subscript adjustment). The only change from DISC is the insertion of line 480.

The series of unequal cash flow type can be taxed in the same manner as the arrears payments above.

```
590 REM SERIES UNEQUAL

 . . .

630 LET N(J1+1)=N(J1+1)+(H1* (1−R5))
```

In line 630 the rental amount H1 is multiplied by one minus the tax rate R5 before being added to the period net cash flow N.

The series of equal cash flow type can be used for more than rentals. Any cash flow that consists of level payments that are either taxable or tax-deductible would be entered as a type 2. From the lessor's viewpoint an example would be a broker's fee that is paid by the lessor over the first five years of the term out of each rental payment. Using the rental of the example lease and assuming the broker's fee is 2% of the rental would result in input data like this.

```
20 2,2,37161.98,0,32
30 2,2,−743.24,0,20
```

Line 20 contains the rental and line 30 the period fee expense. The latter has a negative polarity for it is a cash outflow to the lessor. The program will subtract the after-tax equivalent of the expense item from each period's net cash flow for the term of the fee.

TAXING THE SINGLE CASH FLOW

The single (type 1) cash flow can be used to handle a one-shot cash flow that is taxable income or tax-deductible expense. The multiplier is the same as for rental income, namely one minus the tax rate.

    300 REM SINGLE CF

    . . .

    350 LET N(J2+1)=N(J2+1)+(H1* (1−R5))

Any item entered as a type 1 cash flow will be fully taxed if entered with a positive polarity and fully deductible if entered with a negative polarity. This could be used for the closing costs if they are expensed and not capitalized.

The investment tax credit is a special type of one-shot cash flow that is neither taxed nor deducted. As a credit against the tax bill it is an effective cash inflow and its pretax and after-tax values are the same. The tax rate does not apply to it and it is processed exactly like the single cash flow type before taxes were added. To distinguish it from the now-taxable single cash flow it will be assigned the type code of eight.

    210 GET 1:G1
    220 GOTO 300,400,590,690,960,1100,1950,2030,250 ON G1

    . . .

    2030 REM ITC
    2040 GET 1:H1,J2
    2050 IF B2>=J2 GOTO 2070
    2060 LET B2=J2
    2070 LET N(J2+1)=N(J2+1)+H1
    2080 GOTO 210

If line 210 inputs a cash flow type code G1 that equals eight then line 220 will direct the program to the investment tax credit section at line 2030. Counting the specified line numbers in the GOTO . . . ON statement reveals that branching will occur for nine values of G1. The first three are the same cash flow types as in DISC. The end of data code nine is also the same. The cash flow types four through eight have been added. Of these types six through eight will be developed in this chapter and the loan types four and five will be discussed in the next chapter.

Line 2040 inputs the cash flow amount H1 and the period of occurrence J2. Lines 2050 and 2060 ensure that the total number of periods B2 will be no less than J2. Line 2070 then adds the full amount of the tax credit H1 to the period net cash flow N. The program then returns to line 210 to input the next cash flow.

The input data for the investment tax credit consists of the type code of eight, the dollar amount, and the period of occurrence and for the example lease looks like this:

    30 8,100000,0

Specifying the amount in dollars maintains the flexibility of the program, for it is not tied to any particular percentage of any particular portion of the lease package. Flexibility is also the reason for specifying the time of receipt. As a practical matter the investment tax credit will not be received upon closing at time zero and the user may want to recognize this. And some firms may not be able to use the tax credit immediately because of insufficient taxable income. Because of its relative size and front-end timing the investment tax credit has a relatively large impact on the rate of return and the user may wish to test the sensitivity to timing.

As previously seen the residual is not fully taxed. The undepreciated equipment cost or final book value is deducted before the tax rate is applied. The residual cash flow type will be given the type code of seven.

```
1950 REM RESIDUAL
1960 GET 1:H1,I2,J2
1970 IF B2>=J2 GOTO 1990
1980 LET B2=J2
1990 LET N(J2+1)=N(J2+1)+((H1−I2)*(1−R5))+I2
```

. . .

```
2020 GOTO 210
```

Line 1960 inputs the residual parameters. Variable H1 again refers to the amount in dollars, I2 is the final book value, and J2 is the period the residual is realized. To maintain flexibility J2 is specified rather than having the program refer to the end of the rental term. This way several series of rents and several residuals at various times can be incorporated into one lease package without any constraints on the number of items or the order in which they are entered. Lines 1970 and 1980 ensure that the total number of periods B2 is at least as great as the residual's period J2.

Line 1990 calculates the after-tax cash flow realized from the residual. The excess of the residual amount H1 over the final book value 12 is multiplied by one minus the tax rate R5 to obtain the net income after tax. Then the book value is added back to determine the net cash flow which is added to the period cash flow N. Should the residual value be less than book value (e.g., if there is no market for the equipment and it has only scrap value), then net income will be negative. This is realistic as the book value can be written off against other income.

Line 2020 directs the program back to line 210 to input the next cash flow.

The residual input data for the example lease appears as follows. The amount of the residual is 20% of cost or $200,000, the book value is 10 percentage points less or $100,000, and the cash flow occurs at the end of the term or period 32.

50 7,200000,100000,32

DEPRECIATION

There are several alternative methods of calculating depreciation for tax purposes. The program should be capable of using any one in order to handle all possible cases. Figure 9.2 presents a quarter-by-quarter comparison of five depreciation methods as applied to the example lease. Figure 9.3 presents the same methods on a cumulative basis so that the comparative acceleration, or compression toward the early years, of the various methods can be more readily seen. The present values of the depreciation amounts discounted at 10% appear at the bottom of the figure to further aid in ranking the methods. The asset depreciation range exhibits the greatest acceleration as it has the highest present value. (The assumptions are double declining balance, switch to sum of years digits, with midyear delivery and the half-year convention.) Double declining balance is next, followed by sum of years digits, 150% declining balance, and straight line. The ranking of the double declining balance and sum of years digits methods will vary with the depreciation term with the advantage shifting to the latter method for longer terms.

Lessors will use that method which results in the fastest depreciation. This is because they wish to maximize their book losses in the early years. This will minimize taxes during those years on other income, or income from other leases that have reached the later tax-paying years, and thus provide more early funds for reinvestment.

Lessees would also specify the most accelerated method when using the

DEPRE   8:45   MONDAY JULY 11,1977

COMPARATIVE PERIOD DEPRECIATION -

PER	STRAIGHT LINE	DECLINING BALANCE 150%	DECLINING BALANCE 200%	SUM OF YEARS DIGITS	ASSET DEPRE'TION RANGE
1	32142.86	53571.43	71428.57	56250.00	71428.57
2	32142.86	53571.43	71428.57	56250.00	71428.57
3	32142.86	53571.43	71428.57	56250.00	61224.49
4	32142.86	53571.43	71428.57	56250.00	61224.49
5	32142.86	42091.84	51020.41	48214.29	61224.49
6	32142.86	42091.84	51020.41	48214.29	61224.49
7	32142.86	42091.84	51020.41	48214.29	46768.71
8	32142.86	42091.84	51020.41	48214.29	46768.71
9	32142.86	33072.16	36443.15	40178.57	46768.71
10	32142.86	33072.16	36443.15	40178.57	46768.71
11	32142.86	33072.16	36443.15	40178.57	38265.31
12	32142.86	33072.16	36443.15	40178.57	38265.31
13	32142.86	25985.27	26030.82	32142.86	38265.31
14	32142.86	25985.27	26030.82	32142.86	38265.31
15	32142.86	25985.27	26030.82	32142.86	29761.90
16	32142.86	25985.27	26030.82	32142.86	29761.90
17	32142.86	23426.44	18593.44	24107.14	29761.90
18	32142.86	23426.44	18593.44	24107.14	29761.90
19	32142.86	23426.44	18593.44	24107.14	21258.50
20	32142.86	23426.44	18593.44	24107.14	21258.50
21	32142.86	23426.44	13281.03	16071.43	10544.22
22	32142.86	23426.44	13281.03	16071.43	0.00
23	32142.86	23426.44	13281.03	16071.43	0.00
24	32142.86	23426.44	13281.03	16071.43	0.00
25	32142.86	23426.44	9486.45	8035.71	0.00
26	32142.86	23426.44	9486.45	8035.71	0.00
27	32142.86	23426.44	9486.45	8035.71	0.00
28	32142.86	23426.44	4350.96	8035.71	0.00
TOT	900000.00	900000.00	900000.00	900000.00	900000.00

TIME 1 SECS.

Figure 9.2   Quarterly depreciation by five methods.

program to estimate the lessor's rate of return. When lessees use it to calculate costs however they would use their normal depreciation policy for tax purposes which may or may not be the same as the lessor's.

The five methods provide alternative ways to spread the depreciable amount over the depreciable life of the asset. The depreciable amount is the difference between acquisition cost and salvage value except that tax law permits the asset to be depreciated 10 percentage points below the estimated salvage (residual) value. This amount to which the asset is depre-

COMPARATIVE CUMULATIVE DEPRECIATION

PER	STRAIGHT LINE	DECLINING BALANCE		SUM OF YEARS DIGITS	ASSET DEPRE'TION RANGE
		150%	200%		
1	32142.86	53571.43	71428.57	56250.00	71428.57
2	64285.71	107142.86	142857.14	112500.00	142857.14
3	96428.57	160714.29	214285.71	168750.00	204081.63
4	128571.43	214285.71	285714.29	225000.00	265306.12
5	160714.29	256377.55	336734.69	273214.29	326530.61
6	192857.14	298469.39	387755.10	321428.57	387755.10
7	225000.00	340561.22	438775.51	369642.86	434523.81
8	257142.86	382653.06	489795.92	417857.14	481292.52
9	289285.71	415725.22	526239.07	458035.71	528061.22
10	321428.57	448797.38	562682.22	498214.29	574829.93
11	353571.43	481869.53	599125.36	538392.86	613095.24
12	385714.29	514941.69	635568.51	578571.43	651360.54
13	417857.14	540926.96	661599.33	610714.29	689625.85
14	450000.00	566912.22	687630.15	642857.14	727891.16
15	482142.86	592897.49	713660.97	675000.00	757653.06
16	514285.71	618882.76	739691.80	707142.86	787414.97
17	546428.57	642309.19	758285.24	731250.00	817176.87
18	578571.43	665735.63	776878.68	755357.14	846938.78
19	610714.29	689162.07	795472.12	779464.29	868197.28
20	642857.14	712588.50	814065.57	803571.43	889455.78
21	675000.00	736014.94	827346.60	819642.86	900000.00
22	707142.86	759441.38	840627.63	835714.29	900000.00
23	739285.71	782867.82	853908.66	851785.71	900000.00
24	771428.57	806294.25	867189.69	867857.14	900000.00
25	803571.43	829720.69	876676.14	875892.86	900000.00
26	835714.29	853147.13	886162.59	883928.57	900000.00
27	867857.14	876573.56	895649.04	891964.29	900000.00
28	900000.00	900000.00	900000.00	900000.00	900000.00
===	===========	===========	===========	===========	===========

PRESENT VALUE AT 10%:

TOT	641728.56	681665.66	722703.87	704602.89	732859.24
===	===========	===========	===========	===========	===========

TIME 1 SECS.

Figure 9.3   Cumulative depreciation by five methods.

ciated can be called the final book value, to distinguish it from the declining book value over the term, or the tax residual, to distinguish it from the market residual value. The depreciable life will generally be as short as allowable in recognition of the time value of money but not so short as to endanger receipt of the full investment tax credit. The depreciable life must be consistent with the useful life used in claiming the investment tax credit as the latter is subject to partial or full recapture if the useful life is less than seven years.

The input data for the depreciation cash flow will have six components—the cash flow type code G1 of six, the depreciation method code A1, the equipment cost H1, the final book value I2, and the periods marking the beginning J1 and end J2 of the depreciation term. Instead of automatically using period zero the beginning period is specified in order to accommodate staggered delivery times; that is, cases where discrete items of equipment are delivered and installed at different times. The depreciation method or rate A1 will have the following values. The first three are multipliers of the straight-line rate.

> *Straight line is*   1
> *150% declining balance is*   1.5
> *Double declining balance is*   2
> *Sum of years digits is*   3
> *Asset depreciation range is*   4

The input data for the depreciation cash flow line of the example lease, using ADR, looks like this.

40 6,4,1000000,100000,0,28

STRAIGHT-LINE DEPRECIATION

Straight-line depreciation is the simplest and has no acceleration. The depreciable amount is divided evenly among the years of depreciable life so that book value is a linear function of time. Since each year has the same number of periods each period also has the same amount of depreciation. The total depreciation can therefore be allocated by a simple loop that steps through each period of the depreciation term.

Depreciation for period is S2

```
1100 REM DEPR INPUT
1110 GET 1:A1,H1,I2,J1,J2
1120 IF R5=0 GOTO 210
1130 IF B2>=J2 GOTO 1150
1140 LET B2=J2
```

. . .

```
1170 IF A1=1.5 GOTO 1270
1180 GOTO 1210,1270,1440,1570 ON A1
1190 PRINT "ILLEGAL DEPR RATE."
1200 STOP
1210 REM SL DEPR
1220 LET S2=(H1−I2)/(J2−J1)
1230 FOR T=J1+1 TO J2
1240 LET N(T+1)=N(T+1)+(S2*R5)
1250 NEXT T
1260 GOTO 210
```

Line 1110 inputs the depreciation parameters. If the tax rate R5 is zero, line 1120 will send the program back to line 210 to input the next cash flow, effectively bypassing the entire depreciation section. Since depreciation has no effect on cash flow in the absence of taxes this provision prevents the program from wasting computation time to produce a string of zeros. Lines 1130 and 1140 ensure that the total number of periods B2 will be no less than the depreciation term. Lines 1170 and 1180 direct the program to the appropriate subsection according to the specified depreciation method A1. Line 1170 is required to supplement line 1180 because the GOTO . . . ON statement will operate only on integer values. Lines 1190 and 1200 print an error message and stop the program if the value of A1 does not correspond to any of the five depreciation methods.

If the value of A1 is one the program is sent by line 1180 to the straight-line depreciation subsection at line 1210. Line 1220 calculates the depreciation per period S2 by dividing the number of periods in the depreciation term (J2 − J1) into the total depreciation amount which is the difference between the equipment cost H1 and the final book value I2. Lines 1230 and 1250 form a loop which steps through each period of the depreciation term. Within the loop line 1240 calculates the tax shelter amount by multiplying the period depreciation S2 by the tax rate R5. The result is then added to the period net cash flow N. After exit from the loop line 1260 directs the program back to line 210 to input the next cash flow.

DECLINING BALANCE DEPRECIATION

The declining balance depreciation method may use either of two rates—double the straight-line rate (double declining balance or DDB) and one and a half times the straight-line rate (150% DB). The calculation steps are the same, only the applied rate differs. The particular significance of the 150% declining balance method is that it is the only accelerated method that is allowed for tax purposes for used equipment.

Under straight-line depreciation the amount of depreciation taken each year is determined by the reciprocal of the depreciation term. For a 10-year life one-tenth or 10% of the depreciation is taken each year. The double declining balance method would use twice the straight-line rate or 20%. The 150% declining balance method would use one and a half times the straight-line rate or 15%. The accelerated rate however is applied not to the total depreciation but to the remaining undepreciated cost which is a balance that declines over the term.

The method of calculation will be illustrated by applying the 150% declining balance method to the depreciation parameters of the example lease. These are $1,000,000 equipment cost depreciated over seven years to a final book value of $100,000. The straight line rate is 1/7 or .142857 so the 150% rate is 1.5 times that or .214286. Each year's depreciation is found by multiplying the book value (undepreciated balance) at the beginning of the year by the factor of .214286. For example the book value at the beginning of the first year is $1,000,000. Multiplying this by .214286 results in depreciation of $214,286 for the first year. Subtracting the year's depreciation from the book value leaves a year-end book value of $785,714. The depreciation for the second year is found by multiplying $785,714 by the factor. Each year's depreciation for the whole term is as follows.

150% *Declining Balance Depreciation*

Year	Beginning Book Value	Year's Depreciation	Ending Book Value
1	$1,000,000	$214,286	$785,714
2	785,714	168,367	617,347
3	617,347	132,289	485,058
4	485,058	103,941	381,117
5	381,117	81,668	299,449
6	299,449	64,168	235,281
7	235,281	50,417	184,864
Total		$815,136	

Applying a constant factor to the book value to determine the year's depreciation, which is then subtracted from the book value, results in the depreciation starting at a relatively high value and then declining. The book value also declines but it can never reach zero because it is being reduced each year by only a fraction of itself. The pure declining balance method therefore cannot be used to depreciate equipment to zero. In the above case the book value by the end of the depreciation term is still more than $184,000 which is greater than the desired final book value of $100,000. This is because the total depreciation taken falls short of $900,000 which is the full depreciable amount.

The solution to the problem is to switch to straight-line depreciation at some point during the term. While taxpayers are constrained from shifting freely between accelerated methods they are allowed to shift from an accelerated method to the straight-line method at any tax year. The taxpayer would of course make the switch at the first year for which straight-line depreciation exceeds declining balance depreciation.

The annual straight-line depreciation amount will equal the remaining depreciation divided by the number of remaining years in the depreciation term. The remaining depreciation will equal the book value at that time minus the final book value. For example, the book value at the end of the first year is $785,714 under the declining balance example above. Subtracting the $100,000 tax residual leaves $685,714 as the remaining depreciation. This would be $114,286 per year straight line over the remaining six years. This is less than the $168,367 of depreciation for the second year under the declining balance method so the switch will not be made. The straight-line depreciation must be calculated in this manner each year until the switchover year is reached. From then on the annual depreciation will be the constant straight-line amount. The amount for each year of switchover is as follows.

Straight-Line Depreciation

Year	Book Value Less Tax Residual	Years Remaining	Annual Depreciation
1	$900,000	7	$128,571
2	685,714	6	114,286
3	517,347	5	103,469
4	385,058	4	96,264
5	281,117	3	93,706
6	199,449	2	99,724
7	135,281	1	135,281

Comparison of the depreciation columns of the two tables shows that straight-line depreciation will exceed declining balance depreciation in the fifth year. Therefore the taxpayer will take declining balance depreciation for the first four years and straight-line depreciation for the last three.

	Depreciation Taken:	
Year	Declining Balance	Straight Line
1	$214,286	$ —
2	168,367	—
3	132,289	—
4	103,941	—
5	—	93,706
6	—	93,706
7	—	93,706
Total		$900,001

The total depreciation taken over the depreciation term is now the correct $900,000 (ignoring the manual rounding error). The program will divide each year's depreciation evenly among the year's periods. Several new variables are required.

Year's depreciation is	S1
Year's straight-line depreciation is	S7
Counter for periods of term is	T3
Counter for remaining years is	T4

```
1100 REM DEPR

. . .

1150 LET T3=J1
1160 LET T4=(J2−J1)/B1

. . .

1270 REM DB DEPR
1280 LET A1=(A1*B1)/(J2−J1)
1290 LET S7=(H1−I2)/T4
1300 LET S1=H1*A1
1310 IF S1>S7 GOTO 1330
1320 LET S1=S7
1330 LET S2=S1/B1
```

Line 1150 sets the term period counter T3 to the period marking the beginning of the term J1. Line 1160 sets the years remaining counter T4 to the
number of years in the term, which is equal to the number of periods J2 − J1
divided by the number of periods per year B1. These counters are set in the
introductory section before branching by depreciation method because they
are used by more than one method.

Within the declining balance section line 1280 calculates the annual
depreciation rate. Since the number of years is (J2 − J1)/B1 then the reciprocal B1/(J2 − J1) is the straight-line rate. This is multiplied by the value of
the depreciation code A1, which will be either 1.5 or 2, to obtain the
declining balance rate. Variable A1 is implicitly redefined by the statement
to be the depreciation rate rather than the depreciation code.

Line 1270 calculates the straight-line depreciation S7 for the year by
dividing the number of remaining years T4 into the difference between book
value H1 and the tax residual I2. Variable H1 starts as equipment cost but
declines as the program goes through the years. Line 1300 calculates the
declining balance depreciation S1 for the year by multiplying the book value
H1 by the declining balance rate A1. Line 1310 compares the declining
balance depreciation S1 with the straight-line depreciation S7. If the declining balance amount is not greater than the straight-line amount then line
1320 sets S1 equal to the straight-line amount so that the annual depreciation S1 will be the greater of the two alternatives. Line 1330 then divides the
annual amount S1 by the number of periods per year B1 to determine the
periodic depreciation S2 for the year.

```
1340 FOR T=1 to B1
1350 LET T3=T3+1
1360 IF T3>J2 GOTO 1420
1370 IF H1<=I2 GOTO 1420
1380 IF H1−S2>I2 GOTO 1400
1390 LET S2=H1−I2
1400 LET H1=H1−S2
1410 LET N(T3+1)=N(T3+1)+(S2*R5)
1420 NEXT T
1430 LET T4=T4−1
1440 IF T3<J2 GOTO 1290
1450 GOTO 210
```

Lines 1340 and 1420 form a loop that steps through each period of the year.
Within the loop line 1350 increments the term period counter T3 by one so
that it equals the current period. Ignoring various tests for the moment, line

1400 subtracts the period depreciation S2 from the book value H1. Line 1410 calculates the cash flow effect as the period depreciation S2 times the tax rate R5 and adds it to the period net cash flow N.

Returning to the tests, line 1360 causes the calculations to be bypassed if the period T3 is greater than the end of the term J2. This would apply should the depreciation term be other than a whole number of years.

Under the combination of a high depreciation rate and a high residual value the switch to straight line may not occur. That is, the straight-line depreciation may never exceed the declining balance depreciation. This is the case in Figure 9.2 where the double (200%) declining balance column does not switch since the amount declines every year (every four periods). Compare this column with the 150% declining balance column which does switch as indicated by the figures for periods 17 through 28 being a constant amount. Without the switch the total depreciation is not related to the tax residual and the equipment cost could be overdepreciated. This overdepreciation would have occurred in the 200% column if the final period's amount had been left the same as the first three quarters of the last year. This was prevented by putting a floor under the book value amount by inserting lines 1370 through 1390.

Line 1370 compares the book value H1 with the tax residual I2. Once H1 declines to the value of I2 the program will jump to line 1420 thereby preventing any further deduction from book value and any further cash flow impact. If the book value H1 is still greater than the tax residual I2 then line 1380 tests whether the current depreciation amount S2 will drive it below. If so then line 1390 sets the period depreciation S2 to that amount that will bring the book value H1 down to the desired final book value I2.

After leaving the loop line 1430 subtracts one from the remaining years counter T4. Line 1440 then compares the period T3 with the end of the term J2 and if the final period has not been reached the program goes back to line 1290 to calculate the straight line and declining balance depreciation amounts for the next year. Otherwise line 1450 directs the program back to line 210 to input the next cash flow.

SUM OF YEARS DIGITS DEPRECIATION

The sum of years digits method is another approach to obtaining accelerated depreciation. Each year's depreciation is obtained by multiplying the depreciable amount by a fraction whose numerator is the number of years remaining in the depreciation term and whose denominator is the sum of the numbers representing each year of the term.

Using the depreciation parameters of the example lease the denominator of the fraction is the sum of the years one through seven.

$$1 + 2 + 3 + 4 + 5 + 6 + 7 = 28$$

This calculation could be done in the program by using a short loop that steps through each year of the term. Within the loop the value of the loop counter would be added to the cumulative value. If T4 is the number of years and S4 is the sum of the digits then

```
FOR T=1 TO T4
LET S4=S4+T
NEXT T
```

An alternative approach is to use an algebraic formula. The sum of the digits is equal to one-half of the product of the number of years in the term times the number of years plus one.

```
LET S4=(T4*(T4+1))/2
```

The numerator of the fraction is a declining value equal to the number of remaining years. The numerator for the first year would be seven so that the first year's depreciation would be $900,000 times 7/28 or $225,000. The derpeciation for each year of the term would be as follows.

	Sum of Years Digits Depreciation		
Year	Depreciable Amount	Multi-plier	Depre-ciation
1	$900,000	7/28	$225,000
2	900,000	6/28	192,857
3	900,000	5/28	160,714
4	900,000	4/28	128,571
5	900,000	3/28	96,429
6	900,000	2/28	64,286
7	900,000	1/28	32,143
Total		28/28	$900,000

As before the process is repetitive since each year must be calculated separately. Computational efficiency is improved if as many as possible of the computations are performed before entering the loop as this reduces the number of repetitive calculations. In this case since the depreciable amount is a constant and the denominator of the fraction is a constant then the former can be divided by the latter before entering the year loop. The result will be a constant that can merely be multiplied by the number of remaining years each time to obtain the year's depreciation. In the example this constant would be $900,000/28 or $32,143. A new variable is introduced.

Constant fraction of depreciable amount is S3

Remember that the term period counter T3 and the remaining years counter T4 have already been set before the program enters the sum of years digits section.

```
1460 REM SYD DEPR
1470 LET S3=(H1−I2)/((T4*(T4+1))/2)
1480 LET S2=(S3*T4)/B1
1490 FOR T=1 TO B1

. . .

1550 NEXT T
1560 LET T4=T4−1
1570 IF T3<J2 GOTO 1480
1580 GOTO 210
```

Line 1470 performs two functions. It calculates the sum of the years digits using the formula approach based on the number of depreciation years T4, and it then divides this into the depreciable amount H1 − I2. The depreciation fractional amount S3 is thus obtained in one operation. Line 1480 also performs two functions as it calculates the depreciation for the year by multiplying the depreciation amount fraction S3 by the number of remaining years T4 and then divides the result by the periods per year B1 to obtain the period depreciation S2. Lines 1490 and 1550 form a period loop for the year.

After the periods of the year are processed the program exits the period loop and line 1560 subtracts one from the number of remaining years. Line 1570 then tests whether the period counter T3 has reached the end of the term J2 and if not the program returns to line 1480 to calculate the depreciation for the next year. If the end of the term has been reached then line 1580 directs the program back to line 210 to input the next cash flow.

```
1500 LET T3=T3+1
1510 IF T3<=J2 GOTO 1530
1520 LET S2=0
1530 LET H1=H1−S2
1540 LET N(T3+1)=N(T3+1)+(S2*R5)
```

Within the period loop line 1500 increments the term period counter T3 by one so that it equals the current period. Lines 1510 and 1520 ensure that depreciation will not be taken after the end of the term by setting the period depreciation S2 to zero when the period T3 exceeds the term end J2. This is an alternative way to do the same thing that line 1360 does in the declining balance section.

Line 1530 subtracts the period depreciation S2 from the book value H1. Line 1540 adds the tax shelter cash flow S2*R5 to the period net cash flow N.

Note that the sum of years digits section uses two types of loop, as did the declining balance section. A GOTO loop is used for the years' calculations and within that is nested a FOR / NEXT loop for the periods' calculations. A year FOR / NEXT loop could be substituted for the GOTO loop by inserting FOR T1=1 TO (J2−J1)/B1 between lines 1470 and 1480 and by changing line 1570 to NEXT T1. The disadvantage of the FOR / NEXT loop in this application is that it cannot handle terms that are not whole numbers of years. It cannot handle, for example, a term of six and a half years although the GOTO loop can. However the formula used for calculating the sum of years digits implicitly assumes that the term consists of a whole number of years. As a result the program as constituted will process sum of years digits depreciation for a term that is not a whole number of years but the calculated depreciation amounts will differ slightly from the correct amounts. The problem will be resolved in the next section as ADR depreciation must deal explicitly with terms that are half-year multiples.

ASSET DEPRECIATION RANGE

The Class Life Asset Depreciation Range System (ADR) of depreciation consists of a combination of factors that result in a greater acceleration of depreciation than is usually possible with any of the other methods.

The example lease has a term of eight years and uses ADR depreciation over seven years. The depreciation term is one year less than the lease term. The same seven-year assumption was used in discussing the other depreciation methods so that all methods could be compared over the same term. In practice however all of the methods except ADR would require a depreciation term of no less than the term of the lease. This is because all other methods require that equipment be depreciated over its useful life and it is difficult for a lessor to substantiate a useful life that is shorter than the term for which he or she is leasing the equipment. The ADR system on the other hand is based on a categorized list of ranges of years that vary plus and minus 20% (rounded to the nearest half year) from the class life (asset guideline period). Any depreciation term within the given range can be selected without the need to relate it to actual useful life.

Another distinguishing characteristic is that the ADR system permits a switch from double declining balance to sum of years digits. While straight line, sum of years digits, and double declining balance (with or without switch to straight line) are all allowable, the time-conscious lessor will use the most rapid method available. This would be to start with double declining balance and then switch to sum of years digits in the first year for which the latter provides a higher depreciation amount.

The depreciation computations under the ADR system ignore salvage value but the equipment cannot be depreciated below salvage (less the extra 10%). That is, the depreciation amount is calculated as though the equipment is being depreciated to zero over the depreciation term but depreciation is stopped when the tax residual is reached. This provides a little additional acceleration since the tax residual, if greater than zero, will be reached before the end of the depreciation term as shown in Figure 9.2.

If the taxpayer elects the ADR system then he or she must elect one of two alternative conventions for the first year of service for the equipment. One is the half-year convention which provides that any equipment acquired during the tax year receives half a year of depreciation that year regardless of when it was delivered. The other is the modified half-year convention which provides that equipment acquired during the first half of the year receive a full year's depreciation and equipment acquired during the second half of the year receive no depreciation. The convention that is elected applies to all equipment acquired during that year. Regardless of which convention is elected depreciation for subsequent years is calculated as though the first year were a half year.

The effect of the half-year conventions is to make the depreciation years synchronous with the tax years. The depreciation years under the non-ADR methods begin with the acquisition date and are therefore synchronous with the lease years. Under either half-year convention the lease rate becomes sensitive to the equipment delivery date. This is because the delivery date will affect the amount of depreciation, and thus the net cash flow, taken during the first few periods of the lease. Because of the discounting process, changes during early periods have more impact than those during later periods.

Assume the tax year is the same as the calendar year. Applying the double declining balance rate to the example lease results in initial-year depreciation being calculated as $285,714. Under the modified half-year convention either the full amount or nothing would be taken for the year. If the equipment is delivered on January 1st the full amount would be allocated over the first 12 months of the lease term. If delivery is June 30th then the same amount is allocated over the first six months. And if delivery is July 1st then no depreciation at all is taken for the first six months of the lease.

Under the half-year convention one-half of the full amount or $142,857 is taken for the year regardless of the delivery date. This amount is spread over the first 12 months of the lease for a January 1st delivery date and the same amount is applied to the first *day* of the lease for a December 31st delivery date.

The convention the taxpayer selects for a given tax year must be applied to all equipment delivered during that year. A portfolio lessor who books leases throughout the year might therefore be advised to elect the half-year convention and assume a midyear delivery date for analytical purposes for all leases. This would enable the lessor to quote a consistent lease rate during the year without affecting the average return. It would also avoid surprises arising from a delivery date slipping forward or back from the date anticipated during negotiations.

The following development of the program assumes the half-year convention and a midyear delivery date so that a half-year of depreciation will be taken during the first half-year of the lease term.

Depreciation will start with the double declining balance method. With a seven-year depreciation term the rate will be $2 \times 1/7$ or .285714. Applying this to the equipment cost of $1,000,000 results in a full-year depreciation amount of $285,714. But the half-year convention stipulates that only a half-year of depreciation can be taken for the tax year of acquisition. This amount is $142,857. Since a midyear delivery date was assumed, the end of the initial tax year occurs at the end of the first half of the first lease year. At this time the book value will be $1,000,000 minus depreciation of $142,857 or $857,143. The second tax year will be a full year and depreciation will be .285714 time $857,143 or $244,898. This amount will also apply to a full lease year consisting of the second half of the first lease year and the first half of the second year. Depreciation continues to be calculated on the basis of full years until the end of the depreciation term when again a half-year's depreciation is taken in the first half of the eighth tax year which is the second half of the seventh lease year. This consistent half-year staggering must be borne in mind for depreciation is calculated on the basis of tax years while the discounting of the net cash flows must be based on lease years.

Double declining balance depreciation for each year of the term looks like this.

Tax		Lease		Double Declining Balance		
Year	Half	Year	Half	Beginning Balance	Depre- ciation	Ending Balance
1	2nd	1	1st	$1,000,000	$142,857	$857,143
2	1st		2nd	857,143	244,898	612,245
	2nd	2	1st			
3	1st		2nd	612,245	174,927	437,318
	2nd	3	1st			
4	1st		2nd	437,318	124,948	312,370
	2nd	4	1st			
5	1st		2nd	312,370	89,249	223,121
	2nd	5	1st			
6	1st		2nd	223,121	63,749	159,372
	2nd	6	1st			
7	1st		2nd	159,372	45,535	114,000
	2nd	7	1st			
8	1st		2nd	114,000	16,286	97,714
					$902,449	

After the first half-year calculations of sum of years digits depreciation will have to be made. When the double declining balance depreciation for the year is exceeded by the sum of years digits depreciation then the program must switch to the latter for the remainder of the term.

Since half a year has passed the remaining depreciation term is six and a half years. The sum of the digits is

$$6.5 + 5.5 + 4.5 + 3.5 + 2.5 + 1.5 + .5 = 24.5$$

The same sum can be obtained through a formula by first truncating the remaining term T4 to an integer. The sum of the digits will then be equal to two divided into the sum of the truncated term squared plus two times the truncated term plus one.

```
LET S4=INT(T4)
LET S3=(S4↑2+(2*S4)+1)/2
```

The book value balance after the initial half-year is $857,143. The fraction used as a multiplier is 6.5/24.5 with the numerator being the remaining term and the denominator being the sum of the digits. $857,143 times 6.5/24.5 results in depreciation for the year of $227,405. This is less than the $244,898 calculated by the double declining balance method so the latter is used and the switch to sum of years digits is not made. The sum of years digits depreciation for each year of possible switchover is as follows.

	Tax		Lease		Sum of Years Digits		
					Beginning	Multi-	Depre-
Year	Half	Year	Half		Balance	plier	ciation
2	1st	1	2nd }		$857,143	6.5/24.5	$227,405
	2nd	2	1st				
3	1st		2nd }		612,245	5.5/18	187,075
	2nd	3	1st				
4	1st		2nd }		437,318	4.5/12.5	157,434
	2nd	4	1st				
5	1st		2nd }		312,370	3.5/ 8	136,662
	2nd	5	1st				
6	1st		2nd }		223,121	2.5/ 4.5	123,956
	2nd	6	1st				
7	1st		2nd }		159,372	1.5/ 2	119,529
	2nd	7	1st				
8	1st		2nd		114,000	.5/ .5	57,000

Note that the denominator of the multiplier fraction declines as it must be the sum of the remaining years' digits for comparison testing. Once the switch is made then the denominator is frozen and stays constant. The depreciation actually taken for each year of the lease, starting with double declining balance and switching to sum of years digits after one and a half lease years, is as follows.

		ADR Depreciation	
			SYD	
Lease			Multi-
Year	DDB	Amount	plier
.5	$142,857	$ —	—
1.5	244,897	—	—
2.5	—	187,075	5.5/18
3.5	—	153,061	4.5/18
4.5	—	119,048	3.5/18
5.5	—	53,062	2.5/18
6.5	—	—	1.5/18
7	—	—	.5/18
	$900,000		18/18

Depreciation for year 5.5 would have been $85,034 had depreciation not been stopped when the book value reached the tax residual value of $100,000; that is, total depreciation reached $900,000. Depreciation for the last one and a half years would have been $51,020 and $17,007 which would have depreciated the equipment to zero.

The last column presents the multiplier fraction for sum of years digits depreciation which is applied to a constant $612,246 which is the book value balance at the time of the switchover.

In the program the term period counter T3 is set to the beginning of the depreciation term before the program branches to the ADR section.

```
1590 REM ADR DEPR
1600 LET A1=(2*B1)/(J2−J1)
1610 LET S2=(H1*A1)/B1
1620 FOR T=1 TO B1/2
1630 LET T3=T3+1
1640 LET H1=H1−S2
1650 LET N(T3+1)=N(T3+1)+(S2*R5)
1660 NEXT T
```

Line 1600 calculates the double declining balance rate and names it A1. The equation is the same that was used in the declining balance section except that the constant 2 replaces the input variable A1. Line 1610 calculates the periodic depreciation S2 for the first year as the initial book value H1 times the depreciation rate A1 divided by the number of periods per year B1.

Lines 1620 and 1660 form a period loop that steps through one-half of a year by defining the upper limit of the loop as the number of periods per year B1 divided by two. There is an implicit assumption here that the payment frequency is at least semiannual and is not an odd value such as 13. The loop steps through only a half year because the assumption of the half-year convention and midyear delivery results in half a year of depreciation being taken during the first half-year of the lease.

Within the loop line 1630 increments the period counter T3 by one. Then line 1640 subtracts the period depreciation S2 from the book value H1 and line 1650 adds the tax shelter cash flow to the period net cash flow N.

```
1670 LET T4=(J2−T3)/B1
1680 LET S1=H1*A1
1690 LET S4=INT(T4)
1700 IF T4−S4=0 GOTO 1740
1710 IF T4−S4=.5 GOTO 1760
```

```
1720 PRINT "DEPR TERM NOT HALF-YEAR MULTIPLE."
1730 STOP
1740 LET S3=H1/((T4*(T4+1))/2)
1750 GOTO 1770
1760 LET S3=H1/((S4↑2+(2*S4)+1)/2)
1770 LET S7=S3*T4
1780 IF S1>S7 GOTO 1800
1790 LET S1=S7
1800 LET S2=S1/B1
```

Line 1670 calculates the number of remaining years T4 by dividing the periods per year B1 into the number of remaining periods, which is the difference between the last period J2 and the current period T3. Line 1680 calculates the year's DDB depreciation S1 by multiplying the book value H1 by the DDB rate A1. Line 1690 truncates the number of remaining years T4 to an integer and names the result S4.

Under the ADR system the depreciation term must be either a whole number of years or a whole number plus half a year. The first half-year has just been processed but the remaining term should still be some multiple of half-years. This is tested by lines 1700 and 1710. If the difference between the remaining years T4 and its truncated value S4 is zero then the remaining number of years is an integer and the program goes to line 1740. There the SYD depreciation factor S3 is calculated by the formula that was used in the SYD depreciation section. If the difference between the remaining years T4 and its truncated value S4 is .5 then the remaining term is half a year more than a whole number of years and the program goes to line 1760. There the SYD depreciation factor S3 is calculated by the formula discussed earlier in this section. If the remaining term does not meet either of these two conditions then line 1720 prints an error message and line 1730 stops the program.

Line 1770 calculates the SYD depreciation for the year S7 by multiplying the SYD factor S3 by the number of remaining years T4. Line 1780 compares the year's DDB depreciation S1 with its SYD depreciation S7 and if the former is not greater than the latter then the year's depreciation S1 is switched to the SYD depreciation S7 by line 1790. Line 1800 calculates the periodic depreciation amount S2 by dividing the year's depreciation S1 by the periods per year B1.

```
1810 FOR T=1 TO B1
1820 LET T3=T3+1
1830 IF T3>J2 GOTO 1890
1840 IF H1<=I2 GOTO 1890
```

```
1850 IF H1−S2>I2 GOTO 1870
1860 LET S2=H1−I2
1870 LET H1=H1−S2
1880 LET N(T3+1)=N(T3+1)+(S2*R5)
1890 NEXT T
```

Lines 1810 through 1890 comprise the annual period loop that calculates the new book value and the net cash flow of the depreciation tax shelter. It also cuts off the depreciation when either the end of the depreciation term or the tax residual value is reached. The entire loop is exactly the same as was used in the declining balance section of the program.

```
1900 LET T4=T4−1
1910 IF T3>=J2 GOTO 210
1920 IF S1>S7 GOTO 1680
1930 LET S2=(S3*T4)/B1
1940 IF T4>.5 GOTO 1810
1950 LET S2=S2*2
1960 GOTO 1810
```

Since the program has just emerged from a period loop that covers one year line 1900 subtracts one from the number of remaining years T4. Line 1910 tests whether the end of the term J2 has been reached and if it has then the program returns to line 210 to input the next cash flow.

Line 1920 tests whether the switchover to SYD depreciation has occurred yet. If the year's depreciation just used S1 is greater than the SYD depreciation S7 then the program is still using DDB depreciation and it returns to line 1680. There the DDB and SYD depreciation amounts for the next year will be calculated and compared. If the switchover has occurred then the program goes to line 1930. There the periodic depreciation S2 for the next year is calculated by muiltiplying the SYD factor S3 by the remaining years T4 and dividing by the periods per year B1. Line 1940 tests whether the program has reached the final half-year and if not directs it to line 1810 for reentry into the year's period loop. If the remaining term T4 is only half a year then line 1950 doubles the calculated periodic depreciation S2. This is to adjust for the final depreciation amount being applicable to only half a year's periods rather than the full year that was used to calculate S2 at line 1930. After the adjustment the program returns to line 1810 and reentry to the year's period loop.

If it is desired to recognize the actual delivery date of the equipment and to permit selection of the modified half-year convention then some changes in logic would be required. The basic approach however would be the same. That is the number of payments in the first tax year would be determined and either a full year's, half year's, or no depreciation would be divided evenly among those payment periods. Two additional input data would be required—the selected convention and the delivery month—but these could be piggy-backed upon the depreciation code using polarity and the decimal point. Thus 4.09 could indicate the half-year convention and a September delivery while −4.03 could indicate the modified half-year convention and a March delivery. Entering the ADR code as a simple 4 could cause an automatic default to the half-year convention and midyear delivery assumptions.

CALCULATING THE RENTALS

Once the cash flow inputs have been allocated to the periods on an after-tax basis most of the calculation functions of LEAS will be exactly the same as those of DISC. The present value and rate of return functions will merely be working with a stream of after-tax and not pretax amounts.

The exception is the calculation of unknown payments. The mechanics of calculating payments are the same but the resultant values will be after-tax. They must be converted ("grossed up") to their pretax equivalents for printing of the answers. This will be a simple revision for if the after-tax amount equals the pretax amount *times* one minus the tax rate then by algebraic transformation the pretax amount equals the after-tax amount *divided* by one minus the tax rate.

For the single or one-shot payment (type 1 cash flow) the equation is

LET H1 = ((Z1 − X1)*(1 + R1)↑J4)/(1 − R5)

The difference from the equation in DISC is the addition of the divisor one minus the tax rate.

The more common calculation for a lease program is solving for the rentals which will be a series of equal (type 2) cash flow. The same present value factors E1 through E4 will be used as for DISC and their equations are the same. The difference appears in the statements in which the payments are calculated from the factors. For rentals in arrears one minus the tax rate is inserted into the divisor like this.

LET H1 = (Z1 − X1)/((E1 − E2)*(1 − R5))

For rentals in advance the taxes occur in arrears. This can be handled by subtracting the arrears factor for the taxes from the advance factor for the payments and using the difference as the divisor. If the rentals start at time zero this would be the rental calculation formula.

LET H1=(Z1−X1)/((1+E3)−(R5*E1))

If the rentals start in the future then the factors for the initial nonpayment term must be subtracted from those for the advance rentals and the arrears taxes.

LET H1=(Z1−X1)/((E3−E4)−(R5*(E1−E2)))

The payment H1 will now be calculated as its pretax amount. Since the present value factor E1 is now used for all rental cases the logic sequence

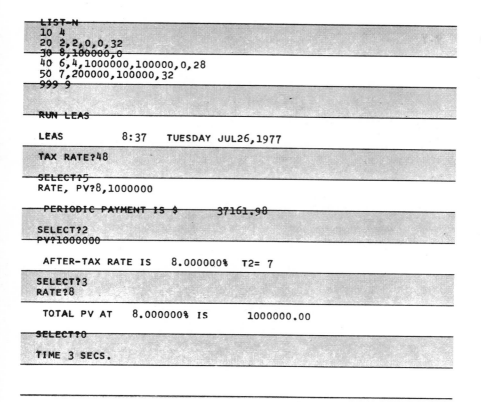

```
LIST-N
10 4
20 2,2,0,0,32
30 8,100000,0
40 6,4,1000000,100000,0,28
50 7,200000,100000,32
999 9


RUN LEAS

LEAS              8:37    TUESDAY JUL26,1977

TAX RATE?48

SELECT?5
RATE, PV?8,1000000

PERIODIC PAYMENT IS $       37161.98

SELECT?2
PV?1000000

AFTER-TAX RATE IS   8.000000%  T2= 7

SELECT?3
RATE?8

TOTAL PV AT   8.000000% IS        1000000.00

SELECT?0

TIME 3 SECS.
```

Figure 9.4   Run of LEAS to calculate after-tax rate.

can be changed slightly so that E1 is calculated before the advance/arrears branching occurs.

The control section that moves the calculated payment in and out of the net cash flows, depending on subsequent selections, must operate on after-tax cash flows. For the single or type one payment this merely requires substituting H1 * (1 − R5) for H1 in the two lines that add or subtract H1 from the period net cash flow N. For the series of equal or type two cash flow no change is required because for this type a subroutine in the input section is used. The input section has already been revised to reflect taxes.

LEAS is now an operating program. Figure 9.4 presents a run to calculate the rentals to yield an 8% after-tax return for the example lease. The rate and present value are then calculated to check the payment calculation.

The program cannot yet handle the case in which the lease is partially financed with debt. This provision is developed in the next chapter.

10

The Leveraged Lease

In the broad sense every lease is a leveraged lease for it is doubtful that any lessor finances leased equipment entirely with equity funds. In the leasing industry however the term "leveraged lease" refers to one whose debt is directly secured by the equipment and without recourse to the lessor. That is, the loan participants look only to the lease rentals to provide their interest and principal payments, are collateralized by a mortgage on the equipment, and base their decisions on the creditworthiness of the lessee and not on that of the lessor. They have no claim on the owner participants. Such a leveraged lease requires one or more trustees to administer the lease in accordance with the defined rights of the various parties and the documentation becomes long and complex.

From the programming viewpoint however a loan is a loan, and the program structure is seldom influenced by the legal structure. This chapter will therefore consider leverage in the general sense of meaning the use of debt financing as a means of increasing the lessor's return on equity. Whether this debt is tied to the specific lease or is raised on the overall credit rating of the lessor is immaterial for calculating and evaluating the cash flows.

The net cash flows of a lease after deducting debt payments and their tax effects exhibits the polarity-reversing pattern that often results in ambiguous rates of return or even two possible rates. This has led to a multitude of proposed methods for calculating the rate of return of a leveraged lease. Two methods have been selected for discussion. The first is the internal rate of return method and requires only the addition of a loan function. The second is the sinking-fund method which requires some relatively sophisticated logic in addition to the loan function.

INTERNAL RATE OF RETURN

The internal rate of return method is the same as that used in DISC and LEAS. It involves finding that discount rate at which the present value of the net cash flows equals the investment; that is, the rate at which the net present value is zero.

Adding debt to the lease analysis reduces the lessor's investment by the amount of the loan and reduces the net cash flows to the lessor by the after-tax amounts of the loan payments. The interest component of the payments is deductible from income for tax purposes while the principal repayment component is not.

Assume that 70% of the equipment cost of the example lease is financed by a $700,000 mortgage-type loan bearing interest at 11%. The cash flows over the term of the lease are as follows.

Rental income	$1,189,183
Depreciation expense	(900,000)
Interest expense	(361,595)
Taxable income	$ (72,412)
Income tax at 48%	34,758
Net income	$ (37,654)
Plus: Depreciation	900,000
Less: Principal repayment	(700,000)
Net cash flow	$ 162,346

The sum of depreciation and interest expenses is greater than the rental income. The lease shows a book loss even over its full term. As a result the income tax is positive, representing the amount by which taxes on other-source income are reduced upon consolidation. Net income is also negative, but the net cash flow from the rentals is $162,346 after adding back depreciation and then subtracting the loan repayment. The lessor also receives the investment tax credit and the after-tax value of the residual, but these amounts are unchanged from those of the nonleveraged lease.

Net cash flow from:	
Rentals	$162,346
Residual	152,000
ITC	100,000
Total net cash flow	$414,346
Less: Investment	(300,000)
Gain from transaction	$114,346

The lessor receives a net gain of $114,346 which is 38.1% of the $300,000 investment. In the nonleveraged case the lessor received a net gain of $302,375 which was 30.2% of a $1,000,000 investment. Using leverage has increased the gain in relation to the investment. Calculating the return on equity investment requires discounting the period-by-period cash flows after taxes and after debt service. The derivation of each period's net cash flow for the leveraged lease is presented in Figure 10.1.

The period net cash flows for the nonleveraged lease in Figure 9.1 were skewed toward the front end but each was positive. Those in Figure 10.1 for the leveraged lease are skewed even further so that the net cash flows are negative during the last three years. During the first year the lessor recovers 69% of the investment and recovers all of it at the ninth quarter. After the fifth year he or she has to reinvest in the lease because the taxes are greater than the excess of the rentals over the loan payments.

The additional skewing is caused by a further acceleration of deductible expenses due to the nature of interest. Interest expense is highest during the early years of the lease when the loan balance is highest and then declines as the loan is repaid. The loan payment is a level cash outflow over the term but the split between the deductible interest component and the nondeductible principal component shifts from favoring the former to the latter. This increases the losses in the early years and thus the tax shelter to other income.

The only required programming change to LEAS to enable it to calculate the rate is to add a loan function.

The LOAN program has the facility to put its loan components into an output file named LCF. The simplest way to add a loan function to LEAS is to have it input the loan cash flows from LCF.

> Inputs from LCF:
>
> | | |
> |---|---|
> | Periods per year is | B3 |
> | Total number of periods is | B4 |
> | Period interest is | L2 |
> | Period principal repayment is | L3 |
> | Period loan balance is | L4 |

The cash flow type code will be five for a loan to be picked up from the LCF file. Since all of the data is in the LCF file no parameters need be entered in the INLEAS file. The loan entry in INLEAS will look like this, assuming the line number is 60.

```
60 5
```

INCREMENT?1
TAX RATE?48

LEASE PARAMETERS:

TERM:	8.00 YEARS	FREQUENCY:	4 TIMES PER YEAR	
RENT:	$	37161.98 IN ARREARS FOR	8.00 YEARS	
ITC:	$	100000.00 AT PERIOD	0	
ADR DEPR:	$	1000000.00 COST TO $	100000.00 OVER	7.00 YRS
RESIDUAL:	$	200000.00 (BOOK $	100000.00) AT PERIOD	32
LOAN:	$	700000.00 AT 11.000% OVER	8.00 YEARS	

CASH FLOW ANALYSIS

PER	RENTALS	DEPRE- CIATION	INTEREST	OTHER	TAXABLE INCOME
0	0.00	0.00	0.00	0.00	0.00
1	37161.98	-71428.57	-19250.00	0.00	-53516.59
2	37161.98	-71428.57	-18867.07	0.00	-53133.66
3	37161.98	-61224.49	-18473.60	0.00	-42536.11
4	37161.98	-61224.49	-18069.32	0.00	-42131.83
5	37161.98	-61224.49	-17653.92	0.00	-41716.43
6	37161.98	-61224.49	-17227.09	0.00	-41289.60
7	37161.98	-46768.71	-16788.53	0.00	-26395.26
8	37161.98	-46768.71	-16337.90	0.00	-25944.63
9	37161.98	-46768.71	-15874.89	0.00	-25481.62
10	37161.98	-46768.71	-15399.14	0.00	-25005.87
11	37161.98	-38265.31	-14910.31	0.00	-16013.63
12	37161.98	-38265.31	-14408.03	0.00	-15511.36
13	37161.98	-38265.31	-13891.95	0.00	-14995.27
14	37161.98	-38265.31	-13361.67	0.00	-14464.99
15	37161.98	-29761.90	-12816.80	0.00	-5416.73
16	37161.98	-29761.90	-12256.96	0.00	-4856.88
17	37161.98	-29761.90	-11681.72	0.00	-4281.64
18	37161.98	-29761.90	-11090.66	0.00	-3690.58
19	37161.98	-21258.50	-10483.34	0.00	5420.14
20	37161.98	-21258.50	-9859.32	0.00	6044.15
21	37161.98	-10544.22	-9218.15	0.00	17399.61
22	37161.98	0.00	-8559.34	0.00	28602.64
23	37161.98	0.00	-7882.41	0.00	29279.57
24	37161.98	0.00	-7186.87	0.00	29975.11
25	37161.98	0.00	-6472.20	0.00	30689.78
26	37161.98	0.00	-5737.88	0.00	31424.10
27	37161.98	0.00	-4983.36	0.00	32178.62
28	37161.98	0.00	-4208.10	0.00	32953.88
29	37161.98	0.00	-3411.51	0.00	33750.47
30	37161.98	0.00	-2593.02	0.00	34568.96
31	37161.98	0.00	-1752.02	0.00	35409.96
32	37161.98	0.00	-887.89	0.00	36274.09
TOT	1189183.36	-900000.00	-361594.96	0.00	-72411.60
RES	200000.00	-100000.00	0.00	0.00	100000.00
TOT	1389183.36	-1000000.00	-361594.96	0.00	27588.40

PER	TAX AT 48.00 %	NET INCOME	ITC	PRINCIPAL REPAYMENTS	NET CASH FLOW
0	0.00	0.00	100000.00	0.00	100000.00
1	25687.96	-27828.63	0.00	-13924.84	29675.10
2	25504.16	-27629.50	0.00	-14307.78	29491.29
3	20417.33	-22118.78	0.00	-14701.24	24404.47
4	20223.28	-21908.55	0.00	-15105.52	24210.42
5	20023.88	-21692.54	0.00	-15520.93	24011.02
6	19819.01	-21470.59	0.00	-15947.75	23806.15
7	12669.72	-13725.53	0.00	-16386.31	16656.86
8	12453.42	-13491.21	0.00	-16836.94	16440.56
9	12231.18	-13250.44	0.00	-17299.95	16218.31
10	12002.82	-13003.05	0.00	-17775.70	15989.95
11	7686.54	-8327.09	0.00	-18264.53	11673.68
12	7445.45	-8065.91	0.00	-18766.81	11432.59
13	7197.73	-7797.54	0.00	-19282.90	11184.87
14	6943.20	-7521.80	0.00	-19813.18	10930.33
15	2600.03	-2816.70	0.00	-20358.04	6587.17
16	2331.30	-2525.58	0.00	-20917.88	6318.44
17	2055.19	-2226.45	0.00	-21493.13	6042.33
18	1771.48	-1919.10	0.00	-22084.19	5758.62
19	-2601.67	2818.47	0.00	-22691.50	1385.47
20	-2901.19	3142.96	0.00	-23315.52	1085.94
21	-8351.82	9047.80	0.00	-23956.69	-4364.68
22	-13729.27	14873.37	0.00	-24615.50	-9742.13
23	-14054.19	15225.38	0.00	-25292.43	-10067.06
24	-14388.05	15587.06	0.00	-25987.97	-10400.92
25	-14731.09	15958.69	0.00	-26702.64	-10743.96
26	-15083.57	16340.53	0.00	-27436.96	-11096.43
27	-15445.74	16732.88	0.00	-28191.48	-11458.60
28	-15817.86	17136.02	0.00	-28966.75	-11830.73
29	-16200.23	17550.24	0.00	-29763.33	-12213.09
30	-16593.10	17975.86	0.00	-30581.82	-12605.96
31	-16996.78	18413.18	0.00	-31422.82	-13009.64
32	-17411.56	18862.53	0.00	-32286.95	-13424.43
TOT	34757.57	-37654.03	100000.00	-700000.00	262345.97
RES	-48000.00	52000.00	0.00	0.00	152000.00
TOT	-13242.43	14345.97	100000.00	-700000.00	414345.97

TIME 3 SECS.

Figure 10.1   Cash flows of a leveraged lease.

When the input section of LEAS inputs a cash flow type G1 with a value of five it will go to the LCF file input section.

```
960 REM LCF IN
970 OPEN 2,'LCF',INPUT
980 GET 2:B4,B3
990 IF B3=B1 GOTO 1020
1000 PRINT "PERIODS/YEAR LCF & LEAS NOT SAME."
1010 STOP
1020 IF B2>=B4 GOTO 1040
1030 LET B2=B4
1040 FOR T=0 TO B4
1050 GET 2:L2,L3,L4
1060 LET N(T+1)=N(T+1)−(L2*(1−R5) )−L3
1070 NEXT T
1080 CLOSE 2
1090 GOTO 210
```

Line 970 opens the input file LCF. Line 980 inputs the general data—the total number of loan periods B4 and the periods per year B3. Line 990 compares the LOAN periods per year B3 with the LEAS periods per year B1. If they are not the same then an error message is printed and the program stops. Lines 1020 and 1030 ensure that the total number of periods B2 will be no less than the number of loan periods B4.

Lines 1040 and 1070 form a loop that steps through each period of the loan. It starts at period zero in case the loan payments should be in advance. Within the loop line 1050 inputs each period's interest L2, principal payment L3, and balance outstanding L4. Variable L4 is not used by LEAS but must be inputted in order to make the next L2 available. Line 1060 calculates the after-tax value of the interest L2 by multiplying it by one minus the tax rate R5, subtracts the result from the period net cash flow N, and then also subtracts the full amount of the principal payment L3.

After leaving the loop line 1080 closes the LCF file and line 1090 sends the program back to line 210 to input the next cash flow.

The advantage of this method of obtaining the loan data is that a wide variety of loans can be accommodated by the LEAS program because the full flexibility of the LOAN program is available to it. A lease may have a floating rental because its debt financing has a floating interest rate. The LEAS/LOAN combination enables such a lease to be evaluated.

The disadvantage is that two programs must be run instead of one. The loan parameters must be entered in INLOAN, then LOAN is run, the lease parameters are entered in INLEAS, and then LEAS is run. Incorporating a copy of LOAN into LEAS would avoid this but it would almost double the size of LEAS and increase the compilation time for each run. This is an inefficient approach for most leveraged leases have a simple debt structure and the full capability of LOAN is not required.

The solution is to retain the loan input file capability of LEAS but to also provide it with an internal loan function that is limited but adequate for most cases. The usual loan structure for a lease is a mortgage-type loan so that the loan payments will have the same level pattern as the rentals. The payments are of the same frequency and timing as the rentals and the loan is fully amortized over the term. Deviations from this typical loan are encountered for lessors have at times shown great ingenuity in structuring the debt either to meet the diverse requirements of several lenders or to enable shaving a few basis points off the rental rate. But a loan function patterned after the typical loan will enable LEAS to be self-sufficient for most cases.

The cash flow type code for the internal loan function will be four. The loan parameters will be entered in INLEAS in the same format as was used for INLOAN and all of the variables will have the same name as they had in LOAN.

```
690 REM MORTGAGE LOAN
700 GET 1:K1,A1,H1,I2,J1,J2
710 IF B2>=J2 GOTO 730
720 LET B2=J2
730 LET A1=A1/(B1*100)
740 IF I2<0 GOTO 830
750 IF K1>1 GOTO 790
760 LET U1=1+( (1−(1/(1+A1)↑(J2−J1−1) ) )/A1)
770 LET U2=I2*A1/(1+A1)
780 GOTO 810
790 LET U1=(1−(1/(1+A1)↑(J2−J1) ) )/A1
800 LET U2=I2*A1
810 LET U3=( (H1−I2)/U1)+U2
820 GOTO 840
830 LET U3=−I2
```

When the program inputs a cash flow type G1 with a value of four it will go to the mortgage loan section at line 690. Then line 700 inputs the loan parameters. Lines 710 and 720 ensure that the total number of periods B2 is no less than the end of the loan term J2. Line 730 converts the interest rate to the periodic decimal form. Line 740 tests whether I2 represents the loan payment, in which case the program goes to line 830 for removal of the piggybacked polarity code. If the loan payment is to be calculated then this is done by lines 760 and 770 for advance payments and lines 790 and 800 for arrears payments. The total payment U3 is calculated by line 810.

```
840 IF K1>1 GOTO 870
850 LET H1=H1−U3
860 LET N(J1+1)=N(J1+1)−U3
870 FOR T=(J1+1) TO J2
880 LET Q1=H1*A1
890 IF T<J2 GOTO 920
900 IF K1>1 GOTO 920
910 LET U3=0
920 LET N(T+1)=N(T+1)−U3+(Q1*R5)
930 LET H1=H1−U3+Q1
940 NEXT T
950 GOTO 210
```

Line 840 tests whether payments are in advance or arrears. If they are in advance then line 850 subtracts the payment U3 from the original loan amount H1 and line 860 subtracts it from the net cash flow N at the very beginning of the term. Lines 870 and 940 form a loop that steps through the periods of the loan term.

Within the loop line 880 calculates the period interest Q1. Line 920 subtracts the payment U3 from the period net cash flow N and adds back the taxes associated with the interest payment Q1. This is algebraically the same as subtracting the sum of the principal payment and the after-tax interest. Line 930 subtracts the payment U3 from the loan balance H1 and adds back the interest Q1. This is the same as subtracting the principal payment. Lines 890 through 910 act together to set the payment amount U3 to zero at the end of the term J2 if the payments are in advance. This operation plus that at lines 840 through 860 are what shift the payments from arrears to advance. After exit from the loop line 950 sends the program back to line 210 to input the next cash flow.

This program section is the mortgage-type loan function from LOAN that has been stripped of such auxiliary features as floating interest rates and rounding. Even so it enables LEAS to handle internally loans with advance or arrears payments, payments that are either given or calculated, loans with breakpoint segments, and multiple loans. The only addition is the inclusion of the tax rate R5 in line 920.

LEAS can now calculate the return on equity of a leveraged lease using the internal rate of return method. Figure 10.2 presents a run in which the return on the $300,000 equity investment of the example lease is calculated as 22.9%.

```
LIST-N
10 4
20 2,2,37161.98,0,32
30 8,100000,0
40 6,4,1000000,100000,0,28
50 7,200000,100000,32
60 4,2,11,700000,0,0,32
999 9
```

```
RUN LEAS

LEAS          9:11   FRIDAY OCT 21,1977

TAX RATE?48
SF MODE (YES OR NO)?NO

SELECT?2
PV?300000

AFTER-TAX RATE IS  22.909161%  T2= 9

SELECT?7
SF MODE (YES OR NO)?YES
SF INVEST RATE (AF-TAX)?3

SELECT?2
PV?300000

AFTER-TAX RATE IS  15.082034%  T2= 9

SELECT?0

TIME 3 SECS.
```

Figure 10.2   Run of LEAS calculating internal and sinking fund rates of return.

SINKING-FUND RATE OF RETURN

The net cash flows for a leveraged lease typically begin positive, turn negative, and then turn positive again upon receipt of the residual. It is the negative cash flows that cause suspiciously high rates and perhaps even multiple rates to be calculated. If these negative cash flows could be stripped away, leaving only a stream of positive cash flows to be equated with the negative outflow of the investment, then a unique and unambiguous rate could be calculated. (Whether it would be a "truer" rate is beyond the scope of this book.)

The sinking-fund rate of return method is one approach to eliminating the negative cash flows. It consists of establishing a hypothetical sinking fund into which is paid some portion of the positive cash flows that occur during the early years of the lease. The sinking fund is assumed to be invested in low-risk securities, such as treasury bills, so that it earns income. When the lease cash flows turn negative during the later years the cash deficits are covered by withdrawals from the sinking fund. The amounts deposited in the sinking fund are calculated so that they plus their earnings are just sufficient to cover the future negative cash flows—neither more nor less.

Assume an investment of $1000 that promises to return $1400 at the end of the first year but requires an additional investment (payment) of $200 at the end of the second year. These two cash flows of $+1400 at period one and $−200 at period two equal the $1000 investment at a discount rate of 24%. The return on investment is therefore 24%.

Assume further that the investor is a conservative investor who wishes to ensure that he will in fact have the funds to pay the final $200 when it becomes due. Upon receipt of the first year's $1400 he immediately deposits $190.48 in a savings account that earns interest at 5% per year. His deposit will earn $9.52 over one year so that it will have grown to $200.00 by the end of the transaction and his terminal obligation is safely covered. The investor has pocketed $1209.52 after the first year for a rate of return of 21%.

Figure 10.3 presents the results of a sinking fund on the example lease, assuming an investment rate for the fund of 3% after tax. The first column shows the net cash flows of the lease and is the same as the last column of Figure 10.1. The second column shows the cash flow to the fund with the negative amounts being withdrawals. The next two columns show the earnings of the fund and its balance at the end of each period. The last column shows the cash flow to the lessor and is the difference between the first two columns.

Deposits into the sinking fund do not start until period eight. After that the lease net cash flows are deposited in their entirety in the fund through period 20. Then the lease net cash flows turn negative and are covered in their entirety by withdrawals from the fund. The net cash flow for the last period is a combination of a $13,424.43 deficit from the last rental and a $152,000 inflow from the residual. The withdrawal from the sinking fund is also $13,424.43 which means that the residual was ignored in establishing the fund. The residual may be either included or excluded from consideration and programs have been written both ways. The author has taken the conservative approach and excluded it on the ground that the residual is a speculative component that should not be depended upon to meet a future tax liability.

```
RUN

LEASSL      8:54   MONDAY AUGUST 1,1977

TAX RATE?48

LEASE PARAMETERS:
------------------
  TERM:       8.00 YEARS        FREQUENCY:  4 TIMES PER YEAR
  RENT:     $      37161.98 IN ARREARS FOR  8.00 YEARS
  ITC:      $    100000.00 AT PERIOD   0
  ADR DEPR: $   1000000.00 COST TO $     100000.00 OVER  7.00 YRS
  RESIDUAL: $    200000.00 (BOOK $     100000.00 ) AT PERIOD  32
  LOAN:     $    700000.00 AT 11.000% OVER  8.00 YEARS
------------------

SF MODE (1=YES, 2=NO)?1
SF INVESTMENT RATE (AFTER-TAX)?3
PRINT SF TABLE (1=YES, 2=NO)?1
INCREMENT?1


                    SINKING FUND TABLE
                    ------------------
```

END PER	NCF BEFORE SINK FUND	CF TO SINK FUND	EARNINGS AT 3.000 %	SINK FUND BALANCE	CF TO EQUITY
0	100000.00	0.00	0.00	0.00	100000.00
1	29675.10	0.00	0.00	0.00	29675.10
2	29491.29	0.00	0.00	0.00	29491.29
3	24404.47	0.00	0.00	0.00	24404.47
4	24210.42	0.00	0.00	0.00	24210.42
5	24011.02	0.00	0.00	0.00	24011.02
6	23806.15	0.00	0.00	0.00	23806.15
7	16656.86	0.00	0.00	0.00	16656.86
8	16440.56	12514.52	0.00	12514.52	3926.04
9	16218.31	16218.31	93.86	28826.69	0.00
10	15989.95	15989.95	216.20	45032.85	0.00
11	11673.68	11673.68	337.75	57044.28	0.00
12	11432.59	11432.59	427.83	68904.70	0.00
13	11184.87	11184.87	516.79	80606.35	0.00
14	10930.33	10930.33	604.55	92141.23	0.00
15	6587.17	6587.17	691.06	99419.46	0.00
16	6318.44	6318.44	745.65	106483.55	0.00
17	6042.33	6042.33	798.63	113324.50	0.00
18	5758.62	5758.62	849.93	119933.05	0.00
19	1385.47	1385.47	899.50	122218.02	0.00
20	1085.94	1085.94	916.64	124220.60	0.00
21	-4364.68	-4364.68	931.65	120787.58	0.00
22	-9742.13	-9742.13	905.91	111951.35	0.00
23	-10067.06	-10067.06	839.64	102723.93	0.00
24	-10400.92	-10400.92	770.43	93093.45	0.00
25	-10743.96	-10743.96	698.20	83047.69	0.00
26	-11096.43	-11096.43	622.86	72574.12	0.00
27	-11458.60	-11458.60	544.31	61659.83	0.00
28	-11830.73	-11830.73	462.45	50291.55	0.00
29	-12213.09	-12213.09	377.19	38455.65	0.00
30	-12605.96	-12605.96	288.42	26138.10	0.00
31	-13009.64	-13009.64	196.04	13324.49	0.00
32	138575.57	-13424.43	99.93	0.00	152000.00
TOT	414345.97	-13835.38	13835.38	0.00	428181.35

```
LESSOR'S INVESTMENT?300000

  RETURN ON INVESTMENT IS  15.082033 %    T2= 6

EQUITY AMORT TABLE (1=YES, 2=NO)?0

TIME 4 SECS.
```

Figure 10.3   Sinking-fund cash flows for a lease.

The cash flows to the lessor in the last column are found by subtracting the payments to or from the sinking fund from the lease cash flows. These represent the equity cash flows and are concentrated in the first two years of the lease. Then they are zero for the remaining six years with a final inflow from the residual. The negative flows have been eliminated insofar as the lessor is concerned. It is the remaining cash flows to equity that are discounted to calculate the return on the lessor's $300,000 investment. Doing so results in a rate of return of 15.1%.

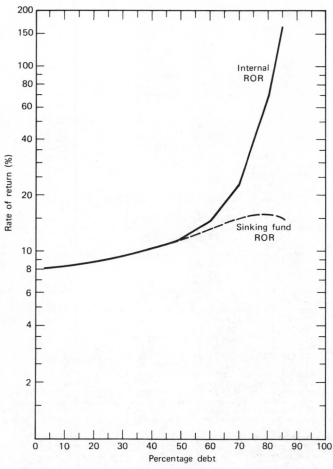

Figure 10.4   Internal and sinking fund rates of return as a function of leverage.

The sinking-fund rate of return is a meld of the internal rate of return of 22.9% and the sinking-fund investment rate of 3.0%. As the sinking-fund investment rate increases so does the sinking-fund rate of return. When the former equals the internal rate of return then the latter will also. This is a demonstration of the implicit assumption of the internal rate of return that its reinvestment rate is the same as the internal rate.

The rates calculated by the two methods differ by almost eight percentage points. The spread is directly related to the proportion of debt used to finance the lease as is shown in Figure 10.4. At the lower levels of debt the internal and sinking fund rates are the same. This is because the debt payments are too low to cause the negative cash flows that require a sinking fund. As the debt approaches 50% the two rates begin to diverge and as the debt exceeds 70% the internal rate of return accelerates dramatically even on a semilog graph. When the debt reaches 85% the internal rate of return is over 160%. The sinking-fund rate of return actually starts to decline at extreme levels of leverage.

The sinking-fund method became popular at a time when it was not uncommon to structure a lease with 80% or more of debt. The resultant high yields were viewed with some skepticism, particularly when it was realized that they could be obtained only if the cash flows were reinvested at the same high rates. The sinking-fund method was developed to explicitly apply a more reasonable reinvestment assumption to at least that portion of the cash flows required to meet the future liabilities of the lease. Today debt of 70% or less is the norm. Thus the problem of unrealistically high returns is now seldom encountered.

Adding a sinking-fund facility to LEAS does not require any change to the basic program structure. LEAS will still discount cash flows in the same manner as before. What is required is a logic section that can convert one stream of cash flows to another. The program should have no less capability with the sinking fund than without it. Therefore, the program should still be able to perform all the prior functions including rental calculations with and without the sinking fund and be able to switch in and out of the sinking-fund mode upon request. Figure 10.5 presents a flowchart of the sinking-fund logic. Some new variables are:

Sinking-fund mode (0 = no, 1 = yes) is   C5
Sinking-fund investment rate is   R7

The sinking-fund logic must be located after the cash flows have been inputted and assigned to their periods. It can be located before or after the select question because either way there will be switching back and forth.

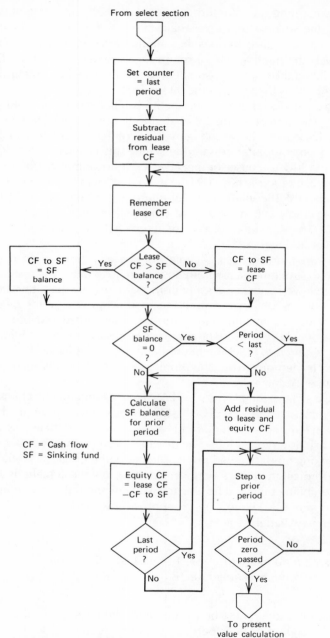

Figure 10.5   Flowchart of sinking-fund logic.

The following development places the input for the sinking fund before the select question and the logic afterwards.

```
2110 REM SELECT SF MODE
2120 IF R5=0 GOTO 2310
2130 PRINT "SF MODE (YES OR NO)";
2140 INPUT E$
2150 IF E$<>"YES" GOTO 2310
2160 LET C5=1
2170 PRINT "SF INVEST RATE (AF−TAX)";
2180 INPUT R7
2190 IF R7>=1 GOTO 2220
2200 PRINT USING 4610
2210 GOTO 2170
2220 LET R7=R7/(B1*100)
2230 GOTO 2310
```

Line 2120 sends the program directly to the select question if the tax rate R5 is zero. In the absence of taxes the sinking fund is inapplicable. Lines 2130 through 2160 determine whether the sinking-fund mode is desired. If not the program goes directly to the select question. If yes then the sinking-fund status C5 is set to one. The literal E$ is used temporarily to enable the user to answer with a familiar word rather than with a numeric code. Actually C5 could be eliminated and the status of the mode could be tested throughout the program on the basis of "yes" or "no." This is merely a matter of programming style. Lines 2170 and 2180 input the after-tax investment rate R7 to be used by the sinking fund. Lines 2190 through 2210 ensure that the rate is in the percentage form, after which line 2220 converts it to the periodic decimal form. Line 2230 then sends the program to the select question.

The program goes through the function select section in the same manner as before. The section that controls the calculated payment status is bypassed in the sinking-fund mode for a new control section will have to be developed for that mode.

To perform the sinking-fund calculations the program will start at the end of the term and work toward the beginning. At the end of the last period the sinking-fund balance must be just sufficient to cover that period's negative cash flow. This amount is determined and then discounted one period at the fund's investment rate to determine the amount that must be in the sinking fund at the beginning of the period. Then the next-to-last period's negative cash flow is added to the sinking-fund balance which is then discounted one period. The program works backward period-by-period, each time adding the period's negative cash flow from the lease to the balance and discounting one period to recognize the fund's earnings.

When the program reaches the early years of the lease the period net cash flows will turn positive. This change in polarity will automatically cause the cash flows to be subtracted from the fund balance each period. Thus the sinking-fund balance starts at zero at the end of the lease term, builds up as the program works toward the beginning, and then declines again to zero.

> *Remember original period cash flow N is*   P
> *Period sinking-fund balance is*   X
> *Cash flow to or from sinking fund is*   S5
> *Residual value after tax is*   F4

The period variables P and X must be dimensioned for the maximum number of periods allowed. This can be done in the same line that dimensions N and V.

```
100 DIM N(360),V(360),P(360),X(360)

. . .

2900 REM SINKING FUND

. . .

2990 LET T=B2
3000 LET N(T+1)=N(T+1)−F4
3010 LET P(T+1)=N(T+1)

. . .

3030 LET S5=N(T+1)

. . .

3080 LET X(T)=(X(T+1)−S5)/(1+R7)
3090 LET N(T+1)=N(T+1)−S5

. . .

3130 LET T=T−1
3140 IF T>=0 GOTO 3010
```

Line 2990 sets the period counter T to the last period of the lease B2. Line 3000 subtracts the after-tax value of the residual F4 from the final period's net cash flow N in accordance with the assumption discussed before. Variable F4 will have been set when the residual was processed in the input section. Line 3010 sets P equal to the lease's cash flow N. The function of P is to remember the original value of N so that N can be reset when required. In the sinking-fund mode, then, P will be the net cash flows before the sinking fund and N will be the cash flows to equity after the sinking fund.

Line 3030 sets the cash flow to the sinking fund S5 equal to the period lease cash flow N. Line 3080 calculates the sinking-fund balance for the prior period X(T) by subtracting the sinking-fund cash flow S5 from the current period's balance X(T+1) and discounting it for one period. The discounting is accomplished by the divisor, one plus the investment rate R7. Line 3090 subtracts the cash flow to the sinking fund S5 from the lease cash flow N so that N becomes the period cash flow after the sinking fund, that is, the cash flow representing return to equity. Line 3130 subtracts one from the period counter so that it becomes the prior period. If the period T has not gone below zero then the program returns to line 3010 and the beginning of the calculations for the new earlier period. When T does go below zero that indicates all of the periods have been processed and the program goes on to the next section for the present value calculations.

```
3020 IF N(T+1)>X(T+1) GOTO 3050
3030 LET S5=N(T+1)
3040 GOTO 3060
3050 LET S5=X(T+1)
```

The above logic controls the amount of the cash flow to the sinking fund S5 for the period in which the cash flow is first diverted from equity to the sinking fund. For any period but the switch period the entire amount of the lease cash flow goes either to equity or to the sinking fund. During the switch period, however, it has to be divided between the two recipients. Line 3020 compares the lease cash flow N before the sinking fund with the sinking-fund balance. If it is not larger, that is, if the sinking fund needs more than the cash flow amount, then line 3030 assigns the total amount of the cash flow to the sinking fund. As the program works toward the beginning of the lease the sinking-fund balance begins to decline. When it reaches the period at which it is less than that period's cash flow then line 3050 sets the cash flow to the sinking fund S5 to that amount necessary to retire the balance X. This "retirement" is in reverse or computational chronology. In actual chronology this is the period in which the first payment is made to establish the sinking fund.

```
3060 IF X(T+1)<>0 GOTO 3080
3070 IF T<B2-1 GOTO 3130
```

Lines 3060 and 3070 together cause the period calculations to be bypassed once the sinking-fund balance X reaches zero and it is not near the end of the lease term. This will keep the balance at zero, the cash flow to the sinking fund will stay at zero, and by default all of the cash flow will go to equity.

```
3100 IF T<B2 GOTO 3130
3110 LET N(T+1)=N(T+1)+F4
3120 LET P(T+1)=P(T+1)+F4
```

The residual value F4 that was subtracted from the cash flow N before the sinking-fund calculations began must be added back to the final period B2 cash flows N and P before the program goes to the next section for discounting. This is done by lines 3100 through 3120.

CHANGE MODE

Now that the cash flows have been calculated net of the sinking-fund payments they can be discounted to find present values and rates of return exactly as before. Additional logic is required for the rental calculation but first a change of mode facility will be added.

The program now asks the sinking-fund mode question before asking the select question and the program always returns to the select question after making a calculation. Thus whichever mode is selected all subsequent selections are performed with the cash flows of that particular mode. To change from one mode to another requires that another selection be made available, namely a change mode selection.

If the program is in the sinking fund mode and a change is requested then the stream of net cash flows has to be converted back to the values before the sinking fund. The change mode selection will have a value for C1 of seven.

```
2110 REM SELECT SF MODE

. . .

2230 GOTO 2310
2240 IF C5<1 GOTO 2110
2250 FOR T=0 TO B2
```

```
2260 LET N(T+1)=P(T+1)
2270 LET P(T+1),X(T+1)=0
2280 NEXT T
2290 LET C5=0
2300 GOTO 2110
2310 REM SELECT FUNCTION
```

. . .

```
2340 PRINT "SELECT";
2350 INPUT C1
```

. . .

```
2380 GOTO 2390,2480,2560,2590,2630,4400,2240 ON C1
```

. . .

```
2460 PRINT "CHNG MODE = 7"
```

After completing any calculation the program returns to line 2310 after which the select question is asked at line 2340. If the answer inputted by line 2350 is seven then line 2380 sends the program to line 2240 in the select sinking-fund section above. That line tests the mode status C5 and if it is zero, indicating the nonsinking-fund mode, then the program goes to the beginning of the select sinking-fund section and asks whether the sinking fund is desired.

If line 2240 determines that the program is already in the sinking-fund mode, that is, C5 equals one, then it goes through a period loop at lines 2250 through 2280. Within the loop line 2260 resets the period net cash flows N to their presinking-fund values as remembered by P. Line 2270 then sets P and the sinking-fund balance X for each period to zero. After exit from the loop line 2290 sets C5 to zero to indicate that the program is no longer in the sinking-fund mode. The program then goes to the beginning of the section where the select sinking-fund question will be asked again.

There is no computational reason for going to the sinking-fund question every time the mode is changed. If the change is from sinking fund to nonsinking fund the program could go directly to the select question. If the change is to the sinking-fund mode then the program could still ignore the sinking-fund question and go to the investment rate question. The purpose of the sinking-fund question in both cases is to leave a printed record of which mode is current.

RENTAL CALCULATION WITH SINKING FUND

The sinking fund acts as a buffer between the lease cash flows and the equity cash flows. This means that the rental payments cannot be calculated with a direct equation while in the sinking fund mode. An iterative approach can be used, however, that is similar to that used for the rate calculation.

When the payment calculation function is selected the program can assume a rental amount for the first trial. The assumed rents will be added to the cash flows, the program will go through the sinking fund, and then calculate the present value of the cash flows to equity. If the present value is less or greater than the desired present value, the amount of the equity investment, then a higher or lower rent will be assumed, the first trial rents will be subtracted from the cash flows, the new trial rents will be added, and the sinking fund and present value calculations will be repeated. After the first two trials an interpolation/extrapolation formula can be used to calculate subsequent trial rentals. When the calculated present value is within tolerance of the desired present value then the amount of the current trial rental will be printed as the answer.

> *Remember last trial rental is*   H2
> *Next trial rental is*   H3

```
2900 REM SINKING FUND
2910 IF C1<>5 GOTO 2990

. . .

2960 LET H1,H2=Z1/((1−(1/(1+R1)↑(J2−J1) ) )/R1)
2970 LET C3=2
2980 GOSUB 450
2990 LET T=B2

. . .


3150 REM PV CALC

. . .


3230 GOTO 2310,3240,2310,3620,3800 ON C1
```

If the selected function is not the payment calculation so that the value of C1 is other than five then line 2910 directs the program to the beginning of the sinking-fund calculations at line 2990. If the payment calculation has been selected then the program goes to line 2960 where the first trial rental is calculated. The formula used is the same as that for calculating the payment amount for a mortgage loan. It will thus produce the amount necessary to amortize the equity investment over the term at the given rate. This will not be the correct rental amount but does give a figure that is related to the investment, the term, and the rate. In practice, simply dividing the invest-ment by the number of periods per year seems to give equally good results but lacks a ready rationale. The primary requirement for the first trial rental is that it be sufficiently high that the sinking-fund balance is reduced to zero before the program works back to the beginning of the term.

Line 2970 sets the payment status C3 to two to indicate that the payment has been added to the cash flows, which it will be shortly, and the program then goes to the subroutine at line 450. The subroutine is the same set of period loops in the input section that are used to add the rentals to the net cash flows. Upon its return the program is at line 2990 and the beginning of the sinking-fund calculations.

After the sinking fund the program goes through the present value cal-culations. Then line 3230 tests the selection C1, finds its value to be five, and sends the program to the payment calculation section at line 3800.

```
3800 REM PMT CALC
3810 IF C5>0 GOTO 4030

. . .

4030 REM PMT CALC SF MODE

. . .

4050 LET T2=T2+1
4060 IF X1−Z1>.01 GOTO 4110
4070 IF X1−Z1<−.01 GOTO 4140
4080 PRINT USING 4590,H1
4090 PRINT "      T2=";T2
4100 GOTO 2310
4110 IF T2>1 GOTO 4170
4120 LET H3=.8*H1
4130 GOTO 4180
4140 IF T2>1 GOTO 4170
4150 LET H3=1.2*H1
4160 GOTO 4180
```

In the sinking-fund mode C5 will equal one and line 3810 will send the program to line 4030 and a special section to calculate rentals in that mode. The first half of this section tests the current trial value and calculates a new trial value in the same manner as was used in the rate calculation. The difference is that the trial values pertain to rental amounts and not discount rates. Line 4050 increments the iteration counter T2 by one for each pass through the section. Lines 4060 through 4090 compare the present value just calculated X1 with the desired present value Z1 and if it is within one cent the trial rental amount H1 is printed as the answer. Then the program returns to line 2310 and the select question.

If the two present values are not approximately equal then lines 4110 and 4140 test whether this is the first trial. If so then lines 4120 and 4150 calculate the next trial rent H3 as a proportion of the old H1. If the calculated present value X1 was too high then the rental is reduced by line 4120. If it was too low then the rental is raised by line 4150. In either case the program moves to line 4180.

```
4170 LET H3=H2+((Z1−X3)/(X−X3) )*(H1−H2)
4180 LET H2=H1
4190 LET H1=H3
4200 LET X3=X1
4210 LET X1=0
4220 IF T2<15 GOTO 4250
4230 PRINT "NO ANSWER BY 15 ITERATIONS."
4240 STOP
```

If the current trial is number two or greater then either line 4110 or 4140 sends the program to line 4170. Here the next trial rental amount is calculated by the interpolation formula that was used for the rate calculation except that the rentals H1 and H2 are used instead of discount rates. The program branches converge at line 4180 where H2 remembers the last trial rental H1. Line 4190 assigns the newly calculated trial rental H3 to H1. Line 4200 uses X3 to remember the present value X1 of the last trial and line 4210 then sets X1 to zero. Lines 4220 through 4240 print an error message and stop the program if fifteen trials have been made.

```
4250 FOR T=0 TO B2
4260 IF K1>1 GOTO 4310
4270 IF T>(J2−1) GOTO 4330
4280 LET P(T+1)=P(T+1)−H2
```

```
4290 LET P(T+2)=P(T+2)+(H2*R5)
4300 GOTO 4330
4310 IF T<(J1+1) GOTO 4330
4320 LET P(T+1)=P(T+1)-(H2*(1-R5) )
4330 LET N(T+1)=P(T+1)
4340 LET P(T+1),X(T+1)=0
4350 NEXT T
```

. . .

```
4380 GOSUB 450
4390 GOTO 2990
```

Line 4250 and 4350 define a period loop whose purpose is to delete the last trial rental H2 from the sinking-fund variables. Line 4260 tests the advance/arrears code K1 and if payments are in arrears then the program goes to line 4310. This line causes the succeeding calculation to be bypassed for the beginning period of the lease term. Line 4320 subtracts the after-tax value of the prior trial rental H2 from the presinking-fund cash flows P. If rentals are in advance the program goes from line 4260 to 4270 which bypasses the succeeding two lines for the ending period of the lease term. It is lines 4270 and 4310 that permit using the same loop for both advance and arrears payments. Line 4280 subtracts the full amount of the prior trial rental H2 from the presinking-fund cash flows P and then line 4290 adds back the relaxed tax amount one period later. This two-step reversal is required because of the rents in advance, taxes in arrears assumption.

Both advance and arrears cases converge at line 4330 where the period net cash flow N is reset to its presinking-fund value P. Line 4340 resets both P and the sinking fund balance X to zero.

Line 4380 uses the GOSUB statement to send the program to the subroutine in the input section of the program. There the new trial rental H1 is added to the period net cash flows N. Upon the program's return line 4390 sends it to line 2990 to calculate the sinking fund with the new rental.

The program can now solve for rentals in the sinking-fund mode. Some control statements must be added however to enable multiple selections. Since a calculated payment will already have been incorporated in the cash flows nothing need be done unless a payment calculation is again selected. In that event the prior calculated rental must be deleted from the cash flows and the sinking-fund variables reset. The payment calculation section already contains the logic to do this so it can be used as a subroutine. The variable C3 will again be used to remember the payment status.

```
2900 REM SINKING FUND

. . .

2920 IF C3<1 GOTO 2960
2930 LET H2=H1
2940 LET C3=1
2950 GOSUB 4250

. . .

4030 REM PMT CALC SF MODE

. . .

4360 IF C3<>1 GOTO 4380
4370 RETURN TO 2950
```

If a payment calculation has not been selected line 2910 sends the program directly to the sinking-fund calculation. Otherwise it goes to line 2920 where the payment status C3 is tested. If no payment has yet been calculated then C3 will equal zero and the program will go to line 2960 to make the first trial rental assumption. If C3 is greater then zero then a payment H1 has already been calculated so the program goes to line 2930 to set H2 equal to H1. This is because the subroutine that subtracts the old rental from the cash flow uses H2. Line 2940 sets the payment status C3 equal to one so this variable can be used to control the program's return. Line 2950 then sends the program to the subroutine at line 4250 in the payment calculation section. There the old rental is subtracted from the cash flows. After the subtraction loop line 4360 tests C3 and finds its value to be one. Then the RETURN statement in line 4370 sends the program back to line 2950. There the program is at the beginning of the first trial rental logic and proceeds to set the first trial rental again, add it to the cash flows, and go through the sinking fund as before.

LEAS has the capability of processing a variety of cash flow types and combining them into a single stream of net cash flows. Other types of cash flows could be developed and added to its repertoire. If the net cash flows could be put into an output file then they would be available for use by other programs. This is particularly useful when a nonrecurring project requires that a set of cash flows be developed and then manipulated in a special way. A temporary program can be quickly written to do the necessary computations but without having to incorporate its own complex front end.

An output to file selection can be added to LEAS and given the code value of six. If six is selected then the program would go directly to the output file logic as no calculations would be required. Output files were discussed in Chapter 4.

LEAS can do everything that DISC can do and more. The two programs could just as appropriately be named DISCSR and DISCJR for LEAS can be used as a general purpose discounting program. For example different depreciation methods or terms could be compared on a present value basis at varying discount rates and tax rates.

Although LEAS is of use to a lessee it was originally developed from the lessor's point of view. The next chapter develops a program that is designed specifically for the lessee.

11

The Lease Versus Buy Program

The lessee desires to evaluate a lease on the basis of how it compares economically to the alternative of purchasing the subject asset. It is assumed that the decision to acquire the asset has already been made so that its effect on revenues or any cost savings resulting from the use of the asset need not be considered. The decision at hand is how the asset should be financed and the analysis will compare the cost of leasing to the cost of purchasing. The buy alternative will include the use of any debt financing.

The name of the program to be developed will be LEASBUY.

DEFINING THE LEASBUY PROGRAM

The comparison between leasing and buying will be in terms of four aspects—rates, present values, cash flows, and impacts on profit. The first two, rates and present values, are derived by discounting the third, cash flows. The profit impact can also be derived from the cash flows and then adjusting for accrual accounting. The first task of the program will therefore be to input the parameters, develop the period cash flows, and categorize them as to whether they apply to the lease or the buy alternative.

The primary cash flow of the lease alternative is the rental, which will be a periodic cash outflow. The rents are tax deductible, so there will be an offset in the form of reduced tax payments. Any other lease-related items such as legal or brokers' fees would also have to be incorporated.

The cash flows of the buy alternative are more complex. Usually the purchase will be financed at least partially by debt. This will require loan payments of which the interest component will be tax-deductible and the principal repayment component will not. Ownership of the asset will entitle the owner to depreciation deductions which will increase cash flow by reducing taxes but will decrease profits. The buy alternative also results in the firm retaining the asset at the end of the term and thus being entitled to its residual value. The owner of the asset receives the investment tax credit so this would be another cash inflow for the buy alternative. However the lessor can pass this to the lessee, for a higher rental rate of course, in which case the investment tax credit would be common to both alternatives. Any other buy-related items, such as maintenance expenses, that might be included in the rental under the lease alternative would also be included.

Under the buy alternative the firm would have the asset for its useful life which would normally be longer than the lease term. For purposes of analysis however both alternatives should have the same cutoff point in time. Since the lease term is contractually fixed it is the term of the buy alternative that should be adjusted. This will involve cutting off the depreciation and loan functions at that time, applying the book value to the residual, and paying off the remaining loan balance.

Once the cash flows are developed the program will calculate the comparative after-tax rates. The after-tax debt cost is found by solving for that rate which discounts the after-tax interest payments plus the principal repayments to the amount of the loan.

The after-tax lease cost is that discount rate which equilibrates the difference between the lease cash flows and the buy cash flows, excluding the debt payments, to the equipment cost. The lease cost components are the after-tax rentals plus the ownership benefits that are relinquished by leasing—the depreciation tax shelter, the investment tax credit, and the residual.

Notice that the debt cost is based on the amount of the loan, which is not necessarily the same as equipment cost. Any difference would be the amount of equity funds required to complete the purchase. While the interest rate of a loan can be determined with some degree of certainty the cost of equity capital is very difficult to determine in practice, particularly if the firm is unprofitable. Since many firms that place heavy reliance on leasing have an unimpressive profit history the cost of capital concept is of limited applicability. One way to avoid the problem is to solve instead for the return on equity of purchasing rather than leasing. A judgment can then be made as to whether the return on equity is high enough, in light of other investment opportunities, to justify purchasing rather than leasing. This return is found by solving for the discount rate that equilibrates the ownership benefits less the debt costs plus the rentals avoided to the equipment cost less the amount of the loan.

It can be seen that the after-tax lease cost to the lessee is based on the same components used by the lessor in calculating the return on a lease before leverage. And the return on equity to the lessee uses the same components used by the lessor in the return on equity calculation for a leveraged lease. The specific parameters however may be different. In the lease/buy analysis the prospective lessee will use his or her own depreciation policy, debt costs, and estimate of residual value.

The most speculative element in the analysis is the estimate of residual value. A way to test the sensitivity of the results to the residual is to calculate the breakeven residual value. This is the value of the residual that would result in the lease cost being the same as the debt cost. It is often easier to judge whether the residual is likely to be more or less than this breakeven value than to estimate the residual with confidence. The program will therefore include such a breakeven residual calculation.

The program should also calculate the present values of the two alternatives at a given discount rate. This is to satisfy those who prefer to think in terms of present value rather than rate.

The program will also have to indicate the comparative impact of the two alternatives on the firm's cash flow and profit over the term. This can be done with a set of tables that show the individual components such as depreciation, interest, and rentals. Their format would be similar to that used in Figure 10.1 except that they should provide for printing on a fiscal year basis. The profit tables will have to be adjusted from a cash basis to an accrual basis to be consistent with the firm's published financial statements.

To reduce terminal time when the individual components are not needed the program can produce a summary table that compares only the net effect on cash flow and profit.

Figure 11.1 presents the master flowchart of LEASBUY and Figure 11.2 presents a sample run. The parameters used are the same as those of the example lease in Chapters 9 and 10 to maintain the consistency of the calculated rates.

DEVELOPING THE CASH FLOWS

LEAS already contains the input logic for the cash flow types required by LEASBUY. The first step would thus be to save a copy of LEAS under the name of LEASBUY and then delete all the lines except those of the input section.

There is a difference in how the cash flows are handled. LEAS immediately reduces each cash flow type to its contribution to a single cash flow stream N. LEASBUY however has to remember the individual components by type so that they can be combined in various ways and can be printed separately in the detail tables. The most direct way to do this is to

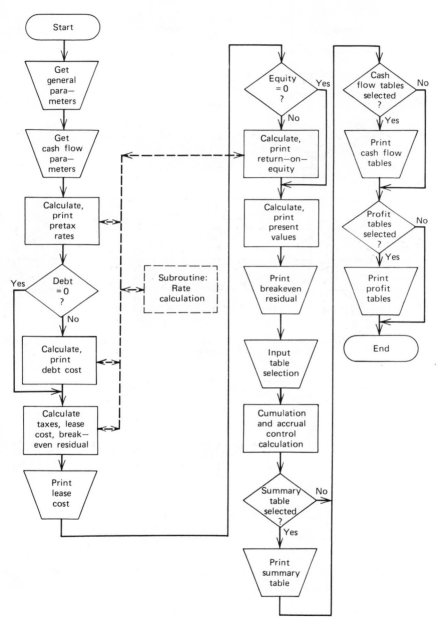

Figure 11.1   Master flowchart of LEASBUY.

```
LEASBUY      8:38   FRIDAY JAN.06,1978

BEGINNING MONTH, YEAR?7,79
TAX RATE?48
DISCOUNT RATE?10

PARAMETERS ($000):
-------------------
COST: $   1000.0  TERM:   8.00 YEARS  FREQ.:  4 TIMES/YEAR
RENT (L):     $      37.2 IN ARREARS FOR  8.00 YEARS
ITC (B):      $     100.0 AT PERIOD   0
ADR DEPR (B): $    1000.0 COST TO $   100.0 OVER  7.00 YEARS
LOAN (B):     $     700.0 AT 11.000 % OVER  8.00 YEARS
RESIDUAL (B): $     200.0 (BOOK VALUE $    100.0) AT PERIOD  32
-------------------
```

```
                      RATE ANALYSIS
                      -------------

                            LEASE        BUY
                          ---------    --------
PRE-TAX RATES:
   NOMINAL RENTAL RATE     4.344 %
   RENTALS + ITC           7.140 %
   RENTALS + ITC + RESIDUAL 10.076 %
   INTEREST RATE                       11.000 %
AFTER-TAX RATES:
   DEBT COST                            5.720 %
   LEASE COST              8.000 %
   RETURN ON EQUITY OF BUY 22.909 %

PRESENT VALUE AT 10.000 % $  -422.2 $   -372.9

PREFER BUY IF RESIDUAL GREATER THAN   -2.1 % OF COST


TABLES: SUMMARY, CASH, PROFIT (0=NO, 1=YES)?1,0,0
1=PERIOD, 2=ANNUAL, 3=TOTAL?2
```

```
                  CASH AND PROFIT SUMMARY
                  -----------------------
```

	CASH FLOW		LEASE BETTER	PROFIT IMPACT		LEASE BETTER
YEAR	BUY	LEASE	(WORSE)	BUY	LEASE	(WORSE)
----	----	----	----	----	----	----
1979	179.5	-38.6	140.8	5.9	-38.6	-44.5
1980	19.1	-77.3	-96.4	-164.5	-77.3	87.2
1981	-12.0	-77.3	-65.3	-130.8	-77.3	53.5
1982	-32.1	-77.3	-45.2	-109.0	-77.3	31.7
1983	-52.6	-77.3	-24.7	-86.8	-77.3	9.5
1984	-88.9	-77.3	11.6	-47.4	-77.3	-29.9
1985	-119.6	-77.3	42.3	-14.2	-77.3	-63.1
1986	-125.4	-77.3	48.1	-7.9	-77.3	-69.4
1987	86.9	-38.6	-125.6	50.6	-38.6	-89.3
TOTAL	-504.0	-618.4	-114.3	-504.0	-618.4	-114.3

```
TIME 6 SECS.
```

Figure 11.2   Run of LEASBUY.

assign a dimensioned variable to each component that must be remembered.

Depreciation (buy) is	D
Investment tax credit (buy) is	I
Other (lease) is	K
Interest (buy) is	L
Principal repayment (buy) is	M
Other (buy) is	Q
Rental (lease) is	R

These variables should be substituted for N for each cash flow type. For example depreciation is a component of the buy alternative and its amount for each period will be remembered by the dimensioned variable D. This merely requires substituting in each depreciation section the expression LET $D(T+1)=D(T+1)+S2$ for the expression LET $N(T+1)=N(T+1)+(S2*R5)$. The tax rate R5 is eliminated because taxes will be explicitly handled later in the program.

Any cash flow type that does not have a separate variable listed above will be classified as either other (lease) K or other (buy) Q. This requires a variable to indicate into which category the cash flow belongs.

Lease/buy category is C5

The variable C5 could be used as an additional input variable for the appropriate cash flows. An alternative is to code an existing input variable, and the obvious choice is the cash flow type code G1. This can be done by adding 10 to the code value for a buy component. As an example the single cash flow (type one) would be one of those considered as a miscellaneous or other income or expense item that might apply to either the lease or buy alternative. If the single cash flow is a lease item its type code G1 will be one. If it is a buy item its type code G1 will have a value of 11.

```
420 GET 1:G1
430 LET C5=1
440 IF G1<10 GOTO 470
450 LET G1=G1-10
460 LET C5=2
470 GOTO 540,630,870,1010, 1330,1520,480,2620,500 ON G1
```

. . .

```
540 REM SINGLE CF
550 GET 1:H1,J2
560 IF C5>1 GOTO 600
570 LET K(J2+1)=K(J2+1)+H1

. . .

590 GOTO 420
600 LET Q(J2+1)=Q(J2+1)+H1

. . .

620 GOTO 420
```

This logic is the same as that of LEAS except that the cash flow is placed in either the lease or buy category. Lines 430 to 460 perform the categorization. The lease/buy indicator C5 is set to one. If the cash flow type G1 is not less than 10 then 10 is subtracted from it and C5 is reset to two. Thus if a single cash flow pertains to the buy alternative it will be entered with a type code G1 of 11 which will be changed to one as the lease/buy indicator C5 is set to two to indicate buy. By this means the branching of the program can continue to be controlled by a GOTO . . . ON statement without exceeding the statement's capacity.

Within the single cash flow section line 560 tests the value of C5 which determines whether the cash flow amount is assigned to other (lease) K or to other (buy) Q. Other cash flow types are handled in the same manner where appropriate.

The loan function must be modified so that any balance outstanding at the end of the lease term is repaid entirely regardless of the loan term. This permits the loan components to be based on the curve of a loan amortized over, say, 15 years and yet to cut off at the end of a lease term that may be only 10 years. The first modification from LEAS is to delete the two lines near the beginning of the loan function that serve to ensure that the total number of periods B2 is no less than the loan term. Next the loan cutoff statements are inserted near the end of the period loop.

```
1010 REM MORTGAGE LOAN

. . .

1200 FOR T=(J1+1) TO J2

. . .

1290 IF T<>B2 GOTO 1320
1300 LET M(T+1)=M(T+1)+H1
1310 LET H1=0
1320 NEXT T
```

When the period counter T equals the final period of the analysis B2 then 1300 assigns the remaining loan balance H1 to the principal repayment M. Line 1310 then sets the loan balance H1 to zero as the loan is paid off.

Provision must also be made to permit the depreciation term to exceed the lease or analysis term. The important thing here is to remember the book value of the asset at the end of the lease term so that it can be deducted from the residual value for the determination of taxable income. The logic presented below for declining balance depreciation also has to be added to each of the other depreciation types. Again the two statements at the beginning of the function that tie the total number of periods B2 to the depreciation term must be deleted.

Final book value of equipment is F5

```
1730 REM DB DEPR
. . .

1900 IF T3<>B2 GOTO 1920
1910 LET F5=F5+H1
1920 NEXT T

. . .

1950 IF T3>=B2 GOTO 420
1960 LET F5=F5+H1
1970 GOTO 420
```

Line 1910 within the period loop remembers the book value H1 at the final lease period B2 and calls it F5. At any other period than B2 the line is bypassed by the test at line 1900. This setting of F5 will occur if the depreciation term is equal to or greater than the lease term. If the depreciation term is less than the lease term then F5 is set by line 1960 after the depreciation term has run its course. This line is bypassed by line 1950 if the final depreciation period T3 is equal to or greater than the lease term B2 for in that event F5 would have been set by line 1910 within the loop.

The mortgage-type loan function copied from LEAS, as well as the facility to pick up other loan types from the output file of LOAN, is applicable when the asset, if purchased, would be financed with a loan taken down specifically for that purpose or if such a loan could be reasonably hypothesized. If the asset would be purchased with general corporate funds however there is a conceptual problem in determining the repayment schedule. The amount of debt financing allocated to the transaction would be determined by the proportion of debt in the firm's capital structure and the interest rate would be the firm's marginal interest rate. But the loan, even through it is only an artificial loan, must be repaid and there is no contractual repayment schedule. One feasible approach to determining the repayment schedule is to tie the principal payments to the depreciation. Depreciation is the accounting for the recovery of the investment in an asset. It would seem appropriate that the financing of an investment be repaid synchronously with the recovery of that investment. This is particularly apt since depreciation is a nontaxable element of cash flow and debt payments are nondeductible expenditures.

> *Original loan balance is*   F6
> *Equipment cost is*   Z2

Provision for tying the principal repayments to depreciation can be accomplished within the existing loan function if a code is provided to control the switching from one repayment method to the other. This can be done by using the cash flow type G1.

```
1010 REM MORTGAGE LOAN
. . .

1255 IF G1=5 GOTO 1284
1260 LET H1=H1−U3+Q1
1280 LET M(T+1)=M(T+1)+U3−Q1
1282 GOTO 1290
1284 LET H1=H1−(D(T+1)*F6/Z2)
1286 LET M(T+1)=M(T+1)+(D(T+1)*F6/Z2)
```

For a mortgage-type loan the principal repayment M equals the total payment U3 minus the interest Q1. This amount is subtracted from the loan balance H1 and added to the period principal repayment M by the old lines 1260 and 1280. For a depreciation-related loan line 1255 directs the program to lines 1284 and 1286 where the period principal repayment M is calculated as the period depreciation D times the ratio of the original loan amount F6 to the equipment cost Z2. Thus if the equipment is financed 60% with debt then the principal repayments equal 60% of the depreciation.

Tying the loan function to the depreciation means that the loan cash flow must be processed after the depreciation. This can be done in either of two ways. The user can be instructed that a depreciation-related loan must have its input line located after the depreciation line in the input file. Or the program can remember the loan parameters when inputted and postpone the loan processing until all of the other cash flows have been processed.

Another addition to the input section is to provide for inputting the commencement date, the desired discount rate, and the selection of tables. In LEASBUY this is done with terminal questions. The only other change would be to provide a summary printout of the transaction parameters in the manner discussed in Chapter 4.

CALCULATING THE RATES

Since several rates are to be calculated the number of statements can be minimized by establishing the rate calculation function as a subroutine. The subroutine will solve for the rate when given a desired present value Z1 and a stream of periodic cash flows N. For each desired rate it will then only be necessary to go through a period loop to define N, set Z1, and then GOSUB.

LEASBUY calculates several pretax rates of which only the interest rate will be illustrated. The interest rate is calculated rather than merely printing the input interest rate in case there are several loans or in case the interest rate varies over the term.

```
2930 FOR T=0 TO B2
2940 LET N(T+1)=L(T+1)+M(T+1)
2950 NEXT T
2960 LET Z1=F6
2970 GOSUB 3530
2980 PRINT USING 4770," INTEREST RATE",R1*B1*100
```

Lines 2930 and 2950 define a period loop that steps through the periods zero to the end of the lease term B2. Within the loop line 2940 sets the period cash flow N equal to the period interest L and period principal repayment M. After exit from the loop line 2960 sets the desired present value Z1 equal to the loan amount F6. Line 2970 sends the program to line 3530 and the rate calculation subroutine. Upon its return line 2980 prints the calculated rate in its annual percentage form.

By next calculating the after-tax debt cost advantage can be taken of the loan components already being in the period cash flows N. It is merely necessary to extract the taxes related to the interest component.

```
3010 FOR T=0 TO B2

. . .

3030 LET N(T+1)=N(T+1)-(L(T+1)*R5)

. . .

3060 NEXT T
3070 GOSUB 3530
3080 PRINT USING 4770," DEBT COST",R1*B1*100
3090 LET R4=R1
```

Within the period loop line 3030 puts the loan cash flow on an after-tax basis by subtracting an amount equal to the period interest L times the tax rate R5. After exit from the loop the program can GOSUB immediately because the desired present value Z1 is still set to the loan amount F6 from the preceding section. Line 3090 remembers the after-tax debt rate as R4 for later use in calculating the breakeven residual.

The next routine will accomplish three things. It will calculate the taxes, the after-tax lease cost, and the breakeven residual.

Period taxes of buy is	C
Period taxes of lease is	H
Present value of lease at debt rate is	X5
Breakeven residual is	F8

The two variables C and H for the period taxes are dimensioned.

```
3110 LET Q(B2+1)=Q(B2+1)+F4
3120 LET D(B2+1)=D(B2+1)+F5
3130 FOR T=0 TO B2
```

```
. . .
```

```
3150 LET C(T+1)=C(T+1)+((Q(T+1)−D(T+1) )*R5)
3160 LET H(T+1)=H(T+1)+((K(T+1)−R(T+1))*R5)
```

```
. . .
```

```
3200 LET F1=Q(T+1)−C(T+1)+I(T+1)−K(T+1)+R(T+1) +H(T+1)
3210 LET N(T+1)=F1
3220 LET X5=X5+(F1/(1+R4)↑T)
3230 NEXT T
```

Line 3110 adds the residual value F4 to other (buy) Q at the end-of-term period B2. Line 3120 adds the final book value F5 to the depreciation D at the final period B2. These two related variables have been remembered separately as undimensioned variables so that they can be readily included or excluded from various combinations of the cash flows.

Within the period loop the period taxes are calculated by lines 3150 and 3160. The period tax for the buy alternative C equals the tax rate R5 times other (buy) Q minus depreciation D. The taxes for the lease alternative H equals the tax rate R5 times other (lease) K minus rentals R.

Line 3200 calculates the net cash flow from which the after-tax lease rate will be determined. It consists of the difference between the buy cash flows (other (buy) Q minus taxes C plus investment tax credit I) and the lease cash flows (other (lease) K minus rental R minus taxes H) and the result is named F1. Depreciation is excluded from the expression because it is a noncash expense whose cash flow impact has already been considered in the calculation of taxes. The loan components have been excluded because the after-tax lease cost is the rate that is compared with the after-tax debt cost for decision purposes. The loan components cannot be in both rates.

Line 3210 sets the period cash flow N equal to the cash flow F1 that has just been calculated.

Line 3220 calculates the cumulative present value X5 of the net cash flow F1 using a discount rate equal to the after-tax debt rate R4.

```
3240 LET F8=((Z2−X5)*(1+R4)↑B2)/(1−R5)
3250 LET F8=F8+F4
3260 LET Z1=Z2
3270 GOSUB 3530
3280 PRINT USING 4760," LEASE COST",R1*B1*100
```

. . .

```
3510 PRINT USING 4790,(F8/Z2)*100
```

After exit from the loop line 3240 calculates the amount required at the end of the lease term B2 which at a discount rate equal to the debt rate R4 would make the present value of the lease cost components X5 equal to the equipment cost Z2. This amount is converted to its pretax equivalent by dividing by one minus the tax rate R5. The expression is the same as that used in LEAS for the payment calculation of a single cash flow. The result is the required increment to the residual to make the lease rate the same as the debt rate. Line 3250 adds the incremental residual to the given residual F4 to determine the breakeven residual F8.

Line 3260 sets the desired present value Z1 to the equipment cost Z2 and line 3270 then sends the program to the subroutine to calculate the rate. Upon its return line 3280 prints the answer as the lease cost rate.

Later in the program line 3510 prints the breakeven residual F8 as a percentage of equipment cost Z2.

With the period cash flow N already set to the after-tax components, excluding the debt, the next step is to include the debt so that the return on equity of the buy alternative can be calculated.

```
3290 REM RETURN ON EQUITY OF BUY
3300 IF Z2−F6<=0 GOTO 3420
3310 FOR T=0 TO B2
3320 LET N(T+1)=N(T+1)+C(T+1)

. . .

3340 LET C(T+1)=C(T+1)−(L(T+1)*R5)

. . .

3370 LET N(T+1)=N(T+1)−L(T+1)−M(T+1)−C(T+1)
3380 NEXT T
3390 LET Z1=Z2−F6
3400 GOSUB 3530
3410 PRINT USING 4770," RETURN ON EQUITY OF BUY",R1*B1*100
```

The amount of the equity investment is the excess of equipment cost Z2 over the loan amount F6. If this amount is zero or less then line 3300 bypasses the return on equity section.

Lines 3310 and 3380 form a period loop. Within the loop line 3320 adds the buy-related taxes C back to the net cash flow N. Line 3340 then reduces the buy taxes C by the amount of tax reduction provided by the interest expense L. Line 3370 deducts the interest payment L, the principal repayment M, and the revised buy taxes C from the net cash flow N. Both the cash flow and the taxes now include the effect of the loan payments.

After exit from the loop line 3390 sets the desired present value Z1 to the equity investment which is the difference between the equipment cost Z2 and the loan amount F6. Line 3400 sends the program to the rate calculation subroutine after which line 3410 prints the return on equity.

The final item in the rate section is the calculation of the present values of the buy and lease alternatives at the given discount rate.

```
3420 REM PRESENT VALUES
3430 FOR T=0 TO B2
3440 LET X9=X9+((Q(T+1)−L(T+1)−C(T+1)+I(T+1) −M(T+1))/(1+R6)↑T
3450 LET X8=X8+((K(T+1)−R(T+1)−H(T+1))/(1+R6)↑T
3460 NEXT T
3470 PRINT
3480 PRINT USING 4780,R6*100*B1,X8,X9
```

Within a period loop line 3440 calculates the present value of the buy alternative X9 and line 3450 that of the lease alternative X8 using the given discount rate R6. The buy cash flow is developed in line 3440 as other (buy) Q plus the investment tax credit I minus interest L, taxes (buy) C, and principal repayments M. The lease cash flow in line 3450 equals other (lease) K minus rentals R and taxes (lease) H. After the loop line 3480 prints the present values X8 and X9 as well as the discount rate R6.

DEFERRED TAXES

Many users of a lease/buy program may not be in a tax-paying position yet taxes are an integral part of the analysis. Such firms may however anticipate a return to profitability and the eventual absorption of the losses they carry forward. For them the tax effects of buying versus leasing are postponed or deferred until some time in the future. This delay will affect the calculated rates.

The effect of deferred taxes is to decrease the cost of leasing and to increase the cost of borrowing. One of the cost components of leasing is the tax benefits of ownership that are relinquished. But the longer taxes are deferred into the future the lower the present value of the ownership tax benefits and therefore the less expensive leasing appears. For a loan the interest payments must be paid in cash when due and if the tax-deduction of these interest payments is deferred then the effective cost of the loan is increased.

This effect is illustrated in the graph of Figure 11.3 which compares the after-tax cost of a lease with that of a loan as taxes are deferred for an increasing length of time. The lease and the loan are those examples of Figure 11.2.

With no tax deferral the after-tax cost of the lease is 8.0% and that of the loan is 5.72%. As taxes are deferred the lease cost declines while the loan cost increases. The lines cross shortly after the fifth year and if taxes are not paid until the end of the eighth year then the lease cost has declined to 6.2% and the loan cost has risen to 7.4%.

Since the lease/buy decision is heavily influenced by the comparison of these two rates LEASBUY will have to provide for deferring taxes. To accomplish this it will be assumed that no taxes are paid or credits received during an initial deferral period. For the rest of the term tax effects will be normal. All of the taxes not paid during the deferral period will be carried forward to be paid at the end of the first period of the tax-paying portion of the term. These will be in addition to the normal taxes of that period.

First taxable period is B5

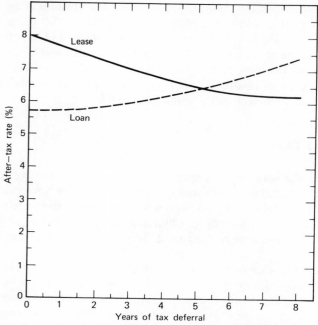

Figure 11.3   Effect of tax deferral on lease cost and debt cost.

The input of the first taxable period can follow the tax rate question. To avoid printing an unnecessary question when there is no tax deferral the program will solicit the information only when the answer to the tax rate question is coded with negative polarity. That is, the entry of a positive tax rate means taxes are not deferred. The entry of a negative tax rate causes the program to ask for deferral information. In the latter case the tax rate will immediately be reversed to positive polarity for computation purposes.

```
200 PRINT "TAX RATE";
210 INPUT R5
220 IF R5<0 GOTO 260

. . .

260 LET R5=−R5
270 PRINT "FIRST PERIOD TAXED";
280 INPUT B5
```

The only other change to the input section is to provide for the deferral of the investment tax credit. Since it is a credit against taxes it cannot take effect until the firm is in a tax-paying position.

```
2620 REM ITC
2630 GET 1:H1,J2

. . .

2650 IF J2<B5 GOTO 2680
2660 LET I(J2+1)=I(J2+1)+H1
2670 GOTO 420
2680 LET I(B5+1)=I(B5+1)+H1
2690 GOTO 420
```

The new lines are 2650, 2680, and 2690. Line 2650 compares the input timing period J2 with the first taxable period B5. If it is less then the program goes to line 2680 and the investment tax credit is assigned to period B5. If it is not less then the investment tax credit is assigned to its specified period J2. If there is no tax deferral then B5 will be zero and J2 could not be less.

This switching between two alternative tax periods must be inserted wherever taxes are calculated.

```
3100 REM AFTER-TAX LEASE COST

. . .

3130 FOR T=0 TO B2
3140 IF T<B5 GOTO 3180
3150 LET C(T+1)=C(T+1)+((Q(T+1)−D(T+1))*R5)
3160 LET H(T+1)=H(T+1)+((K(T+1)−R(T+1))*R5)
3170 GOTO 3200
3180 LET C(B5+1)=C(B5+1)+((Q(T+1)−D(T+1))*R5)
3190 LET H(B5+1)=H(B5+1)+((K(T+1)−R(T+1))*R5)

. . .

3230 NEXT T
```

Line 3140 controls the switching by comparing the current period T with the first taxable period B5. As long as T is less than B5 then lines 3180 and 3190 assign the period taxes C and H to the first taxable period B5. Once the first taxable period is reached then the period taxes are assigned to the current period. Thus any taxes attributable to the deferred portion of the term are carried forward to the first taxable period. This tax deferral provision has to be also added to the return on equity section.

THE SUMMARY TABLE

LEASBUY should have the facility to print all of the components of cash flow and profits for both alternatives. This requires four tables. It should be able to print the tables in three ways—period-by-period, annually by fiscal year, and totals-only. Further the program should be able to print a summary table that presents the net results of the detail tables in case not all of the components are needed.

Only the summary table will be developed here to illustrate the mechanics of compiling the data and controlling the printout. The detail tables would be developed and controlled in the same manner.

The first and basic step is to develop the logic to print the period-by-period data. The profit will temporarily be on a cash rather than accrual basis until the framework is erected. The printing of the title and headings and the IMAGE statements will not be shown as they use the same techniques that were discussed before. Reference should be made to Figure 11.2 for the format used.

> Profit impact of buy for the period is   N1
> Profit impact of lease for the period is   N2

There will also be a series of "V" variables and "W" variables. Each consists of the letter V or W plus a numerical digit. The V variables cumulate the period values between printout lines. The W variables cumulate the V values for the totals line. The digits refer to the column number; for example V1 is used to print the values for the first column within the body of the table and W1 is used to print the total value for the first column. The period or year column is excluded from the above numbering. This type of variable numbering system is a memory aid for the programmer and considerably reduces the confusion when setting up a set of complex tables.

```
4110 REM SUMMARY TABLE

. . .

4220 FOR T=0 TO B2
4230 IF T=0 GOTO 4250
```

```
4240 LET X2=X2+1
4250 LET N1=Q(T+1)−D(T+1)−L(T+1)−C(T+1)+I(T+1)
4260 LET N2=K(T+1)−R(T+1)−H(T+1)
4270 LET V1=V1+N1+D(T+1)−M(T+1)
4280 LET V2=V2+N2
```

. . .

```
4330 LET V4=V4+N1
4340 LET V5=V5+N2
```

. . .

```
4355 IF X2<C2 GOTO 4570
4360 PRINT USING 4730,T,V1,V2,V2−V1,V4,V5,V5−V4
```

. . .

```
4520 LET W1=W1+V1
4530 LET W2=W2+V2
4540 LET W4=W4+V4
4550 LET W5=W5+V5
4560 LET V1,V2,V4,V5,X2=0
4570 NEXT T
```

. . .

```
4600 PRINT USING 4740,W1,W2,W2−W1,W4,W5,W5−W4
```

. . .

```
4620 LET V1,V2,V4,V5,X2=0
4630 LET W1,W2,W4,W5=0
```

Lines 4220 and 4570 form a print loop that steps through each period from zero to the end of the term B2.

The profit impact of buy is calculated as N1 by line 4250. This is equal to other (buy) Q minus depreciation D, interest L, and taxes (buy) C plus investment tax credit I. The profit impact of lease is calculated by line 4260 as N2 and equals other (lease) K minus rentals R and taxes (lease) H.

Line 4270 calculates and cumulates the net cash flow of buy as V1. This is the buy profit N1 plus depreciation D less principal repayment M. Line 4280 cumulates the net cash flow of lease as V2. This is the same as the lease profit N2 since the lease alternative has neither deductible noncash expenses such as depreciation nor nondeductible cash expenditures such as principal repayments.

Line 4330 cumulates the profit impact of buy N1 as V4 and line 4340 cumulates the profit impact of lease N2 as V5.

The body of the table is printed by line 4360. The first column after the time column is buy cash flow V1 and the second column is lease cash flow V2. The third column prints the difference between the lease cash flow V2 and the buy cash flow V1. If the lease cash flow is greater then lease is "better" and if less then it is "(worse)" as indicated by negative polarity. The fourth column prints the effect on profits of buy V4 and the fifth column is the profit effect of lease V5. The sixth and last column prints the difference between lease profit V5 and buy profit V4.

Control of the number of periods cumulated for each print line is discussed below but a few statements are included here to clarify the use of the V and W variables. The basic mechanics are the same as used in previous programs. Line 4240 increments the cumulated periods counter X2 by one for each pass through the loop. However line 4230 bypasses this incrementing for the initial pass at period zero. This is necessary because the first year has one more period than subsequent years because it contains period zero. An alternative method to pick up one more period for the first year would be to set X2 to minus one before entering the loop instead of to zero.

Line 4355 is a temporary insertion for illustrative purposes. This line causes the print line to be bypassed as long as the cumulated periods counter X2 is less than the desired increment C2. In that case the program goes directly to line 4570 and steps the loop. If a sufficient number of periods has been cumulated then the print occurs. Then each totals variable W is increased by the value of the cumulated print variable V in lines 4520 through 4550. Line 4560 then sets the V variables and X2 to zero.

After exit from the loop line 4600 prints the column totals using the W variables. Lines 4620 and 4630 set X2 and all the print variables to zero in preparation for the next table.

PRINT AND ACCRUAL CONTROL

The program should be able to print the tables on a period-by-period basis. But the length of such tables means that this facility is used in practice only for troubleshooting. That is, if the answers appear suspect then the period printout can be helpful to either verify the results or identify the source of error.

Sometimes only aggregate amounts are required, in which case print time is minimized if there is provision for printing only the column totals.

The print frequency used most often will be annual. This reduces the number of lines in the table to the number of years in the transaction, puts all transactions on a common time base, and enables management to visualize the effect of the transaction on the firm's annual financial statements.

As in the previous programs control of the number of periods included in each print line will be achieved by comparing the number of periods cumulated since the last print X2 with the desired increment C2.

```
3810 REM TABLE SELECT

. . .

3900 PRINT "1=PERIOD, 2=ANNUAL, 3=TOTAL";
3910 INPUT C2
3920 IF C2=1 GOTO 3990
3930 IF C2>2 GOTO 3960
3940 LET C2=B1
3950 GOTO 3970
3960 LET C2=B2+1
```

Lines 3900 and 3910 offer the user the choice of three increments. If the period printout is chosen then C2 will be entered as one and line 3920 will send the program to the next section. If the annual printout is selected then C2 will equal two, the tests at lines 3920 and 3930 will be failed, and line 3940 will set the desired increment C2 to the number of payments per year B1. If the totals-only printout is chosen then C2 will have a value of three and line 3930 will direct the program to line 3960 where C2 will be reset to one greater than the total number of periods B2. Thus the desired print increment C2 can have one of only three values—one, B1, or B2+1.

The period and total printouts present no control problem for they require either every period or none to be printed.

The annual printout however requires that the printing be synchronous with fiscal years rather than transaction years. It will be assumed that the fiscal year is the calendar year. The shift from transaction to fiscal years requires that the start date of the transaction be entered as input so that the periods remaining in the first fiscal year can be determined. That is, for a quarterly transaction that starts in June only two payments will occur in the first calendar year—one in September and one in December. This can be achieved by setting the cumulative periods counter X2 to an initial value of two, since two periods have elapsed, instead of zero. It will then reach the desired increment of four with the first two passes through the loop. Since X2 will be set to zero after each print line, all lines (years) subsequent to the first will cumulate four periods.

Beginning cumulation count is   X7
Number of months per period is   B7
Beginning month is   D2

```
3970 REM ANNUAL PRINT AND ACCRUAL CONTROL
3980 IF C2<>B1 GOTO 4090
3990 LET B7=12/B1
4000 LET X7=B1−INT((13−D2)/B7)
```

. . .

```
4090 LET X7=0
```

If the annual printout is not selected then the desired cumulation C2 will not equal the number of periods per year B1 and line 3980 sends the program to line 4090 where the beginning cumulation count X7 is set to zero.

If the annual printout is selected then the number of months per period B7 is calculated at line 3990 by dividing the periods per year B1 into 12. The beginning cumulation count X7 is calculated at line 4000. There the start-up month D2 is subtracted from 13 to give the number of months remaining in the year. This is divided by the number of months per period B7 to give the number of periods remaining in the year which in turn is truncated to give the number of remaining whole periods. This number is subtracted from the number of periods per year B1 which produces the number of periods which have already elapsed at the start-up date. This value is called X7 and will be used to preset the cumulation counter X2.

It is implicit in the above that the beginning month D2 is the first full month of the transaction. At the stage of negotiations at which a lease versus buy program would be used the equipment delivery date would be an estimate, and there is little to be gained from estimating closer than the nearest month.

For a quarterly transaction beginning in July there would be six months or two periods remaining in the calendar year. This means that two periods have elapsed so X2 will be set to two. Only two passes through the print loop will then be required to cause X2 to equal the increment C2 and trigger the print line for the first calendar year.

Profits have so far been calculated on a cash basis. The firm's financial statements however are on an accrual basis. The program will have to adjust the profit impact of the two alternatives to an accrual basis to be consistent with the manner in which profits are normally presented.

For a lease with quarterly rentals in arrears each payment represents rental expense for the preceding three-month period. If the payment occurs

January 31 then only one-third of the rental amount is expense of the current year. The other two-thirds is expense for November and December of the prior year. In its present configuration LEASBUY will assign the total rental amount to the year in which the payment is made. Provision must now be made to allocate the rental to different years when appropriate.

Continuing the above example the other three payments in the current year—April 30, July 31, and October 31—apply in their entirety to expense for the current year. The next payment will not be made until January 31 of the next year but in the interim expense will accrue for November and December. So the rental expense for the current year must include two-thirds of the amount of the first payment in the next year. The total rental expense for the current year thus equals one-third of the first payment, plus the total amounts of the remaining payments made during the year, plus two-thirds of the first payment in the next year. The other profit components such as interest and depreciation are handled in the same manner.

The shift from cash to accrual accounting depends on determining the proportionate split of the first payment in any year between that year and the preceding year. This split will be based on months because the program assumes each transaction begins with a full month. If it were desired to recognize the delivery day rather than the month then the accrual proportions D5 and D6 would be based on the number of days in the year.

> *Accrual proportions:*
> *Proportion of first payment allocated to current year is D6*
> *Proportion of first payment allocated to previous year is D5*

```
3970 REM ANNUAL PRINT AND ACCRUAL CONTROL
3980 IF C2<>B1 GOTO 4090

. . .

4010 IF B1=12 GOTO 4100
4020 LET B6=D2-1
4030 LET B6=B6+B7
4040 IF B6<=12 GOTO 4030
4050 LET B6=B6-12
4060 LET D6=B6/B7
4070 LET D5=1-D6
4080 GOTO 4110

. . .

4100 LET D6=1
```

Line 3980 bypasses the accrual control section if the annual printout is not selected.

Line 4010 tests the periods per year B1 to determine whether the transaction frequency is monthly. If so then the program goes to line 4100 where the proportion of the first payment allocated to the current year D6 is set to one. Its complement D5 retains its initial value of zero. This means that for a monthly transaction all of the monthly amounts will be allocated to the current year with none going to the previous year.

Lines 4020 to 4050 find the number of months into the current year before the first payment is made. The counter B6 is set to one less than the beginning month D2 in line 4020. Then B6 is incremented by the number of months between payments B7 in line 4030. This line and the next one form a short loop that keeps incrementing B6 by the number of months per period B7 until B6 exceeds the 12 months of the year. Then line 4050 subtracts 12 and the result is the number of full months up to the first payment date. Line 4060 divides B6 by the number of months per period B7 to obtain the proportion of the first payment to be allocated to the current year D6. Line 4070 subtracts D6 from one to obtain the proportion attributable to the previous year D5.

ACCRUING FOR THE SUMMARY TABLE

Within the print loop it is now merely necessary to identify each period as to whether it is the first, the last, or an intermediate period of the year. Then the program will be directed to the statement that applies the appropriate proportion D5 or D6 to the values of the profit components.

```
4110 REM SUMMARY TABLE

. . .

4210 LET X2=X7
4220 FOR T=0 TO B2

. . .

4290 IF C2<>B1 GOTO 4320
4300 IF X2=1 GOTO 4380
4310 IF X2=B1 GOTO 4420
4320 REM NONACCRUAL PERIODS
4330 LET V4=V4+N1
4340 LET V5=V5+N2
4350 IF C2>1 GOTO 4470

. . .
```

```
4380 REM FIRST PMT IN YEAR
4390 LET V4=V4+(N1*D6)
4400 LET V5=V5+(N2*D6)
4410 GOTO 4470
```

If the annual printout has not been selected then the desired increment C2 will not equal the periods per year B1 and line 4290 directs the program to line 4320. That line begins the "nonaccrual" section and the statements at lines 4330 and 4340 were discussed before. The print variables V4 and V5 are set to the buy profit N1 and lease profit N2 respectively without any adjustment.

If the annual printout has been selected then line 4300 sends the program to the "first payment" section at line 4380 if the cumulated periods counter X2 equals one. Line 4310 sends the program to the "last payment" section at line 4420 if X2 equals B1 indicating the last period of the year. If X2 does not equal either one or B1 then the current period is an intermediate period of the year and the program defaults to the "nonaccrual" section at line 4320.

If the payment is the first payment in the year then lines 4390 and 4400 multiply the buy profit N1 and the lease profit N2 by the proportion D6 attributable to the current year.

Buy profit for first period of next year is   N3
Lease profit for first period of next year is   N4

```
4420 REM LAST PMT IN YEAR
4430 LET N3=Q(T+2)−D(T+2)−L(T+2)−C(T+2)+I(T+2)
4440 LET N4=K(T+2)−R(T+2)−H(T+2)
4450 LET V4=V4+N1+(N3*D5)
4460 LET V5=V5+N2+(N4*D5)
4470 IF T=B2 GOTO 4490
4480 IF X2<C2 GOTO 4570
4490 IF C2>B2 GOTO 4510
4500 PRINT USING 4730,D3,V1,V2,V2−V1,V4,V5,V5−V4
4510 LET D3=D3+1
```

. . .

```
4570 NEXT T
```

. . .

```
4640 LET D3=D4
```

If the current period is the last period of the year then the year-end accrual must be determined. Lines 4430 and 4440 calculate the buy profit N3 and lease profit N4 respectively for the first payment of the next year. The expressions are the same as for N1 and N2 at lines 4250 and 4260 except that the next period $T + 2$ is specified rather than the current period $T + 1$. Lines 4450 and 4460 add the current period's profits N1 and N2 plus the proportion D5 times the next period's profits N3 and N4 to the cumulative print variables V4 and V5.

The cumulated amounts for the year are printed by line 4500. This is the same as the print line at 4360 except that the year D3 is printed rather than the period T. The print line is bypassed by line 4480 if the cumulated periods counter X2 is less than the desired increment C2 as tested by line 4480. Line 4470 however bypasses the bypass at line 4480 if the current period T is the last period B2 since the final year should be printed even if it is only a partial year. The print line is also bypassed if the totals-only printout was selected as indicated by the desired increment C2 being greater than the total number of periods B2 as tested by line 4490.

After the print line line 4510 adds one to the year D3 thus using it as a year counter. At the end of the summary table section line 4640 resets the year D3 to its original value as remembered by D4.

LEASBUY is now conceptually complete. The detail tables would have the same structure as the summary table but the cumulation variables V would be appropriately redefined. Indeed if all the tables have the same number of columns then they could share the same print loop. This can be done in two alternative ways.

One way is to use a variable whose value indicates which table is currently being printed. Within the print loop section a GOTO . . . ON statement would use that variable to direct the program to alternative headings and to alternative expressions for setting the V variables.

Another approach would be to place the headings and the V variables expressions in separate sections and then use a subroutine for the print loop proper. This would require several GOSUB . . . RETURN combinations for each table as the program must jump back and forth.

A common print loop could be used even if the tables do have different numbers of columns. But then there must be alternative print statements and their test statements. The reason for using one print loop for several tables is to reduce the size of the program by avoiding the duplication of statements as much as possible. As the similarity between the tables decreases the number of alternative statements increase so that the net savings decrease. This makes the multiple-use section increasingly difficult to read and understand. Unless the savings in number of statements is significant it would be preferable to simply and directly use separate print loops.

THE LOGIC BLOCK APPROACH

Throughout this book routines developed for one program have been used in subsequent programs. The mortgage-type loan function developed for LOAN was used in LEAS and LEASBUY. The depreciation functions developed for LEAS were used in LEASBUY. The rate calculation routine developed for DISC was used in LEAS and LEASBUY and could be added to LOAN if it were desired to add a facility for calculating the weighted average interest rate on a package of loans.

Such oft-used routines form discrete blocks of logic that can be assembled in different combinations. As the programmer writes more programs the inventory of logic blocks grows larger. This makes the development of subsequent programs easier and quicker as the proportion of preassembled programming increases.

This process can be systematized by recording these logic blocks on punched paper tape so that they can be entered quickly into the machine when required. The advantage of this method over copying parts of existing programs with editing commands is that it avoids having to remove the special variations required for previous applications. The logic blocks on tape would be in a standard basic form.

The assembly of logic blocks developed at different times for different programs is facilitated if the programmer maintains a consistent vocabulary from program to program—B1 is always periods per year, R1 is always the discount rate, and so on. This avoids having to rename the variables every time a logic block is used in another program.

Each programmer will inevitably develop his or her own techniques and conventions. Programming styles vary widely. But this is to be expected since programming is applied logic and thus each program will reflect the mentality of its creator.

APPENDIX
Dialects of the Basic
Language

As a practical matter the programs developed in this book could be written in but one dialect of the BASIC language, namely IBM's CALL-OS. For the convenience of the reader who may have access to a system using a different dialect this appendix provides a summary comparison of the dialects offered by 23 time-sharing companies and computer manufacturers. Its purpose is to provide a guide for the translation of the book's programs and routines into the alternative dialects surveyed. It is not intended to replace a careful study of the BASIC manual provided by the reader's time-sharing supplier.

The BASIC language was developed as part of the time-sharing system designed in 1964 at Dartmouth College under the direction of Professors John Kemeny and Thomas Kurtz. The project was a cooperative venture with General Electric who provided a GE-225 computer and a communications processor. Funds were provided by the National Science Foundation.

BASIC was conceived as a language with a limited set of instructions that could be learned quickly and easily. The original instructions or statements have been subsequently expanded so that it is doubtful that any BASIC system in use today is not an "extended" BASIC. Some systems have become so sophisticated that becoming familiar with their vocabulary and syntax is no longer a one-day task. Fortunately all of the dialects retain their original Dartmouth roots and thus share a common set of simple statements. The financial programmer who restricts his or her vocabulary, at least initially, will find that he or she has a powerful computational tool that is still easy to learn. Further, the programs can be translated into other versions of BASIC with relative ease.

The BASIC manuals of almost two dozen time-sharing companies and computer manufacturers were reviewed in order to develop a guide for translating the programs in the book from CALL-OS into other dialects and the results are presented in a table below. Manufacturers have developed their own extensions of the language as part of the software packages that they offer in support of their equipment. The time-sharing companies acquire computers from the manufacturers and then sell computer time. They may either use the manufacturer's software or develop their own. This means that any specific BASIC dialect may be represented several times in the table as such duplication was accepted in order to key the table to the names of the retail supplier.

The compared statements are limited to those used in the book's programs and in no case do they exhaust the set of statements offered by any specific supplier.

Twenty-three statements were used in the book if the components of paired statements and the single and multiple assignment forms of the LET statement are counted separately. Fourteen of these are identical for all of the surveyed dialects and therefore do not require translation. These common statements are:

DATA	GOTO	READ
DIMENSION	INPUT	REMARK
END	LET (single)	RETURN
FOR	NEXT	STOP
GOSUB	PRINT	

For all dialects the use of the word "let" in the LET statement is optional. That is LET A=B+C can be written as A=B+C without affecting execution of the program.

Three statements have only two alternative forms. These statements are IF . . . GOTO, GOTO . . . ON, and the multiple assignment form of the LET statement.

For most dialects IF . . . GOTO and IF . . . THEN are interchangeable. That is, both forms are acceptable, either IF A=B GOTO 20 or IF A=B THEN 20. However the manuals used by five companies describe only the IF . . . THEN form and these dialects would presumably require translation from the IF . . . GOTO form used in the book. The IF . . . THEN form is common to all.

Most of the dialects use ON . . . GOTO rather than the GOTO . . . ON form used in the book. Only four companies share the latter form with CALL-OS. Translation would thus be required from GOTO 20,30 ON A to ON A GOTO 20,30.

A majority of the systems use equals signs rather than commas to separate a series of variables being set to a common value. These systems require translation to LET A=B=C from the LET A,B=C form used by CALL-OS and eight other systems. Two of the BASIC manuals make no mention of the multiple assignment LET and translation to those dialects would require replacing each member of the equality series with a separate single assignment LET, thus: LET A=C and LET B=C. Both of these dialects are BBL extensions of BASIC of which more will be said below.

The PRINT USING and IMAGE statements are paired to specify the format of printing at the terminal. Sixteen dialects (but a different 16 for each statement) share a common form of these statements with CALL-OS. The two BBL dialects use a different method based on specifying rows and columns rather than the "picture" method of an IMAGE statement. The abbreviation BBL stands for Basic Business Language and is an extension of BASIC that is specifically designed for the production of reports. It is not a preferred medium for programs such as those in the book but their two suppliers undoubtedly offer a computational BASIC as well. (Other suppliers also offer BBL.) The remaining dialects vary from being very similar to CALL-OS to being distinctly different.

The greatest diversity occurs with the statements relating to external files. The book has used four statements—OPEN, GET, PUT, and CLOSE—to control input and output files. Their manner of use has sometimes been but one alternative among several and often the OPEN and CLOSE statements need not have been used at all. The author however chose to use them in a simple and consistent manner in order to concentrate on computational logic and not file manipulation. Although some systems treat files without distinction, many categorize them according to whether they are accessible to the user directly at the terminal by listing or only indirectly through an intermediary program. They can be further categorized as to whether they are sequential access, in which data are read item by item from beginning to end, or random access, in which one datum can be read in the middle of the data file without reading the other data. Such distinctions are important to the computer professional but are merely annoying distractions to the finance expert who as a casual programmer is primarily interested in answers rather than methods. But the file type will determine the specific program statements to be used in many BASIC dialects. The convention used in the book was to use listable sequential data files for input from the user to the program and nonlistable (binary) sequential files for transfering data between programs. The following discussion and the table assume listable sequential files.

The OPEN statement and its use take many forms. One company uses the same form as CALL-OS, eight use some variation of the word OPEN, and 12 use some variation of the world FILE. Two companies have no equivalent statement, one because it has no provision for data files and the other because the first use of a file will open it automatically. Many of the companies that have the statement also permit automatic opening of files with first use under specified rules. Data files are always in either the read mode (used for input) or the write mode (used for output). Ten dialects require that the mode be specified either by the OPEN statement or by an auxilliary SCRATCH statement. Nine dialects set the mode according to the first use of the file.

Use of the CLOSE statement is optional most of the time since all files are automatically closed when the program reaches its end. Generally it is required only to avoid exceeding the system's limit on the number of open files by enabling one to be closed so that another may be opened. Three companies use the same form for the CLOSE statement as CALL-OS, six use some variation based on the word CLOSE, and five use a form based on the word FILE. Nine companies do not use a CLOSE statement or its equivalent.

The GET statement is used in the CALL-OS form by one company and in a variation of GET by three. Eight companies use a form of READ and 10 use a form of INPUT. One has no equivalent statement.

Many of the dialects distinguish between listable and nonlistable data files through the statement used to access the file. For example some use READ/WRITE for listable files and INPUT/PRINT for nonlistable files. Others reverse the designation.

As an additional translation note two companies, BUR and RCC in the table, use a double asterisk(**) to indicate an exponent in an expression instead of the up-arrow (↑) used in the book. Some other dialects offer the double asterisk as an optional form.

The following table compares the statement form of those statements that are not common to all dialects. An asterisk in the table entry indicates that the form is the same as that of CALL-OS while a dash indicates that the statement is not used. The key to the company abbreviations appears immediately before the table.

KEY TO COMPANIES

Following the company code is the name and address of the company and then the title, publication number, if any, and date of publication of the manual reviewed.

CALL-OS—International Business Machines Corporation, White Plains NY; CALL-OS BASIC Language Reference Manual, GH20-0699-3, July 1972.

BUR—Burroughs Corporation, Detroit MI; B 7000/B 6000 Series BASIC Reference Manual, 5001407, May 1977.

CDC—Control Data Corporation, Minneapolis MN; BASIC Version 2.1 Reference Manual, 19980300, 1975.

CHI—Chi Corportaion, Cleveland OH; CHI 1108 BASIC, CHI-1006, May 1976.

CSC—Computer Sciences Corporation, Infonet, El Segundo CA; CSTS BASIC Reference, E00146-01, May 1974.

CSS—National CSS, Inc., Norwalk CT; see IBM/VS.

CYB—Cybershare, Ltd., Winnipeg, Manitoba; see CDC.

DC—Dartmouth College, Kiewit Computation Center, Hanover NH; BASIC TM075, September 1971.

DL—Dataline Systems, Ltd., Toronto, Ontario; BASIC, BASIC-0375-99, undated.

FD—First Data Corporation, Waltham MA; BBL Introduction, 1973.

GE—General Electric Company, Information Services Business Division, Rockville MD; Mark III Foreground Service Reference Manual Revision F, 3200.01F, July 1973.

IBM/VS—International Business Machines Corporation, White Plains NY; Systems VS BASIC Language, GC28-8303-2, December 1976.

ISC—Interactive Sciences Corporation, Braintree MA; BASIC SYSTEM Reference Manual, June 1977.

MAC—Multiple Access Computer Group, Don Mills, Ontario; see CDC.

POL—Polycom Systems, Ltd., Don Mills, Ontario; see DC.

RCC—Remote Computing Corporation, Palo Alto CA; see BUR.

RD—Rapidata, Inc., Fairfield NJ; BASIC, 10100, 1973.

SBC—The Service Bureau Company (division of Control Data Corporation), Greenwich CT; CALL/370 BASIC Reference Manual, 65-2211-11, May 1977.

SIS—Standard Information Systems, Inc., Wellesley Hills MA; Standard 3600 BASIC AND BASICX, 5M.0315.03, 1972.

TYM—Tymshare, Inc., Cupertino CA; Tymcom-X BBL Basic Business Language, June 1973.

UNI—Uni-Coll Corporation, Philadelphia PA; see IBM/VS.

UCS—United Computing Systems, Inc., Kansas City MO; APEX/SL SUPER BASIC Reference Manual, 6L4-677, June 1977.

WAN—Wang Laboratories, Inc., Wang Computer Services, Tewksbury MA; Wang BASIC Language Reference Manual System 2200, 1976.

XER—Xerox Computer Services, Los Angeles CA; Xerox BASIC for Control Program-Five Operating System Language and Operations Reference Manual, 600002, August 1976.

COMPARISON OF NONCOMMON STATEMENTS

Company	CLOSE	GET	GOTO...ON
CALL-OS	CLOSE 1	GET 1:A	GOTO 20, 30 ON A
BUR	FILE #1, "*"	READ #1, A	ON A GOTO 20, 30
CDC	—	INPUT #1, A	ON A GOTO 20, 30
CHI	FILE #1	INPUT #1, A	ON A GOTO 20, 30
CSC	FILE	INPUT #1, A	ON A GOTO 20, 30
CSS	CLOSE 'NAME'	GET 'NAME', A	*
CYB	—	INPUT #1, A	ON A GOTO 20, 30
DC	—	INPUT #1:A	ON A GOTO 20, 30
DL	CLOSE #1	READ #1, A	ON A GOTO 20, 30
FD	—	READ (20) A	ON A GOTO 20, 30
GE	FILE #1, "*"	READ #1, A	ON A GOTO 20, 30
IBM/VS	CLOSE 'NAME'	GET 'NAME', A	*
ISC	—	READ #1, A	ON A GOTO 20, 30
MAC	—	INPUT #1, A	ON A GOTO 20, 30
POL	—	INPUT #1:A	ON A GOTO 20, 30
RCC	FILE #1, "*"	READ #1, A	ON A GOTO 20, 30
RD	CLOSE:NAME:	INPUT:NAME:A	ON A GOTO 20, 30
SBC	*	*	*
SIS	*	READ (1) A	ON A GOTO 20, 30
TYM	—	READ (1) A	ON A GOTO 20, 30
UNI	CLOSE 'NAME'	GET 'NAME', A	*
UCS	*	INPUT FROM 1:A	ON A GOTO 20, 30
WAN	—	—	ON A GOTO 20, 30
XER	CLOSE:1	INPUT:1, A	ON A GOTO 20, 30

COMPARISON OF NONCOMMON STATEMENTS

Company	IF...GOTO	IMAGE
CALL-OS	IF A=B GOTO 20	: ANSWER IS ##.#
BUR	*	*
CDC	IF A=B THEN 20	*
CHI	*	*
CSC	*	*
CSS	*	*
CYB	IF A=B THEN 20	*
DC	*	LET F$="ANSWER IS ##.##"
DL	*	*
FD	*	(1)
GE	*	*
IBM/VS	*	*
ISC	*	*
MAC	IF A=B THEN 20	*
POL	*	LET F$="ANSWER IS ##.#"
RCC	*	*
RD	*	FMT ANSWER IS ##.#
SBC	*	*
SIS	*	FIELD (11H ANSWER IS ,F2.1)
TYM	*	(1)
UNI	*	*
UCS	IF A=B THEN 20	F=" 'ANSWER IS' ##.#
WAN	IF A=B THEN 20	% ANSWER IS ##.#
XER	*	*

COMPARISON OF NONCOMMON STATEMENTS

Company	*LET* (multiple)	*OPEN*
CALL-OS	LET A,B=C	OPEN 1, "NAME", INPUT
BUR	LET A=B=C	FILES NAME
CDC	LET A=B=C	FILE #1="NAME"
CHI	LET A=B=C	FILE RESTORE #1="NAME"
CSC	LET A=B=C	FILE RESTORE #1=NAME
CSS	*	OPEN 'NAME' IN
CYB	LET A=B=C	FILE #1="NAME"
DC	LET A=B=C	FILE #1:"NAME"
DL	LET A=B=C	FILE #1,"NAME"
FD	—	OPEN "NAME" ON 20
GE	LET A=B=C	FILER NAME
IBM/VS	*	OPEN 'NAME' IN
ISC	LET A=B=C	FILES NAME
MAC	LET A=B=C	FILE #1="NAME"
POL	LET A=B=C	FILE #1:"NAME"
RCC	LET A=B=C	FILES NAME
RD	LET A=B=C	—
SBC	*	*
SIS	*	OPEN 1,"NAME"
TYM	—	OPEN "NAME" ON 1
UNI	*	OPEN 'NAME' IN
UCS	*	OPEN "NAME",INPUTS,1
WAN	*	—
XER	*	OPEN 'NAME' TO :1,INPUT

COMPARISON OF NONCOMMON STATEMENTS

Company	PRINT USING	PUT
CALL-OS	PRINT USING 20,A	PUT 2:A
BUR	*	WRITE #2,A
CDC	*	PRINT #2,A
CHI	*	PRINT #2,A
CSC	*	PRINT #2,A
CSS	*	PUT 'NAME',A
CYB	*	PRINT #2,A
DC	PRINT USING F$,A	PRINT #2:A
DL	*	WRITE #2,A
FD	(1)	PRINT (21)A
GE	*	WRITE #2,A
IBM/VS	*	PUT 'NAME',A
ISC	PRINT USING 20:A	WRITE #2,A
MAC	*	PRINT #2,A
POL	PRINT USING F$,A	PRINT 2:A
RCC	*	WRITE #2,A
RD	*	PRINT:NAME:A
SBC	*	*
SIS	*	WRITE(2) A
TYM	(1)	PRINT(2) A
UNI	*	PUT 'NAME',A
UCS	PRINT IN FORM F:A	WRITE ON 2:A
WAN	*	—
XER	*	PRINT :2,A

Notes: *   Same as CALL-OS
       — Not used
       (1) BBL language, statements not comparable

Index